D1230601

American Commonwealths.

VOLUME 20

WISCONSIN

AMS PRESS

NEW YORK

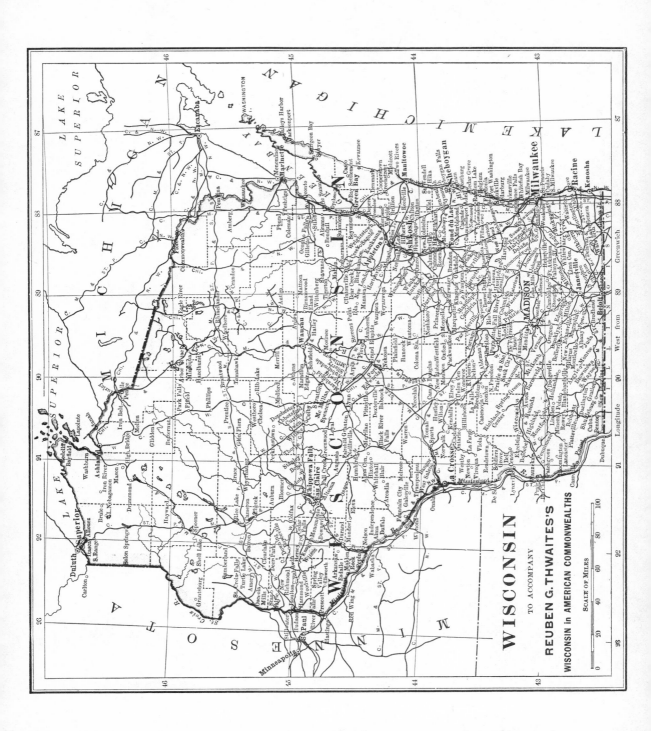

WISCONSIN

TO ACCOMPANY

REUBEN G. THWAITES'S

WISCONSIN in AMERICAN COMMONWEALTHS

SCALE OF MILES

American Commonwealths

WISCONSIN

THE AMERICANIZATION OF A FRENCH SETTLEMENT

BY

REUBEN GOLD THWAITES

BOSTON AND NEW YORK

HOUGHTON MIFFLIN COMPANY

The Riverside Press Cambridge

1908

Library of Congress Cataloging in Publication Data

Thwaites, Reuben Gold, 1853-1913.
   Wisconsin; the Americanization of a French
settlement.

   Original ed. issued as v. 20 of American
commonwealths.
   1. Wisconsin--History. I. Title.
II. Series: American commonwealths, v. 20.
F581.T57 1973   977.5   72-3747
ISBN 0-404-57220-0

Reprinted from the edition of 1908, Boston and New York
First AMS edition published, 1973
Manufactured in the United States of America

International Standard Book Number:
Complete Series: 0-404-57200-6
Volume 20: 0-404-57220-0

AMS PRESS, INC.
New York, N.Y.   10003

PREFACE

THE history of Wisconsin concerns itself with three political régimes — those of New France, Great Britain, and the United States. Its civilization, however, is of the first and third, for the influence of the second was negligible. When, in 1816, American troops first took possession of Green Bay and Prairie du Chien, the country between Lake Michigan and the Mississippi River was still French to the core. Indeed, still another decade was to pass before the Americanizing process began to show results. These came, not by transforming the character or habits of our mild-mannered and non-progressive *habitans* and *voyageurs*, who remained quite unchanged through full two centuries of residence in Wisconsin, but by means of the influx of New Yorkers and New Englanders, who gradually crowded them to the wall. It was nearly twenty years after American occupation began, before the fur-trade, now managed by Americans but almost wholly manned by French, ceased to be Wisconsin's dominating industry.

So far as it differs materially from that of its neighbors, the story of Wisconsin is that of the Americanization of a French settlement, — or rather of a cordon of widely scattered although closely related French fur-trade outposts. Long after the greater part of the Old Northwest had become a vigorous American community, this far northwestern corner, with a history all its own, was practically a foreign land.

During the twelve years of territorial experience (1836–48), the element of growth in Wisconsin was distinctly American. But immediately upon entering the Union, the state became a centre of attraction for German immigrants, and was for a time perhaps better known for its Teutonic than for its native-born population. Norwegians, Poles, Swiss, and other European peoples likewise found in Wisconsin those climatic, industrial, and political conditions favorable to their development. The result was that by 1890 Wisconsin was credited with a larger variety of foreign-born folk than could be found in any other American commonwealth, save perhaps Pennsylvania. In the Americanization of these people, Wisconsin throughout her statehood career has been actively engaged. That this task has been successfully performed is evident to any one familiar with her record. Fortunately, in becoming Americans European immigrants brought from Old-World experiences and culture much that was of use to the life of the young state. The results show themselves in the conservative tendencies of Wisconsin political thought, in the frank welcome here given to mod-

ern ideas, in the generous sustenance awarded to
every form of popular and higher education, in
evidences of a civic patriotism that must work still
larger triumphs for the commonwealth.

Space within the volume has been devoted to the
consideration of these matters rather than to a
marshaling of annals, although I hope that none
of the essentials of the state's history have been
neglected. As for errors of fact or of judgment, no
historical work ever has been or will be free from
them; history is a growing science, ever subject
to new interpretations as fresh material comes to
light, or points of view differ. It will be noticed
that the present treatment of the French and much
of the British régime in Wisconsin differs materially from previous historical writing on this subject; indeed, it must frankly be admitted that
there are herein many statements varying from
what I have myself asserted in earlier writings.
But within the past few years the discovery and
publication of documentary material by the Wisconsin Historical Society has made necessary an
entirely new view of that period, and this volume
has thereby been the gainer. The "deepest deep"
has, doubtless, not yet been sounded, hence to-day's
opinions may still need to be corrected. It would
be strange, indeed, were this not so.

In the preparation of the book, I have been
privileged to receive aid of varying sort from sev-

eral persons, some of whom have even done me the
service of reading the manuscript in whole or in
part. Miss Deborah B. Martin, one of the authors
of that admirable local history, " Historic Green
Bay," has kindly examined those portions having
reference to that ancient town, and much is owing
to her fruitful suggestions. President William
Ward Wight, of the Wisconsin Historical Society,
did for me a similar favor in the matter of Eleazer
Williams, the " lost Dauphin." Dr. Louise P. Kellogg, my editorial assistant on the staff of the
Wisconsin Historical Library, has been especially
helpful in research coöperation, particularly in the
French and British régimes. I have, in occasional
footnotes, acknowledged aid from other sources;
but owing to the popular nature of the work have not
sought to fortify every statement by citations of
authorities.

R. G. T.

Wisconsin Historical Library,
    Madison, *October*, 1908.

CONTENTS

WISCONSIN

CHAPTER I

THE COMING OF NICOLET

In the year made memorable in Jamestown annals through association with the legend of Captain John Smith's rescue by the romantic Pocahontas, twelve and a half years before the Pilgrims landed on Plymouth Rock, Samuel de Champlain, navigator, explorer, and statesman, reared on the gray cliff of Quebec (July, 1608) the stronghold destined to become the capital of New France.

As early as 1498 Devonshire men, " coming out of Bristow [Bristol]," had caught fish and bartered with savages in the fiords of Newfoundland, being soon joined in this profitable undertaking by Spanish Basques, Portuguese, and Normans and Bretons. Throughout the sixteenth century the polyglot fishing village of St. John's was well known as a port of call for maritime adventurers into the western seas, who obtained there water, provisions, and recruits; and later the pioneers of Virginia, New France, and New England not infrequently resorted thither for succor of various kinds.

In 1604 a trading and planting company, under grant from Henry IV of France, founded New France on the mainland of the continent, their initial choice for a site being Port Royal, near the present beautiful little town of Annapolis Royal, in Nova Scotia. Their first winter, however, was miserably spent upon the rocky islet of St. Croix, in Passamaquoddy Bay, on the boundary between Maine and New Brunswick. The river St. Lawrence had in 1534 been ascended as far as the island of Montreal by the French explorer, Jacques Cartier, and a similar expedition had been made by Champlain in 1603. Port Royal had proved too easily accessible to roving English corsairs, jealous of this foreign intrusion upon a domain claimed by their own sovereign, and its facilities for trade with the aborigines were found to be meagre. It was, therefore, determined to remove the capital of the western possessions of the French king to a stronger position. Champlain, now appointed governor of New France, wisely selected the easily defensible rock of Quebec, which lay far from the path of the meddlesome English. It was so situated, also, as to command an apparently unlimited native traffic, and thence might easily be dispatched exploring and military expeditions into the far interior.

The motives that impelled the planting of New France remained to the end its chief characteristics: love of territorial conquest, that which in the political jargon of our day we dub "imperialism;" the missionary zeal of the Catholic Church, eager at any hazard of martyrdom to gather within her fold the heathen savages of the New World; the spirit of commercial enterprise, finding in the fur-trade with North American natives a field at first rich in profits, but in time becoming a gambling venture, beset by enormous risks; and the generous yearning of the French people for adventure in strange lands, in a period when the area of the known world was being rapidly enlarged by the explorations of Europeans, and popular imagination was readily kindled by travelers' tales.

Such were the dominating passions of the enterprise. Subsidiary to these were the hopes of prospectors, who thought in this vast wilderness to discover mines of metals and precious stones; the ambition of army and naval officers, who in the stirring colonial arena sought recognition and rapid promotion; and the cupidity of officials in every branch of service, military and civil, who, in an age far more corrupt than our own, too often deemed public office, particularly in over-sea colonies, but an opportunity for private peculation.

In Champlain's day, —indeed, for nearly a century after he had planted Quebec, — Europeans had small notion of the enormous width of the North American continent. Not until Vitus Bering's exploit in 1741 were they quite certain that it was a continent, and not an outlying portion of Asia. In their many sorry adventures, the Spanish followers

of Columbus were ever seeking an American trans-
continental waterway connecting the Atlantic and
the Pacific. The early Virginians fancied that, once
successfully surmounting the Appalachian mountain wall by way of the James, the Potomac, or the
Roanoke, they might reach the headsprings of
streams flowing directly into the Pacific. Hendrik
Hudson at first thought that he had found the way
through, in Hudson River; he was still more confident when later he discovered Hudson Strait and
Bay. Throughout nearly two and a half centuries
of effort, European navigators one by one exhausted
the possibilities of North American inlets opening
into both oceans; the quest for what came to be
known as the Northwest Passage was thus gradually moved farther and farther up the map, until at
last that mythic waterway, that should shorten the
sea route between Europe and Asia, was consigned
to the impenetrable Arctic.

This prevalent misconception of the width of
North America, the lingering notion that it was a
part of Asia, and the theory that a waterway would
yet be found that directly connected the two
oceans, were three basic facts in the story of the
discovery of Wisconsin. Perhaps equally significant was the circumstance that the sources of rivers
connected with the several divergent drainage systems of the continent in numerous places here
closely approach each other, making it possible for
primitive travelers to proceed from one system to

another, and thus readily traverse the greater part of the country. We shall have abundant opportunity to observe wherein these factors shaped the early history of Wisconsin; indeed, they profoundly affected the course of exploration throughout almost the entire continental interior.

We have seen that in choosing Quebec as the capital of New France, Champlain purposely planted himself well within the continent, upon a great east-and-west drainage trough whose affluents in lake and river were to the adventurous people of New France destined to prove far-stretching highways. Their imagination was easily fired by the prospect of thereby penetrating an immense area of forested wilderness peopled with strange tribes of wild men.

At the head of this trough of the St. Lawrence valley is another low area, extending transversely north and south, practically between the Arctic Ocean and the Gulf of Mexico, with the Mississippi River flowing through the greater part of its enormous length. Now the basin of the Mississippi is separated from that of the St. Lawrence by only a low and narrow watershed running parallel to the Great Lakes. Flowing into these lakes are many short rivers, easily ascended by the light Indian canoes, which the whites soon learned to construct and operate quite as skillfully as the aborigines. Portage paths, varying in length from one mile to ten, and seldom difficult of passage, lead

from these waterways over the height of land to
other, and for the most part leisurely, streams
pouring into larger rivers that in their turn empty
directly or indirectly into the Mississippi. While
possible portages are numerous along this watershed, certain routes had in the course of time been
selected as the most practicable by aboriginal war,
trading, and hunting parties. Well-defined before
the coming of Europeans, they were freely used by
the latter in exploring and exploiting the country.

Proceeding westward, the first of these St. Lawrence–Mississippi routes was one by which the traveler from Lake Erie might, through Lake Chau-
tauqua, gain the waters of the Ohio River, the
Mississippi's great eastern tributary. The Ohio
could also be reached from Lake Erie by way of the
present Pennyslvania town of Erie and French
Creek, a confluent of the Allegheny. The Beaver,
Muskingum, and Scioto (by way of the Cuyahoga),
and the Maumee and the Wabash rivers were also
well-worn trade and war routes between the lower
Great Lakes and the Ohio.

From Lake Erie it was possible to ascend the
Maumee and carry over to the St. Josephs, which
debouches into Lake Michigan, — thus making a
short cut across the base of the lower Michigan
peninsula; or, paddling up the St. Josephs from
Lake Michigan, one might at the present South
Bend, Indiana, portage over to the Kankakee, a
tributary of the Illinois, itself a feeder of the Mis-

sissippi; this route was used by La Salle in 1679, and afterwards became famous as a French highway. Chicago River could be ascended, as it was in 1674 by Marquette, to the swamps closely approaching the Des Plaines, the latter being then followed to the Illinois.

For the French, undoubtedly the favorite path between the Great Lakes and the Mississippi was that of the Fox-Wisconsin rivers, in the heart of central Wisconsin. From Green Bay, the canoeist might work his way up the frequently sluggish but here and there rapids-strewn Fox to where is now the small city of Portage, carry his craft and its cargo across a marshy plain of a mile and a half, and then reëmbark on the swift-flowing Wisconsin, whose current would quickly convey him to the Mississippi. Sometimes the Wisconsin, when in high spring stage, would, as despite modern levees it still occasionally does, leap the scarcely perceptible watershed and pour its flood into the Fox, thus sending to the Gulf of St. Lawrence waters ordinarily flowing toward the Gulf of Mexico. In like manner the Chicago portage plain was sometimes flooded from Lake Michigan, the lake thus seeking a southern outlet through the Des Plaines, — an egress properly its own in an earlier geological era, and in our own day regained through the Chicago drainage canal.

Between Lake Superior and the upper waters of the Mississippi there were, not to mention several minor because more difficult paths, two much-used routes. One followed the narrow and somewhat turbulent Bois Brulé, from whose head-springs there was and still is a carrying path of a mile and a half to the willow marshes whence flows the beautiful St. Croix, an affluent of the great river ; another was by way of the foaming St. Louis, from which can be reached the watery plain of the Mille Lacs, and thence the uppermost pools of the Mississippi. By ascending Pigeon River, on the present international boundary, the traveler might by means of a score or two of portages and a network of lakes ultimately reach Lake Winnipeg ; whence by other interlacing waters could be penetrated the great systems of the Saskatchewan and the Assiniboin, which touch the feet of the Canadian Rockies. Still other portages in the far north and northwest brought him in connection with streams debouching into both the Arctic and the Pacific oceans.

These important geographical facts were but slowly revealed to the French. At first cartographers depended on the vague statements of Indians who sought the lower settlements for purposes of trade ; later, on the reports of explorers, fur-traders, missionaries, and soldiers, who upon their respective errands had followed returning tribesmen into the wilderness, and through close contact with conditions were enabled to extend the bounds of the map of New France.

Champlain was a born rover, and in person conducted several exploring parties, chiefly up the Saguenay, into the country around Lake Champlain, and up the broad Ottawa. The deep trough of the Saguenay led him through picturesque scenes to the north and northeast, into the rich fur-bearing region around Lake St. John, among the rudest of his savage neighbors. His first visit to the Lake Champlain country (1609) resulted unfortunately; for in order to please his Algonkin friends he attacked and routed the confederated Iroquois, who lived for the most part in the northern half of New York State and in northeastern Pennsylvania. Thereby he incurred for New France the undying hostility of the most astute and vengeful warriors among the North American tribes. The effect was, for a century and a half, at times highly disastrous to missionary and trading enterprises throughout the great length of New France, from the Atlantic seaboard to the Mississippi.

Lake Erie was firmly held by these implacable enemies, who long stoutly refused to allow Frenchmen to pass through, so that Champlain's westward exploration must needs be by way of the Ottawa. Stemming its strong flood and portaging around its numerous rapids, the governor ascended to the Mattawan; after tracing that tributary to its source, he followed the Indian portage trail over to Lake Nipissing, and thence descended its many-channeled outlet, French River, to Georgian Bay. Thus in 1615 was discovered Lake Huron, first of the

Great Lakes to be unveiled by the French. Later in the year, Champlain returned by Lake Ontario. We shall find that Lake Michigan was apparently first seen by a Frenchman in 1634, and doubtless Superior also by the same adventurer; while seven years later (1641), Jesuit missionaries at Sault de Ste. Marie wrote familiarly of the "other great lake above the Sault." Erie was seen by the French as early as 1640, but unnavigated by them until twenty-nine years later, save as unlicensed fur-traders conducted an illicit commerce with English and Dutch allies of the Iroquois.

The French had not long been settled at Quebec before news began to reach them of what in later years proved to be the Mississippi River. At first the information brought by Indians, who annually came down in their fleets of birch-bark canoes to barter with the fur-traders on the St. Lawrence, was of the vaguest. It might mean either that in the far-away western country certain "great waters" flowed directly into the Pacific, or that somewhere in what we now call the Middle West might actually be found the coast of the Pacific itself. Savages themselves had necessarily but a limited stock of geographical knowledge. They understood well their particular tribal range for fishing, hunting, trading, and war; the Iroquois at times raided over much of the country north of the Ohio, from New England to the Mississippi. But this was exceptional; to most tribes all beyond their own habitat was apt to be a region of myth, peopled by enemies, man-devouring monsters, and angry spirits. The aboriginal imagination was well developed; tribesmen cowered before the unknown.

Information thus coming at second and third hand, obviously distorted by the fears, superstitions, and personal exaggerations of the tale-tellers, but whetted the curiosity of Champlain. His desire to solve the mysteries of this western wilderness had been accentuated by reports of rich copper mines in that quarter, for among the officials of New France the discovery of mineral deposits ranked only second in importance to the fur-trade. He tells us in his "Voyages"[1] that in June, 1610, an Algonkin chief whom he was entertaining in the neighborhood of Quebec "drew from a sack a piece of copper a foot long, which he gave me. This was very handsome and pure. He gave me to understand that there were large quantities where he had taken this, which was on the bank of a river, near a great lake. He said that they [the savages of those parts] gathered it in lumps, and having melted it, spread it in sheets, smoothing it with stones."

In the light of modern knowledge, it is not difficult to recognize Lake Superior as the home of this historic lump of copper. The governor's guest had, possibly, never been there; the specimen may

[1] Champlain's *Voyages* (Paris, 1613), pp. 246, 247; Prince Society ed., vol. ii, pp. 236, 237.

easily have reached him from the west through
the medium of intertribal barter. North American
savages were keen traders; in intervals between
warfare they held markets with their neighbors,
at certain well-known aboriginal rendezvous (like
Mackinac, Green Bay, or Prairie du Chien), for
the exchange of tribal specialties, and of curiosi-
ties from a distance. By means of this widespread
commerce, European articles, bartered to natives
by early explorers along the Atlantic coast, are
known to have reached the forest camps of the far
interior long in advance of the arrival of white
men themselves.

After his own laborious journey to Lake Huron,
five years later, in search of more definite information concerning the mysterious West, further news
continued to reach Champlain, slowly percolating
through the uncertain channel of savage report.
New France was still weak, both in population and
in resources. In 1629 a predatory English fleet
had secured the unresisting surrender of Quebec.
It was not until three years after (1632) that the
country was restored to its French owners, and the
governor returned to his charge. In the year of
restoration probably not over a hundred and eighty
of the inhabitants of New France might properly
be called settlers, with perhaps a few score military
men, seafarers, and visiting commercial adventurers — during a time when (1627–37) upward of
twenty thousand settlers were emigrating from

Europe to the English colonies. Because of this weakness, exploration in New France long kept at a lagging pace. There were also affairs on the St. Lawrence, among them a protracted hand-to-hand struggle with the exasperating Iroquois, that sapped the slender resources of the province. Not until 1634 could Champlain carry out his long-cherished scheme of dispatching an exploring agent into the country beyond Lake Huron, to make trading treaties with its uncouth tribes, and to bring back what information he might of the great western water and the reputed mines of copper.

In the year of his own visit to Lake Huron, Champlain inaugurated the policy of selecting certain adventurous and vigorous youths of good character and sending them out into the Indian camps to become through years of experience schooled to the forest life, familiarized with aboriginal languages, customs, and thought, and possessed of the confidence of the tribesmen. From among the graduates of this rude seminary he chose his interpreters and explorers: men with fibre toughened to the work before them, adding to the physical endurance of the savage the intelligent persistence and tact of the European.

Among the best of these was Jean Nicolet, who, immediately upon his arrival from Normandy in 1618, being then twenty years of age, was dispatched by the governor to the friendly Algonkins of Allumette Island, far up on the Ottawa River.

The associations and language of this tribe were
in close touch with the West, where men such as
Nicolet were most needed. Says the quaint old
chronicle : [1] —

> Forasmuch as his nature and excellent memory in-
> spired good hopes of him, he was sent to winter with
> the Island Algonquins, in order to learn their language.
> He tarried with them two years, alone of the French,
> and always joined the Barbarians in their excursions
> and journeys — undergoing such fatigues as none but
> eyewitnesses can conceive; he often passed seven or
> eight days without food, and once, full seven weeks with
> no other nourishment than a little bark from the trees.

During his residence with the Algonkins, Nicolet accompanied a party of four hundred of his
forest friends to New York to patch up a temporary peace with the Iroquois, who had recently
been harrying the Ottawa valley. This mission
successfully accomplished, he took up his residence
with the Indians around Lake Nipissing, fifty
leagues farther westward on the route to Georgian
Bay. During the " eight or nine years " that he is
reported to have dwelt among these people, " he
passed for one of that nation, taking part in the
very frequent councils of those tribes, having his
own separate cabin and household, and fishing and
trading for himself. . . . He was able to control
and to direct [the savages] whither he wished,
with a skill that will hardly find an equal."

[1] Thwaites, *Jesuit Relations*, vol. xxiii, pp. 275–277.

It seems likely that Nicolet was even longer than "eight or nine years" among the Nipissings, or perhaps also with their neighbors to the west, on Georgian Bay; for the close of that term would have brought him to the time of the surrender of Quebec, and under the brief English régime there could have been no official employment for Frenchmen of his profession. There is no evidence that he left the woods until the restoration of New France in 1632. In the latter year we find him returning to Quebec, having withdrawn from the undoubted fascination of his wild life — "only in order to secure his salvation in the use of the sacraments," declares the Jesuit "Relation." Here he received employment as agent and interpreter for the Company of the Hundred Associates. To this trading monopoly, directed by Cardinal Richelieu, had been granted almost sovereign jurisdiction throughout the vast transatlantic territory claimed by the French, extending from Florida to the Arctic Circle, and from Newfoundland to the farthest west. Upon the restoration, the company resumed sway, Governor Champlain now being little more than its resident manager.

The route to Georgian Bay, by way of the Ottawa and the Mattawan, Lake Nipissing, and French River, was now fairly well known to the French. Beyond, all was still obscurity. The gift of copper from the Algonkin chief spoke eloquently of the commercial possibilities of the illimitable

West; still more so the rich furs that annually found their way from the upper lakes to the market on the strand of Quebec. But at the time Champlain appears to have been particularly interested in persistent rumors then reaching him, concerning a certain tribe called "Men of the Sea," whose home was reputed to be less than four hundred leagues[1] westward of the Algonkin.

It was reported by the Algonkins that these people had come to their present habitat from a point still farther west, by the shore of a salt sea; that annually there came out of that country, to trade with them, a people without hair or beards, and with manners and dress so described to Champlain as to suggest what he had read concerning the appearance of Tartars or Chinese; and it was confidently asserted that in the course of their coming these western traders traveled upon a great water in large canoes of wood (not bark, the material used by Canadian tribes).

Later knowledge has revealed the fact that the Men of the Sea were but the Winnebago of our day, — a name derived from the Algonkin word *ouinipegou*, meaning "men of the fetid (or stinking) water." When we take into consideration the then prevalent notion that North America, if not

---

[1] The standard French league is about equal to 2.42 English miles; the common league, 2.76. But the early French explorers used the term approximately — it is not safe to hold them too closely to their estimates of distance.

a portion of Asia, was at least a narrow continent washed on the west by a probably narrow ocean that touched Asia; and further, the fact that the widely-diffused Algonquian [1] stock, embracing most of the eastern tribes known to the French, often applied to salt water an adjective equivalent to "stinking," it is not difficult to comprehend why this term was translated into *Gens de Mer*. We understand, also, why the active imagination of Champlain impelled him to accept these unknown Men of the Sea, or their curious visitors, as possible Mongolians, and to hope that through their lands was at last to be found that short route to the Orient sought by Europeans since the days of Columbus, for which they still were searching a century after Champlain's death. Ethnologists now believe that the term *ouinipeg* (stinking water) as applied by the Algonkins to the Winnebago, had no reference to the sea, but to certain ill-smelling sulphur springs in the neighborhood of Lake Winnipeg. Whence the swarthy Winnebago, an outcast and somewhat degenerate branch of the Dakota linguistic stock, are thought to have migrated to the shores of Green Bay by way of the Wisconsin and Fox rivers, — a thin foreign wedge projected into the far-stretching territory of the

[1] Algonkin is the name of a tribe, whose chief seat in the days of New France was the valley of the Ottawa; Algonquian is the name of the linguistic stock, which included the Algonkins and nearly all tribes east of the Mississippi and north of the Tennessee, except the Iroquois, the Huron, and a few of their kindred.

Algonquian race. We now recognize, also, that the "great water" was no other than the Mississippi itself; upon it there came, in long "dug-out" canoes [1] to trade with the Winnebago, many of the Western and Southern tribes, such as the Sioux and the Illinois, to whom the exuberant fancy of the Algonkin attributed physical peculiarities that were intensified as the tale passed from tribe to tribe on its way to the great white chief.

It is a curious etymological fact that as soon as the French discovered that the Men of the Sea were but ordinary Indians, they ceased to call them *Gens de Mer*, thenceforth translating *ouinipeg* into the French word for "stinking," *puant*. Thus in their phraseology the Winnebago early became known as *Les Puants*, [2] or "The Stinkards," — an opprobrious term ill merited by those people, who were quite as cleanly as most of their neighbors.

Jesuit missionaries had first been introduced into New France in 1611, but withdrew after two years of unhappy experiences at Port Royal and Mount Desert Island. In 1615 Champlain invited to Quebec two missionaries of the Recollect order, a branch of the Franciscan "gray friars." For ten years these austere brethren, in cowl and sandals,

---

[1] Dug, or rather burned, out of trunks of trees; the Winnebago of to-day use similar "dug-outs."

[2] Hence La Baye des Puans, by which Green Bay (both the bay itself and the hamlet at the mouth of the Fox) was known throughout the French régime; although generally abbreviated to La Baye.

practiced the rites of the Church in the Canadian woods, all the way from the mouth of the Saguenay to Lake Nipissing, the scene of Nicolet's long and arduous training. But when Richelieu came into control of French policy, it was contended that a mendicant order like the Recollects was unsuited for missionary work among the savages; that the situation required men of a sterner type, with ample financial resources. For this reason the Company (or Society) of Jesus, a highly successful proselyting and teaching agency, then having a strong hold upon the French court, was requested to send representatives to this new and promising field.

In 1625 three of these Jesuit priests arrived, — "black gowns," the Indians called them, from their sombre cassocks, — and immediately the field of missionary operations broadened; although it was in due time to be discovered that the task of promulgating Christian doctrines among the warlike tribes of North America was no holiday undertaking. The work was abruptly closed by the English conquest; but upon the retrocession in 1632 the Jesuits came in larger numbers than before, and rapidly developed the celebrated missions of the interior, the Recollects being thereafter confined to the maritime districts of Nova Scotia, New Brunswick, and much of Maine, an ill-defined region then known to the French by the general term of Acadia.

A great part of what we know concerning the

people and affairs of New France, especially between 1632 and 1673, is obtained from small volumes called " Relations," annually published by the society in Paris, and containing accounts of the far-spread work of the French Jesuit missions in North America. Upon these contemporaneous documents we in large measure depend for our understanding of the circumstances leading to the discovery of Wisconsin, and indeed for not a little of its subsequent history during the French régime.

The several tribes of Indians whom the French called Huron occupied the country to the east and south of Georgian Bay of Lake Huron. Among these people the Jesuits maintained several important stations, which in time were to become scenes of martyrdom for many of the devoted " black gowns ; " for the war-loving Iroquois, although related to the Huron, frequently laid waste the villages of the latter, chiefly because of their adhesion to the French. Ultimately the impoverished Huron, decimated by slaughter, were driven from their scarified lands like autumn leaves before a gale, and, with their surviving French pastors, forced to seek refuge in far distant recesses of the country drained by the upper Great Lakes.

On the first and fourth of July, 1634, respectively, two fleets of birch-bark canoes left Quebec for the confluence of the St. Maurice, where, seventy-seven miles above the capital, was to be laid out, on the northern bank of the St. Lawrence, the

fur-trade and missionary station of Three Rivers,
then the farthest western outpost of the province.
So far back as native tradition went, the site of
Three Rivers had been a favorite rendezvous for
Indian bands when going to or from their winter
hunts. As in many a similar case in North America, this circumstance had induced the French to
establish themselves here; and within the protecting shadow of their little log fort was in due time
reared a hamlet of *habitans* that eventually grew
into the present modern industrial town.

The two companies of Frenchmen borne in these
flotillas consisted about equally of men who had
been dispatched by the Hundred Associates to
build the fort, and a party consisting of the Jesuit
Fathers Jean de Brébeuf, Antoine Daniel, and
Ambroise Davost, with six lay assistants, who
were first to establish a mission to the Indians of
that neighborhood and then proceed to a like service in the country of the Huron. Accompanying
these pioneers of the cross was Jean Nicolet,[1] in-

---

[1] Parkman, in his *Jesuits in North America* (1870), placed
the date of Nicolet's voyage as "in or before the year 1639,"
wherein he but followed Shea in the latter's *Discovery of the Mississippi* (1852). Benjamin Sulte, in his *Mélanges d'histoire et de
littérature* (1876), first showed that the proper date could be none
other than 1634. This was adopted by Butterfield in *Discovery of
the Northwest* (1881), who still more conclusively established that
as the year. Hebberd, in *Wisconsin under the Dominion of France*
(1890), vigorously contends for 1638; but Abbé Gosselin's apparently definitive *Jean Nicolet, 1618–1642* (1893), accepts Sulte's and
Butterfield's conclusion, as does the present writer.

tent upon his assigned task of discovering and treating with the Men of the Sea.

The Jesuits had anticipated meeting at Three Rivers a large party of Huron, expected down the Ottawa to trade with the French; they intended to seek from these savages permission to return with them to their country.

They waited there some time for the Hurons, who did not come down in so great numbers this year as usual, because the Iroquois, having been informed that five hundred men of this nation were moving toward their country to make war upon them, themselves went on ahead to the number of fifteen hundred, it is said; and, having surprised those who were to surprise them, they killed about two hundred of them, and took more than one hundred prisoners.[1]

At first readily granting the request, the fickle Huron soon expressed reluctance at taking these ten Frenchmen back with them, pleading illness and making all manner of flimsy excuses. It was only after much coaxing and present-giving, and a solemn promise that the white passengers should do their full share of paddling, that the tribesmen yielded. It was a toilsome journey against the sweeping currents of the Ottawa — "three hundred leagues to make," says the giant Brébeuf,

---

[1] *Jesuit Relations*, vol. vii, pp. 213-215, being Father Brébeuf's letter to his superior, Le Jeune, in the *Relation* for 1634, upon which we depend for details; but Nicolet is not therein mentioned by name.

"over a route full of horrors." Owing to an outbreak among the savage boatmen of an epidemic
resembling measles, the Frenchmen found that
theirs was indeed the laboring oar. "We start
so early in the morning," writes Brébeuf, "and
lie down so late, and paddle so continually, that
we hardly have time enough to devote to our
prayers; indeed, I have been obliged to finish
this by the light of the fire." At best their food
was of the scantiest, and there were days when
none was forthcoming to the poor missionaries,
who as yet had not so fully accustomed themselves to the privations of savage life as had
Nicolet, to whom both route and conditions were
familiar.

The immediate destination of the Jesuits was
Allumette Island, where Nicolet tarried awhile
with them, among his old friends the Algonkins.
At last bidding his countrymen farewell, the explorer pushed on up the Ottawa, doubtless with
Indian companions, in due course ascended the
Mattawan, whose headsprings lie close to Lake
Nipissing,[1] carried his canoe and baggage over
the easy portage, crossed the stormy lake, and followed its outlet, French River, down into the
beautiful vistas of Georgian Bay. Champlain had
preceded him thither by nineteen years, and probably Nicolet himself, during his long life among

[1] There is evidence that in an earlier geological age Lake Huron here found an outlet to the Ottawa.

the Nipissing, had more than once journeyed to these waters.

Here, apparently at the uttermost limit of French discovery to the west, Nicolet spent some time in parleys with the Huron, cementing their friendly relations with the whites, and from them gaining such information as was obtainable concerning the Men of the Sea and other tribes along the shores of the upper lakes. From the Huron villages, also, he secured seven tribesmen to accompany and assist him upon his voyage. In a long canoe of birch bark, the eight travelers into the unknown threaded their way cautiously among the almost countless islands that fringe the pine-forested shore of Georgian Bay; a region in our time familiar to ever-increasing shoals of summer tourists.

From French River the course lies almost westerly, between La Cloche Island and the Grand Manitoulin, thence through the picturesque archipelago of the North Channel, past Cockburn, Drummond, and St. Joseph islands, and into the tortuous River St. Mary's, the outlet of Lake Superior. Fifteen miles below the foot of that inland sea they encountered the stairlike rapids afterwards named by the Jesuits the Sault de Ste. Marie; and there Nicolet, first of all recorded white men, probably set foot on the soil of what a century and a half later became the Northwest Territory.[1]

[1] The Chippewa village wherein the French mission was later established, was on the east (Canadian) side of the Sault; but

At the Sault he found a considerable village of the Chippewa, engaged in fishing. Here again Nicolet, as an ambassador of the great white chief, was entertained at gluttonous feasts of fish and dog-meat, and engaged in solemn councils whereat prolix oratory and innumerable pipefuls of tobacco were the distinguishing features. It is fair to presume that the traveler's curiosity led him to the great lake above, or at least to its outlet from White Fish Bay, but there is no record of such a visit. Released from Chippewa hospitality, he returned down the St. Mary's with his faithful Huron boatmen, and thence turning to the west and southwest hugged the wooded islands and picturesque headlands lining the north shore of Lake Huron as far as the Straits of Mackinac. Stemming its swift tide, and probably resting for a time with the natives of the richly verdured Island of Mackinac, that divides these narrow waters, Nicolet's canoe was soon dancing upon the green waves of Lake Michigan ; he, so far as we can tell, their first white discoverer.

It was now essential for the explorer closely to skirt the northern coast of this new-found lake, frequently camping upon the sandy edges of its dense mantle of pine, either to await the passage of storms or to refresh his weary crew. Now and then

there is little doubt that Nicolet touched also the Michigan side of the rapids. His approach to the Sault was presumably through the Canadian channel.

they "encountered a number of small tribes in coming and going," [1] for even in aboriginal times Lake Michigan was a somewhat busy thoroughfare between the East and the West, connecting with the Mississippi region by way of the Fox-Wisconsin, the Chicago, and the St. Josephs portage routes. Unfamiliar with the savages west of Georgian Bay, and untaught in their several dialects, Nicolet was obliged to communicate with them by the all but universal Indian sign language in which from his training he must needs have been long familiar. According to the Jesuit chronicler, the strangers "fastened two sticks in the earth, and hung gifts thereon, so as to relieve these tribes from the notion of mistaking them for enemies to be massacred."

Projecting southward from the northwest shore of Lake Michigan is a rock-bound peninsula, some thirty miles in length, terminated by the cliff and reefs of Point Detour. It is presumable that the experienced and therefore cautious Nicolet received good local advice at the Indian villages nestled at wide intervals along this somewhat forbidding coast. No doubt following the route afterwards commonly adopted by the French, and called by them "grand traverse," he proceeded in his frail craft southwestward to Point Detour, thence across the entrance of Green Bay, [2] under shelter of the

[1] *Relation* of 1642–43, which we are now following.
[2] Locally called "Death's Door," because wind, current, and dangerous rocks often combine to render its navigation difficult.

outlying fringe of tree-girt islands, — Summer, Poverty, St. Martin, Rock, Washington, and their lesser fellows, in our day the homes of Icelandic and other hardy fishermen, — and gained the southern mainland at the imposing cliff now known as Death's Door Bluff.

Green Bay is shaped much like a gigantic letter V, opening to the northeast. Fox River enters from the southwest, at the vertex of the angle. The eastern shore of the bay is formed by the Green Bay peninsula, separating it from Lake Michigan — substantially a ridge of Niagara limestone, the same formation that constitutes the basis of Detour peninsula to the north. The connecting string of islands is evidence of a local breaking down of the ledge. Thus the eastern shore of Green Bay is generally high, deeply indented by several small bays, and exhibiting many bold, rocky headlands and abrupt clay slopes, their heights well clothed with both hard and soft woods. Its western banks, however, are low and sandy, with frequent harbors separated by shallow stretches.

It is stated by the Jesuit recorder that the explorer rested at a native camp, doubtless either of Menominee or Potawatomi, two days distant from the Men of the Sea. There was at the time a considerable village of this character on the west shore of Green Bay at the mouth of Menominee River, now a natural boundary between Wisconsin and Michigan ; but it seems improbable that Nicolet

crossed the broad bay to reach it. More reasonable is it to suppose that his tarrying-place was
either on the mainland or upon one of the islands
in the neighborhood of Death's Door Bluff, which
is ninety miles, or two short days' canoe journey,
from his objective. Here the ambassador explained
his errand, and after the manner of the Indians
one of the local tribesmen was sent forward as a
herald, with tidings of the coming of the white
stranger who bore offers of peace and good-will to
the savages of the upper lakes. "Which word,"
says the "Relation," "was especially well received
when they heard that it was a European who carried the message."

About twelve miles down the bay from the mouth
of Fox River, the east shore consists of a long
precipice of reddish clay, rising about a hundred
feet above a broad, pebbly strand. For perhaps a
century past, this conspicuous bluff has locally been
known as Red Banks. In the days of Nicolet it
was surmounted by a large palisaded fort; to the
southward and eastward stretched several hundreds
of acres rudely cultivated in the native manner
and grown to maize, pumpkins, and beans; while
ancient burial and effigy mounds dotted the field,
bespeaking a long-continued aboriginal occupation.
At this vantage point, apparently, was the long-
sought-for village of the Winnebago.

It is probable that these people had long been
on the way thither, from the country beyond Lake

Superior; for migrations of primitive people have usually been by easy stages, dictated by the exigencies of food supply or the pressure of hostile tribes. But it is unlikely that the establishment of the seat of their power at Red Banks antedated Nicolet's arrival by more than a few generations —long enough for the story of their origin to have become shrouded in tradition, and yet not so long that that story and their personal characteristics did not still attract the curiosity of Algonquian neighbors, causing them to be talked about as comparative strangers, and called Men of the Sea.

Little doubt can be entertained that by the time Nicolet had reached Sault Ste. Marie, or in any event Mackinac Island, he had become disabused of the notion that the Winnebago were other than ordinary savages. As he had slowly drawn nearer them, the reports of tribesmen whom he visited must have become more and more vivid concerning the Dakota outcasts. Long before he reached their habitat, their features and characteristics had probably assumed something like definiteness in the mind of this astute student of North American Indians.

When starting on his journey from Quebec, expecting to meet Asiatics in this far-away corner of the continent, the diplomatic Nicolet had placed in his scanty pack " a grand robe of China damask, all strewn with flowers and birds of many colors." There was perhaps little need for displaying so extraordinary a garment among the naked savages of the upper lakes; nevertheless Nicolet well understood the value of ceremonial in appealing to the imagination of primitive peoples, and doubtless his sense of humor was also aroused, for on approaching the palisaded village he donned his gaudy mandarin attire. The Winnebago had sent out several of their most athletic young warriors to meet "the wonderful man," who apparently was the first European to visit these people. In the strong and simple language of the Jesuit "Relation," "they meet him; they escort him, and carry all his baggage." But as the strange procession ascended the cliff by an angling path and entered the excited town, — Nicolet in his variegated gown, his seven breech-clouted Huron companions, and the delegation of young Winnebago burden-bearers, — "the women and children fled, at the sight of a man who carried thunder in both hands; for thus they called the two pistols that he held."

News traveled quickly among Indian tribes. At night signal fires were lighted on the hilltops, and swift runners and canoe-men were dispatched to acquaint neighboring villages verbally of the coming of the great white chief. Soon, says the "Relation," "there assembled" at Red Banks "four or five thousand men. Each of the chief men made a feast for him, and at one of these banquets they served at least sixscore Beavers." Thus, amid much feasting, harangue, and mutual giving of presents,

Nicolet negotiated a solemn treaty with the Men of the Sea, who, having but slight conception of what it all meant, courteously bound themselves to remain the firm commercial and military allies of their new father the King of France, and to consider themselves his most dutiful children.

From their position on Green Bay the Winnebago commanded the Great-Lakes terminus of the Fox-Wisconsin portage route from the Mississippi. There is every reason to believe that they had some knowledge of the latter drainage trough; for although some of the tribes upon the upper Fox and along the Wisconsin may at times have been hostile to them, it is recorded by the Jesuits that in peaceful periods wanderers from toward the Mississippi frequently passed through Green Bay on the road to Mackinac and still farther eastward.

The curiosity of the explorer appears to have led him to ascend the Fox for about ninety miles to an interesting Indian village which we shall find prominently identified with later visits of the French. Its location has been the subject of much dispute, but historians now generally agree that the site was in the immediate neighborhood of Berlin, in Green Lake County. In the Jesuit " Relation " for 1640, Father le Jeune wrote : " Sieur Nicolet, who has advanced farthest into these distant countries, has assured me that, if he had sailed three days' journey farther upon a great river which issues from

this lake [Huron] he would have found the sea." [1]
This is rather enigmatical, and has in our own
time given rise to much speculation. Some allowance, however, must be made for Nicolet's ignor-
ance of languages differing widely from the dialects
with which he was familiar ; for the lapse of six
years between his voyage and the printed account of it ; also for geographical confusion on the
part of his chronicler, Le Jeune, who was not con-
versant with the region. Without here discussing
the matter in detail, it is quite evident to students
in this field that the reference is to Fox River,
despite the fact that that stream flows *into* Lake
Michigan rather than *from* Lake Huron ; that
three days' farther journey from the Indian village,
in the ascent of the Fox, would have brought Nicolet to the Fox-Wisconsin portage, and that four
days' additional canoeing down the west-flowing
Wisconsin would have carried him into the Mississippi.[2]

Just why Nicolet did not pursue his journey to
the supposed Western Sea, which his hosts must
have informed him could be reached within a week,
is of course now unknowable. It is possible that he
considered his mission ended when treating with
the Winnebago and other Fox River tribes ; again,
the autumn must now have been reached, for he

[1] *Jesuit Relations*, vol. xviii, p. 237.
[2] See argument in Butterfield, *Discovery of the Northwest*,
pp. 67–69.

had been subjected to many long and weary delays in protracted pow-wows with the tribes along his route. Certain it is that, in the words of the Jesuit annalist, " The peace concluded, he returned to the Huron, and some time later to the Three Rivers, where he continued his employment as Agent and Interpreter, to the great satisfaction of both the French and the Savages, by whom he was equally and singularly loved." [1]

[1] *Relation* of 1642–43.

CHAPTER II

AFTER wintering with the Hurons, Nicolet returned to Quebec in the summer of 1635. The following Christmas came the death of Champlain, one of the most valorous and enterprising spirits of his time. The new governor, Montmagny, possessed little of his predecessor's enthusiasm for exploration, so that whatever plans Champlain may have entertained regarding the imperial and commercial exploitation of the country of the upper Great Lakes were for a long period allowed to lapse. It must be remembered, moreover, that as the waterways ran, Wisconsin and the Men of the Sea were a full fifteen hundred miles distant from seventeenth-century Quebec — thirty-six hours of passive, luxurious travel upon a modern railway, but two or three months of irksome toil in the primitive days of Nicolet. The long route was beset by a thousand difficulties — powerful currents, swirling rapids, great waterfalls, laborious portages, the dangers of navigating stormy and rock-bound inland seas in frail canoes of bark, the annoyances of extortion and mutinies by savage crews, the often pressing problem of food supply, and deadly perils from hostile tribes who frequently resented with violence the intrusion of a stranger upon their wild domains. Boldly adventurous as were the handful of pioneers of New France, it is small wonder that Wisconsin did not at first tempt many to emulate the enterprising journey of Champlain's agent to the wilderness of this far Northwest.

So far as we are now aware, it was twenty years before a European again set foot upon the soil of our state. But let us not be over-ready to make definite assertions regarding priority of exploration in New France. Under the fur-trade monopoly of the Company of the Hundred Associates (ending in 1663, but followed by governmental control almost equally galling), it was a felony to carry on commerce with the Indians that was not duly licensed by that corporation. Articles needed for barter with the aborigines must be obtained from the company at prices absurdly high ; to it must in turn be sold the resultant furs at such rates as it cared to pay. Every operation of the licensed forest trader was subject to regulations fettering his freedom and curbing his profits, to the advantage of the monopolists.

The man who dared conduct unlicensed trade was styled a *coureur de bois* (wood ranger). Legally he was an outlaw, the lightest punishment he might expect being the liability at any time to lose his property by confiscation. Official attitude towards the *coureurs de bois* varied greatly, however, according to the prevalent temper of the French court at Versailles. Free-traders, who at such risks either openly or covertly defied oppressive commercial restrictions set up by the greed of government favorites, at times constituted perhaps a majority of those engaged in the fur traffic of New France. Among them were many of the most daring and picturesque characters of their day, some of whom are entitled to honorable recognition in any history of our continental interior.

Following Indian bands upon war and hunting trails, and associated with red folk by ties of primitive marriage and genuine comradeship, their travels into strange lands were apt often to be years in advance of official exploration. Even when they possessed the requisite taste and education for making such records, they seldom kept journals of their adventurous wanderings. Neither were they accustomed, these outlaws of the " bush," to talk freely of their affairs when revisiting the small settlements on the lower St. Lawrence ; for their every word might readily be brought to the attention of the king's gainful officials, who, though themselves usually engaged in illicit trade, were too often eager to curry favor at Versailles by reporting the ill deeds of others.

The closer one's study of official documents and ecclesiastical journals of the time, with their often shadowy allusions to the operations of *coureurs de bois*, the stronger grows the conviction that, de-

spite the honors which history showers upon discoveries by the governmental explorers and Jesuit
missionaries of New France, the palm must not
seldom in all honesty be awarded to nameless forest
traders; these men familiarly dwelt, hunted, and
bartered with the aborigines of the upper lakes and
the Mississippi basin long previous to the appearance of those commonly reputed to be first of Europeans upon the savage scene.

By assembling scattered patches of information,
it has chanced that the personality of a few of these
wandering bush merchants has been revealed to us,
and their names added to the slowly lengthening
bead-roll of early Western explorers. Such were
Pierre Esprit, the Sieur Radisson, and his companion and brother-in-law, Médard Chouart, the
Sieur des Groseilliers.

It is recorded in the Jesuit "Relation" for
1655–56,[1] that "On the sixth of August, 1654, two
young Frenchmen, full of courage," and incited
thereto by Governor Jean de Lauson, left Quebec
for the upper lakes, upon "a journey of more than
five hundred leagues," under the guidance of a
party of returning savages from that region, who
had ventured in their canoes down the St. Lawrence
to barter rich furs for the manufactures and gew-
gaws of Europe. The adventurous twain returned
to Quebec "toward the end of August of this year,
1656. Their arrival caused the Country universal

[1] *Jesuit Relations*, vol. xliii, pp. 219 *et seq.*

joy, for they were accompanied by fifty canoes, laden with goods [furs] which the French came to this end of the world to procure."

The travelers related their interesting story to the Jesuit fathers, who eagerly sought news from the farthest wilderness, among other things telling of their visit to " the great Lake of the Hurons, and another near it [Michigan], being as large as the Caspian Sea." In that distant region they had fraternized with the Winnebago, or the Men of the Sea, to whom Nicolet displayed his gorgeous robe; " they also caused great joy in all Paradise, during their travels, by Baptizing and sending to Heaven about three hundred little children." Moreover, the missionary journalist adds in a note of worldly satisfaction, " these two young men have not undergone hardships for naught in their long journey . . . they enriched some Frenchmen upon their return."

Nine years later, Radisson, then at the court of London seeking for his enterprises the patronage of King Charles II, wrote in English for His Majesty's information a curious journal of his adventures, or " voyages," covering the years 1652–64. After nearly two centuries of neglect, this manuscript was purchased by a collector of antiquities and eventually drifted into the Bodleian Library at Oxford.[1] Crude and sometimes chaotic in literary form, as might be expected of an ill-educated

---

[1] A narrative in French of later travels by Radisson and Groseilliers (1682–83) has found a resting-place in the British Museum.

man writing in a language other than his own, generally destitute of dates, abounding in almost hopeless ambiguities and contradictions, and exasperatingly vague as to geography, this remarkable human document was first published two centuries after it was written (1885).[1]

Allowing for the prevalent note of exaggeration as to details, customary in travelers' stories of the seventeenth century, it is but fair to assume that in all essentials Radisson's narrative is to be taken at its face value.

In the record of their earlier wanderings among the savages of the Northwest, he had no reason, now apparent to us, for serious misrepresentation. That Radisson and Groseilliers are identical with "the two young Frenchmen" of the "Relation" of 1655–56, and that the circumstances narrated by the former actually occurred in the main as stated, seems reasonably assured.

By piecing together the "Relations" and the journal of Radisson it would appear that these two adventurers, starting from Quebec in August, 1654, followed the trail of Nicolet up the Ottawa River and over to Lake Huron, where they traded with the Huron Indians; thence proceeding by the way of Mackinac Straits to Lake Michigan, on the west shore of which they wintered with the Potawatomi and visited neighboring tribes.

[1] By the Prince Society, Boston, under the editorship of Gideon D. Scull of London.

We weare every where much made of ; neither wanted
victuals, for all the different nations that we mett conducted us & furnished us wth necessaries. . . . We weare
Cesars, being nobody to contradict us. We went away
free from any burden, whilst those poore miserable
thought themselves happy to carry our Equipage, for
the hope that they had that we should give them a
brasse ring, or an awle, or an needle.

In the spring of 1655 the two traders, still on
the track of Nicolet, seem to have ascended the
Fox River, and to have visited the large native
village upon its upper reaches, where vivid memo-
ries of Nicolet must still have lingered. Exactly
where they wandered after this is uncertain ; but
Radisson quaintly writes, " We ware 4 moneths in
our voyage without doeing any thing but goe from
river to river. . . . anxious to be knowne with
the remotest people." Once they visited a " great
river " with " 2 branches, the one toward the west,
the other toward the South, wch we believe runns
towards Mexico, by the tokens they gave us." Vague
reports reached them that upon this southern-flowing
stream were " men that build great cabbans & have
great beards & had such knives as we have had . . .
wch made us believe they weare Europeans." It is
not difficult for us to believe that the forked river, although unknown to Radisson as such, was the Mississippi with its Missouri affluent, and that these uneasy
wanderers had accidentally discovered the former
eighteen years previous to Jolliet and Marquette.

Returning down the Fox, apparently in the autumn of 1655, the adventurers proceeded to the native fishing villages clustered along the Sault Ste. Marie, there spending the winter, hunting and trading with their hosts, exploring a portion of the southern coast of Lake Superior, making long inland expeditions with the Indians on snowshoes, and even penetrating to far-distant Hudson Bay. The Jesuit chronicler has told us of their reaching Quebec the following August.

The thirst for exploration and wild sport strong within them, Radisson and Groseilliers soon made preparations for another voyage. But there had come a change in official policy, and they were no longer in favor at the governor's house. The Vicomte d'Argenson was then the representative of the king in New France, and warned these unlicensed merchants that they must not again venture into the Northwest. Nevertheless, in the spring of 1659 they contrived to escape governmental vigilance, and clandestinely departed for the upper lakes in the company of a party of Chippewa who were returning to Sault Ste. Marie from the annual fur market at the French settlements. Tarrying for a second time at the village of their hosts, the adventurers paddled westward along the south shore of Lake Superior, accompanied by some twenty-three canoe-loads of Huron and Ottawa tribesmen who were fleeing to the Wisconsin wilds to escape Iroquois raiders, just then ravaging the country to the

east of Lake Huron. Carrying their boats across
the short portage route which nearly bisects Ke-
weenaw Point,[1] the party finally found their way to
Chequamegon Bay, a deep notch in the southern
shore-line of Superior, studded by the beautiful
Apostle Islands.

The savages here left the lake, continuing their
journey over various land and water routes to
camps of their tribesmen in the interior. Huron
and Ottawa had established hiding-places upon the
upper waters of the south-flowing Chippewa, the
Black, and the St. Croix; there, just over the di-
vide, two or three days' journey south of Lake Superior, in a rolling country densely clad with pines
and thickly strewn with inter-communicating lakes
and streams, they felt reasonably secure against
their bloodthirsty enemies from the Niagara frontier. On their part, the two traders remained on
Chequamegon Bay to traffic with the several neighboring tribes who resorted to this shore for fishing,
and who entertained a superstitious reverence for
some of the islands, particularly Madelaine,[2] as the
supposed abode of spirits.

Erecting a rude fortified hut of bushes and logs,
apparently on the southwest shore of the bay, the
coureurs de bois spent a few weeks in becoming

[1] Now completed by a federal canal, which is used by some of
the largest vessels afloat on Lake Superior. This cut-short saves,
to boats following the south shore, a journey of nearly two hundred miles around the peninsula.

[2] Site of the La Pointe village of to-day.

familiar with the country and its people. Then, concealing the greater part of their trading goods in a pit, or *cache*, they set out on a hunt with their Huron and Ottawa friends about the headwaters of the Chippewa. Radisson's narrative is Hogarthian in its realism. We have in his pages a startlingly vivid report of the horrors as well as the joys of the winter's experience. Unusually severe weather set in, game fled before the northern blasts, a famine ensued, even moccasins and robes and bark were boiled for food; so deep was the snow that the hunters traveled only with the greatest difficulty, and five hundred men, women, and children were left dead upon the trail. " If," says Radisson, " I should expresse all that befell us in that strange accidents, a great volume would not containe it."[1]

With the coming of spring and hope, the party set out on a long search for food, penetrating as far west as the Sioux camps stretched along the upper reaches of the Mississippi. At last returning to Chequamegon, they built another small fort, visited some Indians on the northwest shore of Lake Superior, and in August returned to the lower country in a fleet of fur-laden Huron canoes bound for the Montreal market. Their second home-coming, however, was a far different experience from the greeting accorded them four years before. Now treated as outlaws, their furs were confiscated by

[1] The journal, so far as it relates to Wisconsin, is given in full in *Wisconsin Historical Collections*, vol. xi.

the governor, which meant to them an almost complete loss of property, while their great services to New France as explorers were quite ignored.

Angered at this harsh treatment, the adventurers first sought redress from the king, on the plea of having opened to trade new and vast countries in the West; but justice being refused, they turned to England for recognition. It was while in London on this errand that Radisson wrote his now famous journal. Eventually, in 1669, the vengeful explorers piloted an English ship into Hudson Bay, an enterprise which led at once to the organization of the great Hudson's Bay Company, which from that day to this has controlled for England the fur traffic of the far North. The after career of Radisson and Groseilliers was marked by periods of vacillation between adherence to France and England by turns. They finally died in London, ill considered by the English, and by the French dubbed traitors to their native land. Nevertheless, this singular pair were men of elemental genius and uncommon enterprise and daring. To them we owe in large measure the introduction of Europeans to Lake Superior, Hudson Bay, and the vast solitudes lying between.

But while Radisson and Groseilliers were discredited by officials, who were in the interest of the commercial monopoly of New France, their tale deeply interested the Jesuits, who ever were seeking new fields of missionary labor. Some of the

canoes in the fur-trading fleet in which the wanderers had returned to Montreal were manned by
Huron from Black River, in Wisconsin. These
savages spent some ten days at the island settlement, feasting with their customers, and about the
first of September (1660) set out on the long homeward trip, taking with them Father René Ménard,
together with his body servant and seven other
Frenchmen — lay brothers, devoted to the material
interests of the mission.

The first Jesuit representative to penetrate
west of Sault Ste. Marie, Ménard was then only
some fifty-five years of age; but so arduous had
been his long life among the Indians that his hair
was white, he was thickly scarred by wounds, and
" his form was bent as with great age." The long
journey into the Northwest proved too severe a
strain upon one so spent. He suffered much from
exposure to inclement weather, was forced to paddle almost continuously, to carry heavy packs over
the frequent rough portages, and, as usual with
Jesuit guests on similar voyages, was the victim of
many indignities at the hands of his hosts. By
the time the little party had made their weary way
up the Ottawa, through Georgian Bay, around
Sault Ste. Marie, and alongshore as far as Kewee-
naw portage, an accident happened to his canoe,
and he and his fellow Frenchmen were there deserted to shift for themselves.

The winter was passed in a squalid Ottawa vil-

lage, where the father nearly lost his life in a
famine that overtook the natives of the region.
In the spring of 1661 came an invitation to visit
and baptize some starveling Huron, skulking in
the pine forest around the headsprings of the
Black, people who had known the Jesuits while
dwelling in their own country to the east. Thither
Ménard sought them, over a difficult portage route
of a hundred and fifty miles, by way of Lake
Vieux Desert and the Wisconsin River, his companions being his serving man and several returning Huron who had come to trade with the
Ottawa. While portaging around Bill Cross Rapids, not far from the present city of Merrill, on
the Wisconsin, Ménard — bearing his scanty pack
of sacred pictures, silver altar vessels, and camp
kettle, with which every forest missionary was
provided — lost his way in the woods, either falling victim to the club of some covetous savage,
or dying of exposure and starvation; certain it
is, he was never after seen of white men. Thus
miserably ended the career of Wisconsin's pioneer
herald of the Gospel, who fell in the active discharge of duty, as might a soldier on the field of
battle or one of his own martyred brethren in ill-
fated Huronia.

Four years passed before the Lake Superior
mission was reopened. When Father Claude Allouez arrived in 1665, he chose Chequamegon Bay
as the seat of his work, erecting a chapel of bark

on the southwestern mainland, probably not far from the site of Radisson and Groseilliers' first trading-hut. In the neighborhood was an aboriginal village, composed of remnants of eight or ten fugitive tribes that had either been driven westward by the all-conquering Iroquois or eastward by the scourging Sioux of the Western plains. A long, northward-projecting tongue of land, a natural breakwater, bounds Chequamegon Bay on the east, and this object gave name both to the mission and the region, "La Pointe du Saint Esprit," a term soon abbreviated to La Pointe.

Although a successful veteran in the work, Allouez found his present flock singularly obdurate and unmannerly. After four years of fruitless labor, he was, in the autumn of 1669, relieved by a younger and less jaded missionary, Father Jacques Marquette. He himself was dispatched by his superior to Green Bay, and for two years labored zealously among its shore tribes, and as far up the Fox as the large polyglot native village near Berlin, which Nicolet had been first to visit. In the winter of 1671–72 he founded the more favorably situated mission of St. Francis Xavier, overlooking the rapids of De Pere.[1] This, the first obstruction in the navigation of the Fox, had confronted Nicolet and Radisson in their canoe voyages, and

[1] Originally "Rapides des Pères," in allusion to the missionaries stationed there; but under English occupation, this was corrupted to De Pere.

by now was no doubt familiar to many unrecorded Frenchmen who, as wandering fur-traders, had followed them to this distant wilderness.

At St. Francis Xavier, Allouez, with patient toil, achieved considerable success, as success was measured among the wilderness missionaries of New France. To the west, among the Outagami (Foxes), he established the mission of St. Mark, probably near the present New London, on Wolf River, a tributary of the upper Fox; and farther up the latter stream, that of St. James at the village already mentioned. Among wandering bands of many tribes, scattered throughout the broad country between Lake Michigan and the Mississippi River, he painfully toiled along tangled forest paths and by interlocking waterways. In far-away Indian camps, and in his crude chapels of bark and reeds, he baptized many of the red folk, chiefly women and infants, and now and then nominally convinced a tribesman that the white man's " medicine " was more efficient than the machinations of the aboriginal soothsayer. Nominally, we say, for there is room for strong doubt whether, despite the splendidly heroic efforts and not infrequent martyrdom of European missionaries, which illumine the pages of our history, any considerable number of normal North American savages were ever fully converted to the Christian faith.

In due time, Father Louis André came to assist Allouez in these truly arduous labors and frequent

sufferings and perils. They in turn were followed
by Fathers Silvy, Albanel, Nouvel, Enjalran, and
Chardon, — the last-named closing the old Jesuit
régime in Wisconsin; for the uprising of the Fox
Indians, of which we shall read later, came to
make life unendurable for Frenchmen in this region beyond Lake Michigan, that they had so long
exploited for king, commerce, and the Church.

Marquette, who succeeded Allouez at the Chequamegon Bay mission of La Pointe, was a man of
commanding enterprise, as a Jesuit missionary in
New France had well need to be; at the same time,
he was one of the purest souls known to the glowing history of his order, and a preacher of undoubted power and persuasiveness. Yet he won no
greater ascendency over this polyglot flock than had
his predecessor. "They turn Prayer to ridicule,"
he complains to the father superior, "and scarcely
will they hear us speak of Christianity; they are
proud, and without intelligence," and he must fain
content himself with baptizing the sick and dying,
who have not the strength to oppose such procedure.

In view of his future work, however, his time at
La Pointe was well spent. Here he met tribesmen
from the Illinois country, who brought him vague
accounts of the Mississippi, and his letters to
Jesuit headquarters in Quebec breathe deep yearn-
ings to visit the great river of the south, to solve
the puzzle of its course, and to carry to its nations

the gospel of the cross. "This discovery," he writes
with the optimistic spirit of a born explorer, "will
give us full knowledge either of the South Sea or
of the Western Sea." [1]

Marquette's proposal to his superior, to seek
the Mississippi from Chequamegon Bay by means
of the closely connecting waterways abounding in
northwest Wisconsin, was not destined to bear
fruit. In the spring of 1671, the Ottawa and
Huron of La Pointe became embroiled in a serious
quarrel with the Sioux encamped at the extreme
western end of Lake Superior, and with their pastor precipitately fled eastward to escape the wrath
with which they were threatened. The Ottawa
found a home on Manitoulin Island, in the northern waters of Lake Huron. The Huron settled on
the Straits of Mackinac, and with them Marquette
willingly cast his fortunes, for this was the principal pathway toward the Mississippi.

A twelvemonth previous the Jesuits had established upon the turtle-shaped Island of Mackinac
the modest mission of St. Ignace, the advantages
of which are thus set forth by Dablon, father superior at Quebec, in the "Relation" of that year:
"[The island] forms the key and the door, so to
speak, for all the peoples of the South, as does the

---

[1] Marquette doubtless meant the Gulf of Mexico by the term
"South Sea," although this was by most geographers of the time
the name given to the Pacific Ocean, which is here called "Western Sea."

Sault [de Ste. Marie] for those of the North; for in those regions there are only those two passages by water for very many Nations, who must seek one or the other of the two if they wish to visit the French settlements. This circumstance makes it very easy both to instruct these poor people when they pass, and to gain ready access to their countries." The "Relation" of 1671–72 also refers to the island as "the great resort of all Nations going to or coming from the North or the South."

We have seen that from the earliest days of New France, Frenchmen had been thinking much of the Mississippi River and the road thither. Champlain had dreamed of reaching its banks, but after venturing as far as Lake Huron, was drawn homeward by colonial affairs. Nicolet closely approached the goal. There is strong probability that Radisson and Groseilliers were upon the great river in the summer of 1655. Some have thought, but in our opinion on insufficient evidence, that La Salle traded for furs on the Mississippi as early as 1670. In that same year Fathers Dablon and Allouez were at the Indian village on the upper Fox, only a short distance from the Wisconsin — "a beautiful river," writes the latter in the "Relation" for 1669–70, "running southwest without any rapid. It leads to the great river called Messisipi, which is only six days' sail from here." The matter of definite exploration of the valley, so long the object of profound popular curiosity, was, among a roving people like those of New France, merely a question of time and of the proper men.

When Marquette, twenty-nine years of age, arrived at Quebec from France in 1666, he found there at the Jesuit house, in training for the priesthood, Louis Jolliet, eight years his junior. The two became fast friends, but Jolliet appears soon to have abandoned his theological studies and entered the field of professional exploration, in which Nicolet had won such marked success. A man of adventurous spirit and fine physique, he, like Nicolet, rapidly acquired a considerable number of Indian dialects, and through arduous training became a master of woodcraft and aboriginal diplomacy. At the time when Marquette was sent by his superior to La Pointe mission, Jolliet was dispatched by the governor of New France to accompany, as interpreter and Indian expert, an official party engaged in prospecting for copper in the Lake Superior region. He remained for several years in the country of the upper Great Lakes, and we find him frequently referred to in official and Jesuit reports from that quarter as possessed of discretion, bravery, and unusual ability. His maps and statements concerning the Northwest did much to renew ecclesiastical and official interest in the discovery of the Mississippi, concerning which he, like Marquette, assiduously collected information from many sources.

Great was the delight of Marquette, at the lonely

mission of St. Ignace, now removed to Point Ignace on the northern shore of Mackinac Straits, when, on the 8th of December, 1672, — the day of the feast of the immaculate conception of the Virgin, to whom the father had vowed to dedicate his long-proposed mission to " the Nations who dwell along the Missisipi River,"— " Monsieur Jollyet arrived with orders from Monsieur the Count de frontenac, Our Governor, to accomplish This discovery with me. I was all the more delighted at This good news, since I saw my plans were about to be accomplished." Jolliet was likewise the bearer of Marquette's marching orders from the father superior. Jesuit missionaries were under the strictest discipline, and might undertake no enterprise without specific authority from headquarters.

The long northern winter was spent by the two comrades in careful preparations for the hazardous journey to which, as the result of their petitions, they had at last been assigned by their respective chiefs. The exciting news of the proposed expedition spread quickly and widely among the tribes of the district. The intending explorers were visited by all manner of aboriginal delegations, eager to give of their meagre geographical knowledge, or more often to caution the adventurers against unduly risking their lives in this strange enterprise into unknown lands abounding in nameless horrors, and among strange peoples reputed to be in league with the spirits of evil.

Writes Marquette in his journal:

We obtained all the Information that we could from the savages who had frequented these regions; and we even traced from their reports a Map of the whole of that New country; on it we indicated the rivers which we were to navigate, the names of the people and of the places through which we were to pass, the Course of the great River, and the direction we were to follow when we reached it.[1]

With the earliest canoes from the lower country, came young Father Philippe Pearson to succeed Marquette at St. Ignace. A few days later, upon the 17th of May, 1673, the epoch-making expedition set forth — "Monsieur Jollyet and myself, with 5 men, in 2 Bark Canoes, fully resolved to do and suffer every thing for so glorious an Undertaking." Following the path broken by Nicolet and Radisson and Groseilliers, and no doubt by several other of their compatriots, the discoverers voyaged cautiously along the north shore of Lake Michigan and past the dangerous bluffs of Point Detour, crossed Death's Door with its swirling tide, and ascended Green Bay and Fox River to De Pere, where they no doubt tarried briefly at the Jesuit mission of St. Francis Xavier. Thence alternately portaging and paddling up the Fox, and stopping

[1] The original of what apparently is this map rests in the archives of St. Mary's College, Montreal. It is published in *Jesuit Relations*, vol. lix, where also will be found the full text of Marquette's journals of both his 1673 and his 1674 expeditions.

for three days at the native village near Berlin, they found their way to the broad and picturesque Wisconsin, which was rapidly descended to its mouth, near the present Prairie du Chien. On the 17th of June their canoes emerged from the flood-washed delta of the Wisconsin into the broad, sweeping current of the Mississippi, at this point nearly a mile in width. With "a Joy that I cannot Express," writes the gentle Marquette, they gazed on one of the noblest scenes in America. At last they had found the object of their quest.

However, their dangerous journey was still far from its end. After numerous adventures, many of them pleasing because of the fresh charm of the country, but now and then alarming from the hostile attitude of several of the native villages along the shores, the little flotilla reached the mouth of the Arkansas. It was now the middle of July. Heat and mosquitoes sadly vexed the adventurers; the opposition of the tribesmen was intensifying as they proceeded southward; it was at last evident that the river flowed neither into the Pacific nor into the waters of Virginia, but "into the florida or Mexican gulf;" reports of Spaniards on the lower reaches or along the gulf shore became daily more pronounced; and "Finally," writes the black-gowned journalist, " we had obtained all the information that could be desired in regard to this discovery."

Upon the seventeenth, two months after they had bidden farewell to Pearson at St. Ignace, and one after the discovery of the great river at Prairie du Chien, the explorers took formal leave of their treacherous Arkansas hosts and turned homeward. The canoes, heretofore gliding easily, now made slow progress against the strong descending current; the mosquito pest was well-nigh unbearable; malaria beset the wearied travelers, who were scorched by day and chilled by night fogs; hostile savages often compelled them to sleep in their anchored canoes; camps had frequently to be made without fires that might betray their presence, — so that they were in a sorry plight by the time the Illinois River was reached. Learning that this route to Lake Michigan was shorter than the Fox-Wisconsin, they ascended the Illinois, where Marquette preached in the numerous native villages and Jolliet discoursed bravely of the power of New France and the advantage of its fur-trade. Reaching either the Chicago or the Calumet River over a portage path that traversed the scarcely perceptible watershed, the explorers descended to the great lake. Thenceforth they painfully worked their way for three hundred miles northward along the whitish clay bluffs lining the Wisconsin shore, crossed over to Green Bay by means of the Sturgeon Bay portage route,[1] and at the end of September were warmly welcomed by the Jesuit missionaries at De

[1] Now penetrated by a federal canal.

Pere, to whose house Marquette had by this time been formally assigned.

The party had been much enfeebled by the long and hazardous journey, and were pleased enough thus early to settle down in peace for the protracted winter. The two leaders occupied themselves with their respective reports and maps. Marquette's simple narrative was addressed to his superior, Father Dablon, at Quebec; Jolliet's, doubtless more detailed, to his chief, the governor of New France. In the spring (1674) Jolliet, the stronger of the two, bade farewell to his still ailing colleague, and with their boatmen set forth in high spirits upon his long voyage homeward. He had successfully compassed the many dangers of lake navigation and those of the turbulent Ottawa, and was gayly shooting the great rapids at La Chine, above Montreal, when his canoe upset, his crew and his papers were lost in the tumultuous waters, and he barely escaped with his life. The poor fellow was in a sorry plight on his return to the diminutive capital of New France, with little to show of his great discovery. He was, however, promptly seen by Father Dablon, who managed to catch the mail for France with a hurried report of the trip,[1] " put together after hearing him converse, while waiting for the relation, of which father Marquette is keeping a copy."

In due time Marquette's narrative reached Da-

[1] Jesuit *Relation* for 1674.

blon, doubtless by the hands of an Indian messenger descending the St. Lawrence in one of the annual trading fleets to Quebec. It is this report that has come down to us as the only journal of the famous expedition, which accounts for the fact that Marquette's name has in history become much more intimately connected with the discovery than that of his almost forgotten companion. The good father, however, went to his grave quite unconscious of the fame that had been thrust upon him. In the brief life remaining to Marquette he could never have known of the sad fate of Jolliet's papers. Dablon's "interview" with the latter was not published in the "Relations" until the missionary was dying in the land of the Illinois; his own priceless journal did not see print until six years after he himself had passed away.

Marquette did not rally at St. Francis Xavier, to the extent he had expected. Fretting continuously with a desire to be again at work among the simple Illinois tribesmen, who had clamored for his return, the good father was obliged to remain thirteen months in enforced idleness. At last, consent having arrived from his superior, he ventured forth at the close of the season, although still but a physical wreck.

Starting from De Pere on the 25th of October (1674), with two French servants, he experienced a cold, stormy voyage of a month along the Wisconsin coast, and early in December entered Chicago River, " which was frozen to the depth of half a foot." His ailment, a chronic dysentery, returned in vigor, and he was obliged to pass the remainder of a peculiarly severe winter in a wretched cabin erected by his men, " near the portage, 2 leagues up the river." In April, scarcely able to sit in his canoe, he nevertheless persisted in penetrating to the great village of the Illinois, near the present city of Peoria, where " he was received as an angel from Heaven." But his disease increased in severity, soon impelling him to hurry back either to De Pere or Mackinac in order to obtain from his brethren the last sacrament. His servants carried him tenderly by way of the Chicago portage and down the east side of Lake Michigan, that the canoe might gain advantage of the north-setting current which sweeps that shore ; but the dying missionary finally yielded up his life on the 18th of April (1675), at their camp near the site of the modern Michigan town of Ludington, and was there buried. The following year a party of Mackinac Indians reverently visited the grave of their black-gown friend, and with native ceremonial removed his bones to St. Ignace. To-day these relics are divided between the old church at St. Ignace and the Jesuit university in Milwaukee, which latter is proud to bear his name.

It is idle in our day to inquire to whom should be awarded the greatest credit for the discovery of the Mississippi, — De Soto in the South, or Radisson or La Salle or the heroes of our present chapter, in the north. Nothing came of the De Soto expedition; it was as inconsequent as the landing of Leif, son of Eric, at the North American Vineland, nearly five centuries before the coming of Columbus. If Radisson's journal be rightly interpreted as indicating his early visitation to the Mississippi, that chance voyage was equally fruitless for civilization. La Salle's possible priority of presence on the great river was far more significant than that of Radisson or De Soto; but the claim in his behalf is based on the merest surmise.

There is some reason to believe that an inquisitive Virginian traveler, Abraham Wood, may, previous to 1670, have penetrated as far westward as the Mississippi — indeed, the story of early English exploration in the trans-Alleghany has yet to be written; but even if the tale be accepted, nothing came of Wood's exploit.

Jolliet and Marquette went about their famous task unsuspecting possible European predecessors. So far as they knew, the region was a mysterious wilderness, untrodden by white men. Persistently and systematically they sought information concerning it, and proceeded upon their journey in the spirit and the manner of true explorers. They wrote their narratives with care, and prepared excellent maps for publication, and the announcement of their discovery at once resulted in the opening of the re-

gion to commerce, missionary enterprise, and settlement. They were as much the real discoverers
of the Mississippi as was Columbus of the New
World.

CHAPTER III

FRENCH EXPLOITATION

WE have seen that Nicolet piloted the way to
Wisconsin. Radisson and Groseilliers, and doubtless many another adventurer now unknown, proved
the capabilities of the fur-trade in the broad region
westward of Lake Michigan. With that zealous
fortitude that makes men martyrs, the Jesuit missionaries here planted seed that was slow of growth
and uncertain as to fruit, but through the medium
of the much-thumbed " Relations " they familiarized Europeans with this heathen wilderness. Jolliet and Marquette opened a highway through the
land, and showed the Fox-Wisconsin route to be
in many respects the most feasible path to the interior of the continent. Their adventure practically
closed the era of exploration ; the period of French
occupation promptly followed.

In June, 1671, two years before the departure
of the expedition of discovery from Mackinac,
Saint-Lusson, a political agent of New France,
with much ceremony took possession at Sault Ste.
Marie, in the name of King Louis, of the entire
Western country. In the fashion of the day, his
procès-verbal was broad enough in its terms to em-

brace all lands "as well discovered as to be discovered, which are bounded on the one side by the
Northern and Western Seas and on the other side
by the South Sea including all its length or
breadth."[1] In his train were several Jesuit missionaries, including Dablon and Allouez; but perhaps the most interesting character in this little
company at the Sault was their guide and interpreter, Nicolas Perrot.

It is known that Perrot, following closely the
footsteps of Radisson and Groseïlliers, had wandered into Wisconsin as early as 1665, when but
twenty-one years of age. As a fur-trader, he attained remarkable influence over the wild tribes,
which power was frequently utilized by the Quebec
government in winning over Northwest Indians
to the acceptance of French exploitation of their
country. Twenty years later (1685) he was appointed French "commandant of the West;"
doubtless, as was generally the case on the frontiers of New France, wholly maintaining himself
and his small corps of twenty soldiers from the
profits of his trade with the natives.

Through the winter of 1685–86 we find Perrot
quartered in a little log stockade on the eastern
bank of the Mississippi, near the modern village of
Trempealeau, exchanging Paris-made beads, brass
and silver ornaments, and tools and arms of iron
for the buffalo and other fur peltries brought to

[1] Text in *Wisconsin Historical Collections*, vol. xi.

his gates by the bargain-loving Sioux. Others of his fortified trading-posts were Fort Perrot, on the Minnesota side of Lake Pepin, Fort Nicolas, in the outskirts of the Prairie du Chien of to-day, and one lower down the Mississippi to guard a lead mine near Galena, which he discovered and worked. The beautiful silver ostensorium which in 1686 he presented to the Jesuit mission at De Pere, has, after some curious adventures, at last found a resting place in the museum of the Wisconsin Historical Society at Madison, where it is treasured as probably the oldest historical relic in the trans-Alleghany, that bears upon it a contemporaneously engraved date.

Perrot appears to have been a man of excellent character, of unusual bravery and enterprise, and to have displayed rare diplomatic capacity in treating with the Indians of the Northwest; but he was, also, the victim of violent passions, and ruled his turbulent wards after the manner of an Asiatic despot. His haughty temper, while doubtless in general a source of strength to a man in his rude situation, sometimes brought him into trouble, and among his many thrilling adventures were not infrequent attempts upon his life; more than once he narrowly escaped death by torture at the stake. In the closing year of the seventeenth century the uprising of the Fox Indians led, as we shall see, to the withdrawal of French garrisons from the Western posts, and Perrot returned to the lower country a poor man. His military expenses had far outrun his fur-trading profits, a not unusual experience among the captains of the great Louis who were serving him upon the far-away frontiers of North America.

Another French adventurer whose name is closely linked with that of early Wisconsin was Robert Cavelier, Sieur de la Salle, one of the most remarkable characters in our Western history. In partnership with officials at Quebec and Montreal, he conducted a far-reaching but seldom profitable fur-trade with the savages of the interior, and incident to the extension of the bounds of that commerce won lasting repute as an explorer.

After some experience as a Jesuit novice in France, where he was born of a wealthy Rouen family, La Salle had come to Canada in 1666, when but twenty-three years of age. Befriended by Governor Frontenac, a man of lofty ambition but of kindly nature, young La Salle promptly entered upon the one field in New France that gave promise to a fellow of spirit, that of explorer and fur-trader. Hard study made him master of several of the difficult Indian dialects, and an expert in savage customs and methods. He was soon wandering widely upon hunting and prospecting trips, with both native and French companions. It has been claimed, but not proven, that in 1671 he was, earliest of known white men, at the Falls of the Ohio (Louisville), and about that time discovered the Mississippi.

In 1673 he first set out upon the several recorded expeditions toward and in the Mississippi
basin, that have made his name one of the most
famous in American history. In that year, as
Frontenac's representative and partner, he established the fur-trading post of Fort Frontenac
(Kingston) at the outlet of Lake Ontario. After
a voyage to France, seeking royal favor and encouragement, we find him in 1676 strengthening
this fort, and building vessels for trade upon the
lake. The following year he was again in France,
receiving from the king a patent of minor nobility
and a license to conduct a far Western trade in
buffalo wool and skins, as well as to build posts in
the valley of the Mississippi, concerning which
Jesuit reports of the adventures of Jolliet and
Marquette had greatly quickened public interest.
But in his operations in that wonderful land,
"through which would seem that a passage to
Mexico can be found," the Sieur de la Salle was
cautioned not to involve the crown in expense, nor
trade with tribes trafficking direct with the settlements on the lower St. Lawrence. Like Perrot, he
was to recoup himself from his fur-trade monopoly
in the region to be explored.

Better than any royal license, however, was his
acquisition of a lieutenant in the person of Henri de
Tonty, a young Italian soldier of fortune, who had
lost his right hand at the battle of Libisso, and
thereafter wore one of metal, which he kept gloved.

Tonty's was a bold, adventurous spirit, like that of his chief; but, unlike his cold, hard, and domineering leader, who had few friends, the Italian was of a tactful, sunny temperament. Under the thousand trying circumstances incident to wilderness travel, he only of the two could hold their followers together.

La Salle and Tonty arrived at Niagara in January, 1679, with material, supplies, and crew for a ship to be constructed above the cataract, for the navigation of the upper lakes. In the first week of August the Griffon sailed, and in twenty days arrived at Mackinac, to the consternation of the free-traders assembled there, for La Salle's wholesale and organized methods seemed to spell ruin to the calling of the *coureurs de bois*. At an island rendezvous in or near Green Bay the vessel found a rich cargo of peltries awaiting her, gathered by La Salle's buyers, who had preceded him to Wisconsin. Clearly he was here violating the terms of his agreement with the king, for the Ottawa and other tribes around the foot of Lake Michigan were certainly in the habit of trading direct to Montreal. However, the question was never raised; for soon thereafter the Griffon was, with her entire freightage, lost in a gale on the great lake.

La Salle and Tonty having themselves left the vessel on its approach to Green Bay, it was many months before they heard of the disaster. With fourteen men, the former voyaged up Lake Michigan along the Wisconsin shore, while Tonty led a like contingent by the east bank. The two parties, reuniting at St. Josephs River, descended to Illinois River by the Kankakee portage, and celebrated New Year's Day (1680) at the great village of the Illinois on Peoria Lake, where Marquette had ministered six years before.

Here Fort Crèvecœur was built, with Tonty in command, and late in February La Salle returned to Fort Frontenac for supplies to fit out a vessel for the exploration of the lower Mississippi. A few days before his departure he dispatched a small party to report upon the upper waters of that river. This branch expedition was headed by Michel Accau and his lieutenant, Antoine Augel, in their company being Father Louis Hennepin, a Franciscan friar, who was consumed by a most unchurchly appetite for roving and for wild adventure. It was customary in New France, as we have seen, for priests to accompany explorers, in order not only to meet their spiritual needs, but to instruct such heathen aborigines as might be encountered. Hennepin was not only the pastor but the journalist of the expedition; indeed, this first Western enterprise of La Salle is largely known to us through the medium of Hennepin's narrative. The lively but sadly braggart and often unveracious account of the friar's many remarkable experiences, which lost nothing in the telling, was published two years later in France, and became one of the most widely-read books of the day. Well it might; for despite glaring inaccuracies it remains one of the most valuable, as it is one of the most entertaining, contemporary records of travel and observation in seventeenth-century North America.

Accau's party reached the Falls of St. Anthony, the site of the modern Minneapolis, some five hundred miles above the mouth of Illinois River. Taken prisoners by the Sioux, who objected to the intrusion, they were kindly treated by their captors; but, as not infrequently was the case in Indian camps, food was sometimes so scarce that the Frenchmen were inadequately nourished. After extended wanderings in northwestern Wisconsin and northeastern Minnesota, they were rescued by Tonty's cousin, Daniel Greysolon Duluth, who, with a small band of followers, was then trading among the Sioux in behalf of Frontenac. Duluth accompanied the explorers down the Mississippi, and by way of the Fox-Wisconsin route to Mackinac, where the Jesuits entertained them until spring, when they could proceed down the lakes to Niagara and Fort Frontenac.

In a later work (1697), published after La Salle's death, Hennepin unblushingly claimed that his party — he always pretended to be the leader — had, during their sojourn on the Mississippi, not only explored its upper waters, but descended the great river to its mouth, thus preceding La Salle himself by two years. But this impossible tale was soon discredited, as it should be, and Hennepin's last ten years were spent in neglect and obscurity.

The gallant Tonty had an unfortunate experience during the absence of his chief. Most of his men, corrupted by rival fur-traders, deserted during the spring and summer. When a large force of Iroquois raiders appeared before his new fort of St. Louis, on Starved Rock, a high cliff on the Illinois River, he had but four white companions. With these he retreated to Lake Michigan, descending along the Wisconsin coast to the Jesuit mission at De Pere, which was reached in December. At the same time, La Salle, well stocked with supplies, was advancing up the Michigan coast to his lieutenant's relief, but missed him. On reaching the Illinois the leader found nothing but traces of disaster, and retired to his fort on the St. Josephs.[1] The next spring (1681) he had news of his distressed companions and rejoined them at Mackinac, whence the reunited party returned to their base at Fort Frontenac.

In August, with credit now stretched to the utmost, for his disasters had resulted in debts of enormous proportions, La Salle again ventured forth into the West, with Tonty and a party of

[1] La Salle's Fort Miami, built in 1679, was at the mouth of St. Josephs River, where it debouches into Lake Michigan. The later French and English fort on the St. Josephs was sixty miles up stream, near the present South Bend, Indiana, and guarded the portage of half a league to the Kankakee.

fifty-two others. In two sections they reached the
Illinois by both the Kankakee and Chicago portages, and entered the Mississippi on February 6
(1682). On March 9, while among the Arkansas,
— Jolliet and Marquette's southern limit, — the
great adventurer formally took possession for his
sovereign of the entire Mississippi basin, a ceremony repeated with great solemnity on April 9 at
one of the mouths of the Mississippi.

But the lower reaches were found to be unhealth-
ful, food was scarce, the Indians hostile, and for
forty days La Salle lay ill with malarial fever.
Once more the expedition dragged its way back to
far-away Mackinac. With the coming of autumn,
however, the commercial explorers were again on
the march and descended to their old haunts on
Illinois River, where, amid a population of six
thousand natives, they for a year conducted a
gainful trade in buffalo hides.

But there had been a change in the political control of New France. La Salle's fur-trade partner,
Frontenac, was replaced as governor by La Barre,
who disliked and sought to ruin the austere and
ambitious fur-trader who dreamed of a great commercial empire in the West. When La Salle was
on his way in the autumn of 1683 to visit, and if
possible to propitiate, the new governor, he met
along the east coast of Lake Michigan Chevalier
de Baugis, who had been dispatched to seize La
Salle's forts and succeed him as military command-

ant in the Illinois. With more tact than he was
accustomed to display, the latter sent by De Baugis
a note to Tonty to yield gracefully, and soon La
Barre's traders were monopolizing the district.

On reaching Quebec, La Salle, paying slight attention to the governor, departed at once for France
to lay his case before the throne. Hennepin's first
book, with its glowing reports of Canada and the
vast interior, was just then being eagerly read by
court and people. The great explorer, freshly returned from the farthest wilds of that wonderful
land, was everywhere welcomed, and found eager
audiences. The king promptly ordered La Barre
to restore to the adventurer his several forts, —
Frontenac, St. Josephs, and St. Louis. The hero
of the day was further authorized to found colonies
throughout the broad tract then known as Louisiana, and to wield military control all the way from
Lake Michigan to the Gulf of Mexico. To assist
him in carrying out this imperial enterprise, the
court sent with him four ships and four hundred
men.

Exultantly La Salle left Rochelle (July 24,
1684), heading an expedition at last befitting his
lofty ambition. But a bitter quarrel soon arose between him and Beaujeu, his principal ship captain.
The Spanish captured one of the vessels ; the other
three, through lack of good charts, failed to find
the mouth of the Mississippi and rendezvoused to
the westward, in Matagorda Bay (January, 1685).

Here one of the ships was soon wrecked. In miserable plight the leader landed his ill-equipped pioneers, most of their tools having been lost with the vessel, and built another Fort St. Louis. Beaujeu now left the wretched colony to its fate, and sailed home to France in one of the two remaining ships; later in the year, the last of the craft was lost in a wreck.

The strength of the squalid and fever-stricken settlement, feeble at best, was soon wasted in expeditions through the neighboring forests and swamps, in vain search for the great river's mouth. Desertions were frequent, a mutinous spirit arose, disorder was rampant. Early in January (1687), the commander and sixteen ragged, half-starved, and for the most part desperate followers, set out for Canada overland, leaving behind them about twenty men to garrison the little palisaded fort. On March 19, on Trinity River, La Salle, whose harsh and overbearing temper had made him bitterly hated by the majority, was murdered by some of the disaffected, who fled into the wilderness, leaving his handful of friends to pursue their way as best they might. These eventually reached Starved Rock, whence the grieved and despairing Tonty had dispatched numerous toilsome expeditions to find the chief to whom he himself appears to have been passionately devoted. Outfitted by the lieutenant, the miserable refugees at last reached Mackinac and Quebec. Two years later Spanish ex-

plorers, coming overland from Mexico, discovered
the ruins of Fort St. Louis on Matagorda Bay.
Several of the garrison had been killed by Indians
and the rest imprisoned ; these latter were promptly
ransomed by the Spanish, thus closing one of the
most tragic chapters in the checkered story of
American exploration.

We have alluded to the fortunate meeting between Duluth, the cousin of Tonty, and Father
Hennepin's exploring party, captive among the
Sioux. Duluth was a picturesqne personage in our
history. Born about 1647, in a little village near
Paris, he was in his youth a member of the Royal
Guard, a command composed exclusively of gentle-
men, and later won a captaincy in the marines, to
which corps was committed the military protection
of French colonies. Retiring from this service, on
half pay, Duluth entered the broader field of the
fur-trade, and in the autumn of 1678 left Montreal
for the far West. For several years he wandered
and trafficked among the Sioux, Assiniboin, and
other tribes beyond Lake Superior.

It was while thus roving that in June, 1680, he,
with four men in his employ, ascended the Bois
Brulé from Lake Superior, and portaged over to
Upper St. Croix Lake, the headwaters of St. Croix
River. Arriving at the mouth of the latter, he heard
of the French prisoners, and descending the Mississippi for some two hundred and forty miles visited the camp of the captors, there meeting Accau,

Augel, and Hennepin. The friar he had possibly met in Holland, six years before, at the fierce battle of Seneffe, wherein Hennepin was an almoner and Duluth a squire to the Marquis de Lassay. The fur-trader's dominance over his savage customers was well evinced in his ability to secure the release of his countrymen, whom, as we have seen, he escorted to Mackinac by way of the Fox-Wisconsin route.

While at Mackinac, Duluth learned that he had incurred the enmity of officials on the lower St. Lawrence. He was accused of being a *coureur de bois*, and of heading a combination of nearly eight hundred free-traders roaming through the upper country. What was still worse, he was said to be trading with the English, who, from Albany as their commercial base, were now boldly operating along the Ohio River and its branches. By means of higher prices and better goods, they were attracting a large share of the native trade which New France deemed to be legally and morally hers.

This news determined Duluth to go to France and have it out with the minister of the marine. He appears to have convinced this official that he was a regular trader, that he had at his own expense won the Indians over to favor French dominion, and that up to this time his followers had been an insignificant handful. He returned to Canada with license to traffic among the Sioux by way of Wisconsin River, and to their country he at once repaired; although La Salle vainly protested that the Wisconsin was clearly within his own assigned territory, and might not properly be invaded by a rival merchant.

In the first week of May, 1683, Duluth was again at La Baye (the Green Bay of our time), with thirty men, and valiantly helped to defend that place — apparently the mission stockade at De Pere — against an incursion of the Iroquois, just then raiding the tribesmen who had fled to Wisconsin from the neighborhood of Lake Huron. Thence proceeding to the north shore of Lake Superior, he built forts near Lake Nepigon and at the mouth of the Pigeon; the latter being called Kaministiquia, and afterwards serving as the eastern base of a long line of fortified places by way of Lake Winnipeg and the Saskatchewan, collectively called the "Post of the Western Sea." By means of this cordon, the French sought commercially to connect Lake Superior and the Pacific Ocean, overland: hoping thus to cut off interior trade from the English Hudson's Bay Company, which strenuously claimed the "whole, entire, and only liberty of Trade and Traffick" in the vast northwestern wilderness which the English then called "Rupert's Land."

Three years later (1686) we find Duluth erecting a fort near Detroit, to bar the proposed entrance of English traders into the upper lakes. Thereafter, he was prominently connected with

various French military enterprises between Detroit and Montreal, several of them involving rare
enterprise and daring. He died in 1709, the victim
of diseases induced by prolonged hardships suffered in behalf of New France, no doubt well earning the encomium of Governor Vaudreuil, who,
in notifying the government at Versailles of the
decease of this battered veteran of the frontier,
declared that " He was a very honest man."

Another Frenchman to leave his mark on the
pages of Wisconsin history was Pierre Charles le
Sueur. Coming from France to Canada in his
youth, he also joined the ranks of the Western fur-
trade adventurers. As early as 1683, ten years
after Jolliet and Marquette, we hear of his jour-
neying from Mackinac to the Mississippi over the
Fox-Wisconsin route, ascending to St. Anthony's
Falls, whither Hennepin had preceded him by
three years, and trafficking with the Sioux about
the headwaters of the Mississippi.

In 1689 Le Sueur, then prominent among the
licensed traders of the Northwest, and evidently a
man of talent and unusual enterprise, was one of
the witnesses to Perrot's act of taking possession
for France of the region of the upper Mississippi,
on Lake Pepin. Four years later (1693), by order
of Governor Frontenac, he built a stockaded fort
on Madelaine Island, in Chequamegon Bay, overlooking the site of Radisson's landfall of twenty-
four years previous, and another long fortress on

an island in the Mississippi, some eight miles below the mouth of the St. Croix. The purpose of these posts was to keep open for French trade, as against possible raids by the now rebellious Fox Indians, the Bois Brulé–St. Croix route, Duluth's favorite highway between Lake Superior and the great river. This Mississippi River fort soon became an important rendezvous for tribesmen having furs to offer for barter, and is alluded to by the Jesuit historian Charlevoix as "a centre of commerce for the Western parts, and many French of Canada pass the winter here, because it is a good country for hunting."

Thus far, Le Sueur had been strong in favor with Frontenac, but in time their commercial interests clashed, and friction naturally arose. In 1697 the former had obtained from the ministry permission to work certain lead mines and colored earths on the Mississippi and copper deposits on Lake Superior, which he had discovered. Delay in the execution of his project, however, resulted from the capture by an English fleet of the vessel on which he was returning to New France, and he was imprisoned in England until the conclusion of King William's War, later in the year. When released, he obtained a new royal commission (1698) and again started for Canada. Frontenac, then all-powerful, now represented to the court that these mines were too far away from the lower St. Lawrence to be of any use to Canada ; that Le Sueur could support himself in that distant country only through a license to trade in beaver skins, there being no small game; and if he did this it would exclude others from that profitable traffic. "I think," slyly suggests the governor to the minister of marine, "that the only mines he seeks in those regions are mines of beaver skins."

Thus repulsed by the Canadian authorities, Le Sueur again went to France and obtained fresh permission from the court to go out to America; this time to join his gallant relative, Iberville, who, in February, 1699, had founded at Biloxi the new colony of Louisiana, which La Salle had failed to establish.

Le Sueur arrived in Louisiana during the first week of December. At the head of twenty-nine prospectors and miners he was promptly dispatched up the Mississippi by Iberville, to investigate more fully the deposits of metal and colored earths concerning which he had reported. After visiting mines in Illinois, near the present Galena, and having numerous conferences with the Indians, the adventurers passed the mouth of Wisconsin River on the first of September (1700). Later they ascended to the Falls of St. Anthony and built a wintering fort on Blue River, a branch of the Minnesota, a league above the present town of Mankato. Here they conducted a profitable fur-trade with the Sioux, and discovered what Le Sueur took to be a copper deposit. Some three thousand

pounds of this supposed ore were transported in
their slender craft to Biloxi, which was reached in
February, 1702. But, like the miners at Jamestown colony, in the previous century, Le Sueur
was doomed to disappointment; for on arrival in
France the cargo that had cost so much to procure
proved to be but worthless greensand. This practically closed the career of the now discredited Le
Sueur; eight years later he died, while crossing the
ocean. However, the lead deposits discovered by
him in northwestern Illinois, and probably in
southwestern Wisconsin and in adjacent districts
to the west of the Mississippi, continued to be
worked at intervals throughout the French régime,
being of the highest importance to the fur-trade of
the entire Mississippi basin; for without bullets
the firearms of the white men were of small avail.

Conditions of life under the French régime
upon the rude frontiers of Canada and Louisiana
— and we shall see that southwestern Wisconsin
was, for a time, considered a part of the latter province — were such as to foster strong personalities.
Conspicuous among them was Louis-Armand de
Lom d'Arce, known to history as Baron de Lahontan. His father was a famous French engineer in
Gascony, whose once ample fortunes had, about the
time of his son's birth (1666), been wasted through
legal strife, so that the boy inherited only a title
and a shattered estate. When but seventeen years
of age he went out to Canada as a petty officer in

a company of the marine corps sent from France to chastise the turbulent Iroquois. Engaged in two rather exciting Iroquois campaigns, the young Gascon acquired a close knowledge of Indian languages and customs, and won repute as a fellow of spirit. Despite his caustic temper and his cordial hatred of the priests, — he was an avowed agnostic, — he came to be regarded as a valuable man-at-arms, particularly when engaged upon somewhat desperate enterprises. At heart he was a wanderer, as well as a cynic, and the ready victim of ennui.

Dispatched in 1687 to command the little stockade of Fort St. Joseph, "at the strait of Lakes Huron and Erie," — one of Duluth's chain of forts, — Lahontan went out in the company of Duluth and Tonty, who tarried with him a few days at his new station, the two cousins then disappearing into the farthest West. For a year the restless commandant, paying little heed to his post, roamed through the region of Mackinac and Sault Ste. Marie, ostensibly in search of corn for his garrison, among the Indians, but really in quest of adventure. Late in the summer of 1688 he declared St. Joseph untenable because of Iroquois encroachment, and abandoning the fort retreated with his detachment to Mackinac.

From here, so he claimed in after years, he made, in the autumn and winter following, an extended journey with his men and some Indian allies westward to Green Bay, over the Fox-Wisconsin route

to the Mississippi, and a long distance up an alleged
westerly affluent of the Mississippi, which he called
River Long. On this apocryphal river, which cor-
responds to no stream on the maps of to-day,
Lahontan claims to have visited the wonderful nations of Eokoros, Esanapes, and Gnacsitares, from
whom he learned of still other strange tribes beyond, and of a river flowing westward into a large
salt lake. That he actually was at Green Bay and
on Fox River, there seems no reason to doubt;
but relative to the Wisconsin and the country westward, his published account is vague, and evidently
based on second-hand information.

Leaving these nations of the West, whose idyl-
lic life he describes in glowing terms, which may
have given a hint to Swift for "Gulliver's Travels,"
Lahontan reports that he and his companions descended to the Mississippi, reached Lake Michigan
by way of the Illinois-Chicago route, and returned
to Mackinac; whence — and this is established history — the commandant, in the company of some
Ottawa savages, proceeded to Montreal in canoes,
by way of Ottawa River. The following autumn
(1690) his friend Frontenac sent him to France,
with dispatches reporting the withdrawal of the
discomfited English from the St. Lawrence. Two
years later he was again ordered to France, to present at Versailles in person a sagacious plan of his
own invention, for defending the upper-lake region
from the Iroquois. His vessel stopping at New-

foundland en route, he was conspicuous in repulsing a British naval attack on Plaisance, and once
more was the bearer of welcome news to the ministry.

Overlooking his cherished scheme for guarding
the upper country, the court ordered him back to
Newfoundland as lieutenant of the king for that
island and Acadia, a highly honorable but to him
distasteful task; for his heart was in the free, roving life of the Western frontier. At Plaisance he
quarreled with the governor, De Brouillon, who
seems to have been almost insanely jealous of the
young lieutenant who had been thrust upon him.
Pretending to be in danger of his life, the latter
fled in a fishing vessel to Portugal, and was thereafter an exile from France, for his government
would not countenance this desertion of a post of
duty.

In 1703 the poor fugitive, beset by ill fortune,
drifted between Portugal, Holland, Germany, and
England, and published his "Voyages to North
America." It was a racy work of travel and philo-
sophical reflection, filled to the brim with well-told,
stirring adventures among a people and in a land
concerning which there was then universal curiosity; it abounded, also, in satirical references to the
governments and priests of Europe, and throughout
breathed the fierce spirit of a social democrat and
religious agnostic. The vogue of this heterodox but
fascinating publication was immediate and wide-

spread; its various editions in several European languages must, if properly managed, soon have replenished his slender purse. Dying about 1715, the closing years of this unfortunate adventurer were marked by ill health and popular neglect, save that a few choice spirits, like the philosopher Leibnitz, at Hanover, held him in high esteem.

It has long been the fashion for historians to condemn Lahontan's book as a tissue of falsities; but with the one exception of his fanciful account of the country and people of the River Long — which he seems to have introduced as a medium for lampooning the European civilization of his time — the " Voyages " constitutes one of the most valuable contemporary descriptions of the North American wilderness in the later decades of the seventeenth century; for this reason, deserving far better treatment than it has been accorded. Further, as laying bare to us the heart and motives of one of the most gallant and picturesque of early American adventurers, it is a human document of the greatest value.

CHAPTER IV

In their exploitation of Wisconsin, through which lay diagonally the favorite Fox-Wisconsin trade route between the upper Great Lakes and the upper waters of the Mississippi, it must not be supposed that the French were meeting with no aboriginal opposition. Instead, Fox Indians long pestered commercial operations by the Canadians; in the end their enmity brought about a condition of affairs that did much to disrupt French dominion over the continental interior.

The royal charters of English colonies on the Atlantic coast, in the easy land-grabbing temper of European monarchs of that time, carried their bounds indefinitely westward. At first, however, Englishmen, busy in settling the coastal plain, cared little for the hinterland, which was not yet needed. Meanwhile, the adventurous French, pushing their inquiring way up the Ottawa, early reached the upper Great Lakes. We have seen Champlain's commercial agent, Nicolet, setting foot in Wisconsin and learning of the great Mississippi, at a time when the Mayflower child was but a lad of fourteen; Radisson, early exploring the Lake Superior

region; Saint-Lusson, Perrot, and La Salle, by supreme right of discovery, each in his turn, formally taking possession of the entire Mississippi
basin for the king of France; Jolliet and Marquette, Duluth, Hennepin, and Le Sueur exploring
vast areas heretofore unknown to Europeans; Jesuit
missionaries building bark chapels and rearing
huge log crosses in the widely-scattered villages of
the tribesmen; fur-traders ranging everywhere to
the west of the mountains; military commandants
building cordons of log posts along vast stretches
of connecting lakes and rivers; and even mines of
lead and copper being worked in the name of
France.

Not only in Canada: but with the coming of
Iberville there was founded the southern province
of Louisiana, which, joining hands with New France
on the north, now claimed French mastery over the
whole of the trans-Alleghany. And it seemed in all
fairness, despite paper claims by the English, to
belong to the great Louis, by virtue of both discovery and occupation. His ambitious scheme of
North American empire needed for its validity,
however, in that predatory age, the backing of
power; and France in America was lamentably
weak. The entire population of New France was
at the time of King William's War (1689–97)
not greater than twelve thousand, whereas New
England and New York alone supported a hundred
thousand inhabitants — although it must be said

that the English colonists were torn by dissensions and their militia system lacked organization; whereas New France possessed in her hardy peasantry a well-trained fighting corps that might readily be mobilized.

But Quebec and New Orleans were separated by a vast wilderness, only laboriously to be traversed by canoes and batteaux; the little waterside stockades were for the most part days distant from each other, and looked more formidable on the map than in reality; much dependence was placed on Indian support, but in need the savages often proved but fair weather allies. Moreover, the officials of New France and Louisiana were often at loggerheads, with conflicting trade and military interests, and with ill-defined bounds to their respective provinces. For a time, it was claimed that Louisiana extended northward to the mouth of the Wisconsin; at others, New France governed not only all of Wisconsin, but the whole of the Illinois country. Almost universal official corruption, also, was a besetting weakness in the over-sea dominions of the king; and this was encouraged by the penurious folly, long persisted in, of obliging explorers and military commandants to recoup themselves from the fur-trade of their several districts. Opposition to the exacting fur-trade monopoly bred hundreds of free-traders, who lawlessly roamed the farthest streams and forests with bands of half-savage retainers; seeking better prices and cheaper goods, these rovers oftentimes carried peltries to thrifty English merchants operating from either Albany or Hudson Bay, whose commerce with Western savages it was the policy of France to repress at every hazard.

Plymouth was about sixty years old before Americans on the seaboard, slowly spreading into the western uplands, began to bestir themselves relative to their claims beyond the Alleghanies. In 1686 Governor Denonville of New France reported to Versailles that New York was displaying "pretensions which extend no less than from the lakes, inclusive, to the South Sea [Pacific] ; " and that traders from that province had already penetrated to Mackinac to purchase furs from "our Outawas and Huron Indians, who received them cordially on account of the bargains they gave." But Denonville's plea that such irregularities should harshly be checked, was vain. As usual, Versailles waited.

During the next thirty years English explorers and traders, with *Wanderlust* at last strongly developed within them, advanced boldly through the trans-Alleghany, as far south as the Creek tribes, all through the Ohio basin, and even to the upper lakes. Duluth's strongholds could not stem their progress. In 1721 Governor Keith of Pennsylvania desired the lords of trade at London to "fortify the passes on the back of Virginia," also to build forts upon the Great Lakes, in order to "interrupt the French communication from Quebec to the River Mississippi." Official England would not hurry, however; she, also, played a waiting game. In due time, of growing strength came action, and France was compelled to release her weak hold upon the transmontane hinterland that American borderers to the east of the range, eager for new pastures as well as for trade with the Indians, had now come to demand as their heritage under the royal charters.

In this long and glowing struggle for racial supremacy on the North American continent, Wisconsin waterways and Wisconsin Indians played a significant part. It has been shown that French supremacy could not permanently exist in the interior of the continent without free communication by boat between the divergent drainage systems of the Great Lakes and the Mississippi River. Only by this means might New France and Louisiana be kept in touch, and their commercial and military expeditions maintained from the bases of Quebec, Montreal, and New Orleans. The Fox-Wisconsin trade route being early recognized as in many respects the most feasible connection between the two systems, Wisconsin was the keystone of the arch of French occupation, and thus essential to the integrity of the plan. Interruption of this highly strategic path to the Mississippi was bound to weaken the fabric by forcing Frenchmen to attempt other and less satisfactory portages —

from the lower lakes over into the Ohio, from Lake Michigan to the Illinois, or from Lake Superior to the upper Mississippi.

It is probable that the Fox Indians, then in control of the Fox River of Wisconsin, once dwelt in the valley of the St. Lawrence, but from various economic reasons slowly drifted westward together with other Algonquian peoples. We first hear of them, in historic times, in lower Michigan; but by 1665 Father Allouez met Foxes on Lake Superior, whither they had, like so many of their linguistic family, retreated before the advancing scourge of the Iroquois. But in fleeing to the protection of our inland lakes and rivers they had lost nothing of their independent, warlike temper. French traders and missionaries found them haughty, ungovernable, vengeful, and of stronger fibre than their neighbors.

Forest merchants of any race are quite apt to include men of vicious temperament. From a combination of untoward incidents the Foxes came bitterly to detest Frenchmen of this type, almost the only whites of their acquaintance. Moreover, these tribesmen were almost continually embroiled with the Sioux of the West, who also were born fighters. Frenchmen passing up Fox River, so called because the seat of the Foxes, were trafficking with the Sioux and carrying to the latter firearms which were being used against Fox warriors. It is small wonder, as the culmination of long-continued friction, that the Foxes sought at first to interrupt the trade of the obnoxious French, by levying toll; next, to close to the latter the gateway between East and West, of which they held the key; then to harry the Chippewa, Ottawa, and other tribes remaining in the French interest, and in time boldly to hold council with the French-hating Iroquois.

Duluth had contrived to keep these fiery savages on Fox River in some measure of control. The astute Perrot attained a considerable mastery over them. Nevertheless, the Jesuit mission at De Pere was burned to the ground in 1687, causing the black-gowns to retreat to Mackinac, and towards the close of the century the Fox-Wisconsin water-way became unsafe even for armed traders. It was for this reason that Le Sueur had been ordered (1693) to keep open Duluth's old route between Lake Superior and the Mississippi, via the Bois Brulé and the St. Croix.

With the death of Frontenac (1698), who had kept a strong hold upon the outlying military posts of New France, there came a period of govern-mental weakness, during which garrisons on the upper lakes were withdrawn. Emboldened by lax-ness, the Foxes carried matters with a high hand. In 1699, for instance, Father Saint-Cosme, a Sul-pician missionary bound for the Illinois, found the Fox-Wisconsin closed to him, and reported much plundering of such French traders as had been allowed to pass through. He was compelled to proceed with his little flotilla of canoes southward by the Wisconsin shore of Lake Michigan, stopping among the Potawatomi, probably at the site of the present Sheboygan, and visiting a considerable population of Mascoutin, Foxes, and Potawatomi on the shores of Milwaukee Bay. His journey was continued over the Chicago portage.

In the year of Saint-Cosme's adventure, orders were issued from Versailles to establish a fort at Detroit, under Antoine la Mothe, Sieur de Cadillac, its purpose being the familiar one, to prevent the Indian trade of the upper lakes from being won by Englishmen, whose allies were the dreaded Iroquois. It was just then a feature of French policy to concentrate the Western Indians in large numbers at Detroit, where they might be under surveillance and their trade confined to the French. At first the Foxes refused to go, but finally a large body of them yielded to continued solicitations (1710), and after a long march overland from Wisconsin planted themselves in a rather defiant mood before the gates of the little Michigan fortress. But Cadillac had by this time gone to be governor of Louisiana; his successor, Dubuisson, represented a different governmental policy, and was much annoyed by the turbulent strangers, whom he invited to return to Wisconsin — a wish converted into a command by Governor Vaudreuil. In the early months of 1712 the unheeding Foxes, now strongly fortified, were set upon by the combined Indians of several tribes, aided by the French, and in the course of nearly three weeks of active hostilities the greater part of the Wisconsin visitors suffered slaughter.

However, there were still many of their kind remaining in the forests of Wisconsin, and with much skill these organized a confederacy of neighboring tribes, which soon inaugurated a reign of terror for the French from Mackinac to the Mississippi. In 1715 Marchand de Lignery was sent out with an expedition designed to operate in two columns against La Baye. But the attempt was mismanaged, and a failure. It was followed next year by a more formidable party under La Porte de Louvigny, starting from Montreal and gathering strength from whites and reds as it proceeded up the lakes, overawing the Iroquois on the way. Composed at last of eight hundred men, the column worked its toilsome way up and around the rapids of the lower Fox River, and found the Foxes intrenched near Petit Lake Butte des Morts. Louvigny's two small cannon and a grenade-mortar had slight effect on the moated palisade of the savages, who defended themselves with much military skill, and finally secured quite favorable terms of surrender; practically buying themselves off for the time, with the opportunities for a profitable trade in beaver skins, which they afforded the French invaders.

The only lasting result for French arms was the

establishment at La Baye (in 1717) of the first permanent fort at that early outpost of New France. No doubt the Jesuit mission at De Pere was surrounded by the usual palisade for the protection of the little company of whites against marauding tribesmen. It is fair to presume, however, that the more formidable fortification now erected was placed at some point lower down the Fox; probably on or at least near the west side site, a half league above the river mouth, whereon we know that in later days were built successive outposts of France, Great Britain, and the United States.

No sooner had the thrifty Louvigny withdrawn than the neighborhood confederacy rapidly grew into a widespread aboriginal intrigue against French domination, which seems to have extended as far as the Chickasaw on the south and included the Sioux and Omaha of the trans-Mississippi plains; but the Illinois remained true to their French allegiance. The Sioux alliance with the crafty Foxes was particularly distressing to the officials of New France, for the trade of the former was of the greatest importance, and they held the Mississippi and the inland routes westward. Numerous overtures were made to them through the post on Chequamegon Bay, but for a long time without success.

The possibility of finding a water route through the American continent, by which Europe might be in close touch with eastern Asia, excited the

ambition of every New World explorer from Columbus until well along in the eighteenth century.
In 1720 the Jesuit historian and traveler, Father
Pierre François Xavier de Charlevoix, came to
New France to prospect for a suitable trade route
to the Pacific. He visited Wisconsin and the Illinois, and made to the government at Versailles
two suggestions: first, an expedition up the Missouri, thence to follow some westering waterway
to the ocean — the scheme which Lewis and Clark
realized eighty-five years later; second, to establish a line of fur-trade and missionary posts among
the Sioux, and thus gradually to creep into and
across the interior.

In accordance with this last proposition there
was constructed (1727) Fort Beauharnois, on the
Minnesota side of Lake Pepin, with René Boucher
de la Perrière in charge, and the Jesuits Guignas
and De Gonnor to look after the missionary field.
But a fresh uprising of the Foxes threatened to
cut these men off from their base on the St. Lawrence, and the post was soon abandoned — so also
the entire project for reaching western tidewater
by way of the trans-Mississippi plains.

Throughout the protracted troubles with the
Foxes, Western officials of New France did not
appear averse to Fox raids on the Illinois, thus destroying the fur-trade of upper Louisiana, so long
as their own beaver traffic at Detroit, Mackinac,
and La Baye was undisturbed. Royal commands

were issued in 1724, sharply directing that such
raids be punished; but without effect until four
years later, when Lignery, then considered the
most competent of the frontier officers, appeared
on Fox River with a considerable convoy, found
that the Foxes had retreated before him, burned
their villages and cornfields, and on his return
destroyed La Baye fort as no longer tenable — a
singularly futile expedition, in which Lignery has
been suspected of bad faith.

A new officer was then (1729) sent to the country of the Foxes, Pierre Paul la Perrière, Sieur
Marin, who soon displayed energetic ability, and
two years later rebuilt the stockade at La Baye.
The allies of the Foxes were now falling away, for
Indian conspiracies have seldom been of long duration, and this last was displaying undoubted signs of
weakness. Soon after Marin's arrival, a large body
of the unfortunate tribesmen appear to have attempted an escape to the Iroquois in the east, by
way of northern Illinois and Michigan. But they
were overtaken south of Lake Michigan, by hastily
summoned French commands from St. Josephs,
Miami, and the Illinois, and put to rout with great
loss of life.

In the winter of 1731–32, a band of mission
Indians from Canada were allowed to proceed to
Wisconsin and slaughter no less than three hundred of the miserable remnant of the Foxes, who
by this time seem to have completely lost their

allies. Kiala, head chief of the distracted nation, and evidently a man of unusual ability among them, now appeared at La Baye and freely offered his life that the remainder of his people might be spared. He might have saved himself the sacrifice; for De Villiers, now in command, triumphantly carried the poor headman to Montreal, whence he was transported to Martinique, where this once proud Demosthenes of the far northern forests became one of a chain-gang and soon fell a miserable victim to unaccustomed labor under a tropical sky.

It was thought that at last the Foxes had been brought to their knees. Disregarding the compact with Kiala, their complete extermination was promply ordered from headquarters in Montreal. But other tribes began to pity the weary Foxes and to see in their fate a presage of their own. Their kinsmen and neighbors the Sauk, in particular, harbored some of the fugitives. Upon De Villiers going among the former to ask that these be surrendered to the vengeance of the French, he and his youngest son were killed; the brother pursued the murderers and fought them for an entire day at their village near Lake Petit Butte des Morts, with heavy losses on both sides. Thereafter Sauk and Foxes, deserting the valley of the Fox, were as one nation; fresh allies sympathetically came to them from the West, and the fugitives took their stand in the lead-mine district of south-

west Wisconsin, along Rock River, and in eastern
Iowa. Their prestige, however, was never fully regained.

Henceforth Frenchmen had free passage over
the Fox-Wisconsin route, although there continued
until 1750 to be more or less serious trouble with
the recalcitrants, marked by the plunder and murder of traders within their country, and now and
then a flickering flame of outright rebellion. The
details we have not here space to follow, although
they are often of much interest.[1]

A tragedy of another sort attaches itself to La
Baye of this period. During the winter of 1749–50
the commandant of the fort, young Lieutenant
Pierre Mathurin, the Sieur Millon, who in 1744
had served as an ensign at Crown Point, was out
alone in a canoe on Green Bay and lost his life in
a squall.

By 1750, as a result of prompter and more efficient punitive expeditions from Mackinac, La
Baye, and the several forts on the upper Mississippi and in the Illinois, something like peace was
restored. Occasionally thereafter we find Sauk
and Foxes arrayed, with other large bodies of Wisconsin Indians, under the French standard, in
expeditions against English borderers and their
Indian allies. Under the skillful command of
young Charles Michel Langlade of Mackinac, by

[1] See L. P. Kellogg, "The Fox Indians during the French
Régime," in Wis. Hist. Soc. *Proceedings*, 1907.

this time famous throughout the West as both fur-trader and officer in the French militia, Sauk and Foxes joined with their neighbors in many a fierce foray, from Pickawillany (1752) to the death struggles before Quebec and Montreal (1759–60).

To the Western military officials of New France, the cessation of the prolonged and vexatious Fox War brought a sense of relief, and probably they looked forward to a long term of security. With the Fox-Wisconsin route open, the fur-trade at La Baye post once more became extremely profitable. As was the fashion in New France, Marin and his colleagues promptly proceeded to feather their own nests through the double medium of private trade and official thievery. No wonder Marin complacently declared that " peace is more profitable than war." In 1753, in token of his military efficiency, he was ordered to the Ohio to superintend the building of a chain of forts designed to restrain the rising tide of English exploitation of the West. Upon his retirement from La Baye, the post was leased to François de Rigaud, a brother of Governor Vaudreuil, who, at an enormous advance, promptly re-leased it to a company of traders.

In 1757, Captain Bougainville, aide-de-camp to General Montcalm, made a detailed report on the military status and resources of New France, in which he alluded to La Baye as " an established post. It is farmed for nine thousand francs, all at the cost of the lessee. The commandant (Coutrol, lieutenant) is an officer interested in the lease and who runs it for his own profit and that of his associates. He has two thousand francs of gratification." The Indians who assemble at the post to trade are the Sauk, Foxes, Winnebago, Mascoutin, Kickapoo, and the Sioux of the prairies and lakes. "There come from there," continues Bougainville, "in an ordinary year, five to six hundred packages" of furs.[1] Two years later (1759), for the family were thrifty, Rigaud obtained a life grant of the revenues of this profitable enterprise, which in the same season was advantageously leased to two merchant adventurers named Sieur Jacques Giasson and Ignace Hubert, whose compensation was to be a third of the profits.

The powers of New France were tested to their utmost in the seven years' titanic struggle for the mastery of our continental interior, which opened in 1754. In Acadia, along the St. Lawrence, and upon the back of the English frontier settlements of Pennsylvania and Virginia, the French and Indian War waged hottest. Wisconsin fur-traders, with following of half-breeds and savages from their several forest neighborhoods, hurried to the front and did effective service in a cause predestined to fail.

But the upper country itself again fell into neglect. The cherished cordon of forts, supposedly guarding the upper lakes and the Mississippi,

[1] Bougainville's memoir in *Wis. Hist. Colls.*, vol. xviii.

proved of small importance in this great crisis. The long and weary Fox insurrection had disrupted the coveted connections of the West, practically isolating Canada from Louisiana. There had been no time in which to recover, between the tribal subjugation culminating in 1750 and the outbreak of the greater contest with the English. France was irretrievably weakened at the arch of her inter-communication in the Northwest, a fact contributing in no small measure to her defeat; for she had lost the confidence of a large mass of her Western savage allies,[1] and, with the centre of her line of defense broken, could not long have withheld British attack in this quarter. With the lower St. Lawrence lost, the slender fabric of French occupation readily collapsed.

[1] In 1758, for instance, an outbreak of Menominee at La Baye resulted in the killing of several Frenchmen and the pillaging of the post.

CHAPTER V

As employed in the earliest contemporary French documents, the term "La Baye" was regional rather than local. It meant, at first, all of the far-stretching shore of the great western arm of Lake Michigan. Gradually, however, the name came to refer specifically to the six miles of Fox River bank, between the mouth of that stream and the De Pere rapids.[1] Although now two municipalities, this district should in any historical account of Wisconsin in the seventeenth and eighteenth centuries be considered as an entity; we shall not here attempt to distinguish between them. The boundaries of the modern cities of De Pere and Green Bay practically touch, and there is to-day a continuous line of prosperous settlement, urban and suburban, between the rapids and the river mouth.

La Baye lay at the entrance of the principal canoe route to the Mississippi. The presence of the rapids, the first interruption to the navigation

[1] In 1820, when the boundaries of French claims on Fox River were being established, the federal commissioner reported that those at Little Kaukauna, twelve miles above the fort, were also "considered to have been comprehended within the settlement of Green bay."

of the Fox, necessitated the portaging of canoes
and cargoes, bound either up or down; and as
usual at such obstructions, fish were abundant.
Both strategically and economically important, the
river banks hereabout undoubtedly were occupied
by aborigines long before the coming of the French,
who found this vicinity one of the most important
native trading centres of the Northwest. In consequence, white men trafficking for furs appear to
have early established themselves in the neighborhood — intermittently at first, but soon with some
approach to continuity.

After Father Allouez opened a Jesuit mission at
De Pere rapids (1671–72), particularly at the time
of Duluth's defense of the place in 1683, and the
coming of Perrot (1685) as military commandant
of the West, it is fair to assume that there was not
only a forest mission here, but at least a desultory
French trading settlement; undoubtedly feeble as
to numbers, but probably protected by a palisade.
The earliest documents of the French régime in the
upper country [1] not infrequently contain casual references to the presence at the mouth of the Fox
of adventurous traders; for instance, the lawless
company whom Allouez found on his arrival in the
winter of 1669–70, and the advance agents of La
Salle, who collected at La Baye (1679) the Griffon's rich cargo of Wisconsin furs. Certainly by
1717, when what appears to have been the first per-

[1] Published at length in *Wis. Hist. Colls.*, vols. xvi–xviii.

manent fort was erected near the river mouth, this far Western outpost of New France seems to have been fairly well planted.[1] During the protracted Fox War, life in Wisconsin was at times intolerable for Frenchmen, and they occasionally deserted La Baye; but it is evident, as related in the preceding chapter, that with each return of military protection white residence was resumed.

Practically every little waterside stockade designed to protect the interior fur-trade of New France was girt about by a tiny hamlet of *habitans:* boatmen, tillers of the soil, mechanics, according to bent or necessity. At the head of society in this rude settlement was the military commandant; next in social precedence the Jesuit father, whose tiny chapel usually lay just within the gate. Visiting the frontier fort were always wandering traders, each at the head of a band of rollicking voyageurs, jauntily clad in fringed buckskins and showy caps and scarfs, with a semi-savage display of bracelets, dangling earrings, and necklaces of beads. The *coureur de bois,* with his sprightly party of devil-may-care retainers, was not an infrequent caller, upon unheralded expeditions here and there through the dark woodlands and along sparkling waters. Freely mingling with this varied company

---

[1] A manuscript of 1718, in the Colonial Archives at Paris, published in *Wis. Hist. Colls.*, vol. xvi, p. 371, says of La Baye: "It is settled by the puants [Winnebago] and folleavoines [Menominee]; there are some French also."

were bands of half-naked, long-haired Indians and half-breeds, glistening with oils and tricked out with paint and feathers. Such a fortified trading colony was, no doubt, La Baye of the first two-thirds of the eighteenth century.

The combined genius of General Wolfe and Admiral Saunders had compelled the surrender of Quebec (September 17, 1759). This practically ended French dominion in North America; but New France at large, now grown to seventy-three thousand souls, was not actually abandoned until after the fall of Montreal (September 8, 1760).

Among the officers of the colony, assisting Governor Vaudreuil in the defense of Montreal, was Lieutenant Charles Langlade, then second in command at Mackinac. Five days before the surrender, Vaudreuil sent Langlade back to his fort, together with an Indian contingent from the upper lakes and two companies of deserters from the British army, on their way to Louisiana by way of Mackinac. He also carried with him Vaudreuil's instructions to the former's chief, Captain Louis de Beaujeu de Villemonde, to evacuate that post and retire to the Illinois, leaving Langlade in charge until the arrival of the British. Accordingly, in October, Beaujeu retired " with 4 officers, 2 cadets, 48 soldiers and 78 militia." It is probable that he picked up on the way whatever garrison may still have remained at La Baye. While on Rock River the party were caught in the ice, and obliged to

winter there among the Sauk and Foxes, from
whom they obtained supplies at exorbitant rates as
measured in trading goods belonging to Beaujeu
and his partners, for which the owners advanced a
claim against the French government amounting to
65,387 livres. It was six months before they arrived
at their destination.

Robert Rogers, prominent throughout the French
and Indian War as a daring and successful leader
of English provincial rangers, was sent up the
Great Lakes to enforce the capitulation of French
outposts in the West; and during the winter and
following year secured the transfer of Forts Miami
and Detroit.

From Detroit, Rogers dispatched Captain Henry
Balfour, of the Eightieth (Light-Armed Foot)
Regiment, to make similar visits to the posts on
Lakes Huron and Michigan — Mackinac, La Baye,
and St. Josephs; at each of which he was to leave
a small garrison of regulars from both his own
regiment and the Sixtieth (Royal American Foot).[1]
Lieutenant William Leslie, of the Sixtieth, was stationed at Mackinac with twenty-eight men, while
Balfour, accompanied by Ensign James Gorrell, a
young Marylander, also of the Sixtieth, continued
on to La Baye, where they arrived the 12th of Oc-

---

[1] Raised in 1757 for frontier service, chiefly among the English and German colonists in New York and Pennsylvania.
While mostly officered from Great Britain, several of the minor
officers were of American birth.

tober (1761), a year after Beaujeu's retreat, to find it almost deserted. Together with nearly all of their Indian neighbors, the French traders resident at the place had already left upon winter hunting parties up Fox River and as far west as the Sioux country.

At the end of two days Balfour left the ensign with a force of one sergeant, a corporal, fifteen privates, and a French interpreter, together with two British traders, one McKay of Albany and one Goddard of Montreal. Later, five additional Albany traders arrived and operated among Wisconsin Indians — Garrit Roseboom, Teunis Visscher, William Bruce, Cummin Shields, and Abraham Lansing; the last named being killed by two of his French employees.

It was a dismal outlook for poor Gorrell. The old and neglected French fort, which Balfour had promptly rechristened Edward Augustus, was " quite rotten, the stockade ready to fall, the houses without cover, our fire wood far off, and none to be got when the river closed." [1] His was the only British force in the great wilderness west of Lake Michigan. To the northeast, two hundred and forty miles away, across a gloomy stretch of stormy waters abounding in strong currents, lay his base, the shabby little trading hamlet of Mackinac — not now, as in Marquette's first year and in our own time, on the island of that name, but clustered

[1] Gorrell's Journal, in *Wis. Hist. Colls.*, vol. i.

within a cedar-wood stockade some two leagues distant, on the south shore of the strait, not far west of the Mackinaw City of to-day.[1] In the country of the Illinois, eight hundred miles of canoe journey to the southwest and south, were a half dozen small French villages ranged along the Mississippi and the Wabash, having in all a shifting population of perhaps twenty-five hundred. To the westward of the Mississippi lay the great province of Louisiana, which France had conveyed to Spain by a secret treaty signed (November 3, 1762) just previous to the cession of New France to Great Britain. Between La Baye and St. Josephs, the only other civilized community accessible from Lake Michigan, stretched a dangerous water route of four hundred miles.

Here and there, on the bank of a lake or stream,

[1] The term Mackinac, like La Baye and La Pointe, in the earliest period indicated a district in the neighborhood of a particular mission, fort, or settlement. There have been, in chronological succession, at least three distinct localities specifically styled Mackinac. (1) Between 1670 and 1672, Mackinac Island was the seat of the Jesuit mission to the Ottawa. (2) From 1672 to 1706, the Mackinac of history was at Point Ignace, on the north shore of the strait. Between 1706 and 1712 there does not appear to have been any French establishment hereabout. (3) From 1712 to 1780, Mackinac was on the south shore; the mission was in 1738 removed from Point Ignace to L'Arbre Croche, but later the present Franciscan mission was opened on the old Jesuit site at Point Ignace. In 1780, the British commenced the erection of a fort on Mackinac Island, and in 1781 removed their garrison thither; thenceforth, the island has been the seat of military power in the district.

at the foot of a rapids, or beside some portage path, were clustered wretched Indian villages, with both long and conical wigwams of bark or matted reeds, architecture and materials varying with the tribe, — Chippewa, Menominee, Potawatomi, Winnebago, Sauk, Foxes, Kickapoo, Iowa, or Sioux. Hard by were their fields of corn and pumpkins, rudely cultivated in the summer by women or boys, or perhaps by Pawnee slaves obtained in barter from the man-hunting nations of the South. Not infrequently, either in the dark solitudes of waterside forests or boldly exposed on cliffs and hill-tops, were to be seen curious earthworks left by preceding and forgotten tribes: conical mounds in which they had ceremoniously buried their dead, interspersed with those shaped crudely to resemble the birds and beasts that were the armorial emblems or totems of their several clans — the Bear, the Buffalo, the Eagle, the Squirrel, or the Elk. Gorrell estimates in his journal that in what we now know as Wisconsin there were then some eleven hundred warriors; and to the west of these, he thinks, perhaps eight thousand Iowa and thirty thousand Sioux, making a total of some thirty-nine thousand savage men dependent on him for supplies, to say nothing of their women and children — a census doubtless much overestimated.

News traveled swiftly among the aborigines, being borne by tribal runners or by ubiquitous forest merchants and their *voyageurs*. The recent radical

change in the political mastery of the wilderness
was freely discussed around winter camp-fires of
savage hunters and their friends the French traders.
The latter lost no opportunity of poisoning the
minds of the red men toward the newcomers, and
thus nullifying the friendly overtures of Gorrell,
whom Sir William Johnson, British superintendent
of the northern Indian department, had scantily
supplied with belts of wampum and other appropriate peace-offerings. Johnson had particularly
instructed him to please the natives at all hazards;
but with the limited supply of presents furnished
to him, this was a difficult task to perform.

Now and then small squads of the tribesmen
came straggling into La Baye, spies sent to feel
the British pulse. Being well treated, they seemed
invariably to return in high spirits to the woods,
to pave the way for an era of good feeling. The
same fair words and judicious distribution of gifts,
together with good prices for furs and honorable
business dealing, — in this last respect, better
treatment than was often accorded them by their
comrades the French Canadians, — appeared to out-
weigh the well-founded suspicion of the mercurial
Indians, that the fastidious English were at heart
contemptuous of barbarians. Towards the end of
June (1762) there appeared at the fort a young
American officer, Ensign Thomas Hutchins, in after
years famous as a cartographer and long geogra-
pher-general of the United States, who came to

"inquire after Indian affairs," and promised the tribesmen flags, medals, and wax-sealed military commissions such as their French father had so liberally distributed among them. In such manner was won the nominal allegiance of the roving bands. The time thenceforth went pleasantly with feasting, present-giving and receiving, and floods of polite Indian eloquence, in whose easy and obvious symbolism English officials soon came to be adept; until the Pontiac uprising in 1763 rudely disturbed these apparently friendly relations with their wily neighbors, and revealed to the English the volcano on which they rested.

The union jack was now floating over a few widely isolated palisades through the Northwest. But before Englishmen could enter into full possession of the country of the Ohio and the upper lakes, from which they had ousted French garrisons, the Western savage allies of New France must be pacified. Seemingly they had been, as at Fort Edward Augustus. But until the news of the actual terms of the treaty of Paris (February 10, 1763) at last reached the forest councils, the aborigines were hardly aware of the meaning of the victory and of the humiliating terms of peace accepted by their French friends, whom they now taunted with cowardice. To savage minds it was incomprehensible, the more they thought of it, that the frontier stockades, which they considered stout strongholds, should supinely be surrendered, without the firing of a gun — simply because of a message to that effect from the great French chief across the wide water, whom few if any of his American officers had ever seen, and who, so far as any one could find out, had never exposed his own precious body upon the war-path. As for themselves, there were those among them who objected bitterly to being handed over like so many baskets of corn to the rule of the hated Big Knives, as they termed the English. Leading these malcontents was Pontiac, head-chief of the Ottawa, a considerable tribe whose home was in Michigan and about the northern shores of Lake Huron. His motives were in part patriotic, but he was also largely actuated by a wish to avenge certain private wrongs.

So accentuated was the democracy of the North American Indians, that their attempts at concentration were almost invariably weak. Moreover, as individuals they lacked self-control and steadfastness of purpose. Children of impulse, they soon tired of protracted military operations; their strength as fighters lay in their capacity for personal stratagem, in their ability to thread the tangled thickets as silently and easily as they would an open plain, in their powers of secrecy, and in their habit of making rapid, unexpected sallies for robbery and murder, and gliding back into the dark and almost impenetrable forest. Moreover, tribal jealousies were so intense that intertribal relations were seldom possible. Thus lacking cohesion, Indians generally yielded before the whites, who better understood the value of adherence in the face of a common foe. Here and there in our history there have been formidable Indian conspiracies for entirely dispossessing the whites, such as the Virginia scheme (1622), King Philip's uprising (1675), and now the Pontiac War. In later days, we find several other such plots ; for example, those centring around the names of Cornstalk, Tecumseh, Red Jacket, and Sitting Bull. These were, however, the work of native men of genius, who had the gift of organization highly developed ; but their uprisings were short-lived, because they could not find material equal to their skill.

The conspiracy, breaking out in April, 1763, was active all the way from the Alleghanies and Niagara on the east to the upper lakes and the Mississippi on the west. With a persistence almost unique among savages, Pontiac and his numerous allies besieged the English forts throughout the long summer. While Fort Pitt (Pittsburgh) and Detroit successfully withstood protracted assaults, several of the others succumbed and their garrisons were massacred — notably Presqu'isle, Le Bœuf, Venango, Mackinac, Sandusky, St. Josephs, Miami, and Ouiatanon (near Lafayette, Ind.). The Louisiana posts of Vincennes and Chartres had not yet passed into English possession. A reign of terror existed along the western borders of the American colonies, hundreds of backwoods families were slaughtered, outlying plantations and hamlets were burned, forest traders were browbeaten or killed, and for a time the outlook for English trans-Alleghany settlement was gloomy enough.

The story of the massacre of the garrison of Mackinac (June 2) is a familiar page in Western history. Captain George Ethrington, of Delaware, then in command, together with Lieutenant Leslie and eleven other Englishmen, were saved in the mêlée by friendly Ottawa and taken in canoes to the native village of L'Arbre Croche, some fifty miles away on the northeastern shore of Lake Michigan, and then the seat of the Jesuit mission to the Ottawa.

As early as the 18th of May, Gorrell (who in March, 1762, acquired a lieutenancy) had learned of a conspiracy to attack Fort Edward Augustus, but by adroit management he continued temporarily to satisfy the natives. He had, however, just been informed of a fresh plot, when on the 15th of June there arrived, by the hand of a delegation of French and Ottawa, a note from Ethrington, dated four days previous, conveying news of the Mackinac tragedy and commanding him to evacuate his post and with the English traders join his superior on the east shore of Lake Michigan.

Of all his various neighbors, — Menominee, Sauk, Foxes, and Winnebago, — Gorrell placed most reliance on the Menominee. But Ethrington having wisely instructed him not to acknowledge that his purpose was retreat, he confided to his savage friends the information that he desired only to restore order at Mackinac, and on their part they promised to care for La Baye fort and its supplies during his absence.

The proposed departure of the garrison attracted general attention, and native delegations swarmed to the post to learn more about it, drawing heavily on Gorrell's fast-waning store of Indian presents. Pontiac's emissaries were active, and opposition to the movement began to develop. Affairs were in this critical stage when a contingent arrived from the trans-Mississippi Sioux, enemies of the Chippewa, who of the Wisconsin Indians were most attached to Pontiac's plans. Fortunately, the warlike visitors from the West espoused Gorrell's cause, and threatened with punishment those who opposed him. This attitude at once changed the situation, and thereafter was noted only a general solicitude to further the commandant's wishes; while the friendly Ottawa, who had brought the news, were sent back to inform Ethrington of Gorrell's approach.

On the 21st of the month the lieutenant and his English traders — the latter were leaving behind them, at the mercy of the Indians, large quantities of goods [1] — sailed from Fort Edward Augustus in

---

[1] Evan Shelby and Samuel Postlethwaite of Frederick County, Maryland, a large supply firm for the Indian trade, had in 1762

their canoes and bateaux, for escort having ninety of the neighboring barbarians, gaudily appareled as for a gala day. It was the 30th, after a fair passage across Lake Michigan, before they effected a junction with Ethrington. Protracted Indian councils now followed, day by day, the Chippewa opposing the proposition of the English officers that they be allowed to descend with their men to Montreal; but the La Baye Indians, renewing their old-time allegiance with the Ottawa, insisted with the latter that Gorrell and his friends should be allowed to depart in peace, and eventually their counsel won. On the 18th of July, after allowing three of the traders (Bruce, Visscher, and Rose-boom) to return to La Baye with their Indian friends, the detachment set forth under Ottawa and Menominee guidance, in a fleet " consisting of forty canoes of soldiers, traders, and Indians." After a tedious journey by the old route of the French and Ottawa rivers, the party reached Montreal in safety on the 13th of August. The following year Mackinac was reoccupied by regulars, but not until the brief invasion of 1814 was the English flag again seen waving over a Wisconsin fort.

A few weeks after the retreating garrisons of King George had reached Montreal, there was

outfitted Edmond Moran, a trader at La Baye. As all unsold goods were, on Moran's departure, appropriated by the natives, the firm's loss was between six and seven thousand dollars, for which doubtless they were reimbursed by the British government.

issued from Whitehall (October 7) a royal proclamation relative to the government of those portions of North America surrendered by France
through the treaty of Paris, signed the previous
February. The newly acquired territory was divided into "four distinct and separate governments, stiled and called by the names of Quebec,
East Florida, West Florida, and Grenada." In
general terms, the province of Quebec embraced
Canada and that broad triangle lying between the
Great Lakes and the Mississippi and Ohio rivers,
which in history is called the Old Northwest —
this latter term having reference to the subsequent
American ."Territory Northwest of the River
Ohio."

In this proclamation the king solemnly commanded his "loving subjects" not to purchase or
settle lands to the west of the mountains " without
our especial leave and license." Several considerations appear to have prompted this reactionary
policy. It seemed at London as though Pontiac and
his followers, who were seriously objecting to the
presence of Englishmen, might thus be appeased;
the fur-trade with the Indians was enormously profitable, it being with the English, as with the French,
practically the only commerce possible in the interior
of the continent; and were the trans-Alleghany kept
as a preserve for fur-bearing animals, certain powerful London merchants would profit thereby; possibly His Majesty thought, also, to check the

westward growth of his wayward American children, lest they slip beyond his reach, commercially as well as politically. But this injunction, like many another attempt at governmental regulation in far-off America, was futile; the irresistible expansion of the colonies was not for a day checked by a proclamation the news of which probably did not reach the borderers themselves until after the spirit of revolt had gained such head among them that any royal command as to their movements was but idle speech.

The Pontiac uprising greatly disturbed trans-Alleghany settlement and the fur-trade. It did more. The weakness displayed by Pennsylvania in resisting Indian attacks on her western border settlements — even Virginia and Maryland were but fairly active — called forth from the commander-in-chief, General Amherst, angry protests against her " infatuated and stupidly obstinate conduct," and served to justify the maintenance in America of a standing army for the protection and regulation of the obstreperous Americans.

But, as was to be expected, the savages in time wearied of their confederacy, and were discouraged by frequent defeats. Under French influence, Pontiac in 1765 sued for and readily obtained peace. Thenceforth, until the formal opening of the Revolution, eleven years later, the spread of the English colonies into the coveted West met only with accustomed local opposition from tribes that guarded the passes of the Appalachians.

Prominent among French traders at Mackinac were the Langlades, who figure largely in the history of the upper lakes during the last half of the eighteenth century. Their operations extended throughout the hinterland of these inland seas, particularly Michigan and Superior, and like many of their calling they exercised a strong influence over the tribesmen of this broad area, with whom they were connected by bonds of marriage. In his young manhood, Augustin, the senior, had served with Lignery in the latter's punitive expedition against the Foxes in 1728; and in 1731, with his brother Didace Mouet, had been one of a company for exploiting the Sioux post on the upper Mississippi. His son, Charles Michel, more noted than he, was born at Mackinac of an Ottawa mother, in May, 1729. Charles was employed in the militia of New France throughout the French and Indian War, often leading against the British and their Indian allies large parties of tribesmen and half-breeds from the Northwest. The English-sympathizing Miami felt his strong arm at Pickawillany (1752). At Braddock's defeat (1755), his hybrid contingent took prominent part in the fearful slaughter. He defeated Robert Rogers on Lake Champlain (January, 1757), later led the Western Indians against Fort William Henry (May), and in the following autumn was appointed second officer at Fort Mackinac, where he remained until summoned to aid in the Quebec campaign (1759). Appointed lieutenant in 1760, we have seen that Langlade participated in the defense of Montreal, returning to Mackinac in time to help Beaujeu escape with the garrison ; and later he surrendered the fort to Balfour and Leslie.

Peace being declared, the Langlades, in common with other Mackinac merchants, now made numerous trading voyages to the Western interior. It seems probable that he and his father had for some years, among their several ventures, maintained a commercial branch at La Baye, possibly as early as 1746.[1] Attracted by its situation, and its importance as a centre for inland traffic with the Indians, they had arranged to remove thither with their families in the spring of 1763, to make this their permanent home ; but, owing to the outbreak of Pontiac's conspiracy, remained in Mackinac. It would appear that those Englishmen who were saved largely owed to Charles's powerful intercession their lives as well as the permission to depart to Montreal. Captain Ethrington left the post in charge of the experienced Langlade, who retained possession until the arrival of regulars in September, 1764. Either in the same autumn, or during the following year, his family at last carried out their plan of settling at La Baye, and at once be-

---

[1] In a document in *Wis. Hist. Colls.*, vol. xvii, pp. 450, 451, Governor Beauharnois and Intendant Hocquart notify the French minister of the marine (September 22, 1746), that they have allowed " two private individuals to Fit themselves out at Michilimakinac for the said Place of La Baye, on condition that they pay 1000 livres each."

came the leading landowners and merchants in the Fox River valley.[1]

Pontiac and his fellows having subsided, the region beyond Mackinac was again safe for Englishmen and English sympathizers seeking traffic with the savages. Henceforth we have abundant evidence that not only the Langlades but many others, both traders and travelers, roamed freely through the wilds of Wisconsin. But with English as with French explorers of the primitive West, few have left records by which their wanderings may now be traced. It is but occasionally, as the result of memoirs published by or for them in later life, or from chance allusions in contemporary official documents, that we catch glimpses of a few types of those serving as our earliest pioneers. Conspicuous among these was Alexander Henry, a fur-trader who spent the winter of 1765–66 upon Chequamegon Bay, conducting an extensive traffic with the Chippewa, who maintained here their principal market.

Henry had been a young soldier in the British army at the reduction of Montreal, and immediately thereafter ventured into the far West as a trader,

[1] The Langlades have long been credited with being the " first permanent settlers in Wisconsin;" but documents published in *Wis. Hist. Colls.*, vol. xviii, conclusively establish that they did not settle at La Baye until some twenty years after tradition places them there. Even had 1745 been the date of their arrival, as stated in tradition, it has been shown that the hamlet was a fixture long previous thereto. It is quite impracticable to say who was Wisconsin's first " permanent " settler.

with an outfit from Albany. From his headquarters at Mackinac, where for a time he was imprisoned by Indians engaged in the massacre of 1763, he and his representatives made wide journeys through the country of the upper lakes. In 1765 he obtained from the military authorities a monopoly of the Lake Superior trade, sharing it with Jean Baptiste Cadotte, who later established himself permanently at Chequamegon Bay.

Ever since the days of Radisson and Groseilliers, who built their rude trading shanty on the mainland shore near the Washburn of our time, this charming bay, a favorite fishing resort of tribes in northwest Wisconsin, and convenient to the principal portage routes between Lake Superior and the Mississippi River, had at times been resorted to by adventurous Frenchmen bartering with the savages for furs. While originally applied merely to the site of the Jesuit mission, near Radisson's landfall, the term "La Pointe" came in time to have regional significance, having reference to the bay at large. It is not clear when Madelaine Island first became, in preference to the mainland, the seat of power at Chequamegon. Apparently it was not until the time of Le Sueur (1693), who was safeguarding the northern approaches to the Mississippi, that an insular stronghold came into favor.

In 1717, the year of La Baye's first permanent fort, we hear of a stockaded trading station at

La Pointe. A year later, Captain Paul Legardeur Saint-Pierre, whose mother was a daughter of Jean Nicolet (first of known white men to set foot in Wisconsin), was sent to command this important outpost, succeeded by his chief lieutenant, Ensign Linctot. Documents of the fourth decade of the eighteenth century contain numerous references to one of its commandants, Louis Denis, Sieur de la Ronde. In his day, La Ronde, with his son and partner, Philippe Denis de la Ronde, were the principal merchants on Lake Superior. They built for their commercial operations a bark of forty tons, accredited with being " the first vessel on the Great Lake, with sails larger than an Indian blanket."

The La Rondes were particularly interested in copper mining. As early as 1665 Allouez had reported that this mineral was found in masses on the shores and islands of Lake Superior, being rudely mined by the savages, and by them fashioned not only into utensils and implements, but into idols which they greatly reverenced. Five years later Father Dablon made a still more detailed report on this subject. We have seen that in 1700–02 Le Sueur was discovering copper deposits on the upper Mississippi. The elder La Ronde secured much detailed information concerning native mines on the south shore of the great lake, and induced the government at Versailles to send out two German experts, who reported (1739)

favorably on deposits at Ontonagon and on the
Iron and Black rivers, which he was working in a
small way. Whereupon the Chequamegon commandant proposed to the king that he be permitted
to operate his mines on a larger scale, and ship the
ore in vessels down the lakes. But war breaking
out between the Sioux and Chippewa, the entire
upper country was for a time embroiled, and La
Ronde died before he could secure important results.

In 1750, Sieur Marin, then commandant of La
Baye, built a post on the upper waters of the Mississippi, and no doubt, like Le Sueur, maintained
communication with La Pointe by way of the Bois
Brulé–St. Croix trade route ; for he was connected
with the widespread operations of Legardeur Saint-
Pierre, who in 1749 had succeeded the Vérendryes
in conducting the " Post of the Western Sea,"
an ambitious cordon of fortified trading stations
stretching westward from Lake Superior to the
upper Saskatchewan.

Hertel de Beaubassin, the last French commandant at La Pointe, was, about 1758, summoned
to Lower Canada with his Chippewa allies, to do
battle against the English. Thereafter, until the
coming of Henry, who reopened the trading station, we hear little of the place, save that sometimes there wintered on this lonely, pine-clad
island nameless traders on their way to and from
the west end of Lake Superior.

In some respects, the best known of the explor-

ers of Wisconsin during the British régime was
Jonathan Carver of Connecticut. An ignorant
shoemaker, — not a physician, as claimed in his
" Travels," — he enlisted as a private in a Massachusetts company of rangers serving in the French
and Indian War. Although later dubbing himself
captain, there is no evidence that he ever held any
military office.

Under pretense of seeking the Northwest Passage by way of the upper waters of the Mississippi,
Carver appears to have left Boston in June, 1766,
proceeding westward through Albany and Niagara.
There is ground for suspicion that he was in some
manner connected with the shady operations of
Robert Rogers, the famous ranger, then commandant at Mackinac. Rogers was not only somewhat
mysteriously engaged in the fur-trade, for which
he supplied Carver with a small stock of goods,
but was suspected of carrying on an intrigue for
the delivery of his fort either to the French or
the Spanish. Imprisoned on a charge of treason,
he eventually obtained acquittal because of a lack
of evidence, although this did not quiet suspicion.
As Carver seems to have joined Rogers in London,
after this episode, and was himself a common adventurer who could hardly be interested in mere
geographical discoveries, it has been surmised that
in some unexplained manner he was acting as a
tool of the Mackinac intriguer.

Carver claims, in his " Travels," to have reached

Green Bay on September 18, to find that Fort Edward Augustus, which Gorrell had abandoned three years before, was now in a ruinous condition. Within the stockade there lived " a few families," while, " opposite to it " (on the east shore), were " some French settlers, who cultivate the land and appear to live very comfortably."

Passing up the Fox, the traveler visited a Winnebago town of fifty houses on Doty's Island, ruled by a chieftess picturesquely named " Glory of the Morning," widow of a French trader, De Corah, who had fallen in the defense of Quebec. From this man fully half of the Winnebago tribe of to-day, in Wisconsin and Nebraska, claim descent. Passing over the Wisconsin portage, where he found an intelligent French trader whom he calls " Mons. Pinnisance," Carver visited the loghouse village of the Sauk on Sauk Prairie, " the largest and best-built Indian town I ever saw ; " and later, an almost deserted Fox camp, probably near the present Muscoda.

Arriving at Prairie du Chien on October 15, he found an Indian community of three hundred families, who owned " many horses of a good size and shape," obtained in barter with far Southern tribes, who had acquired them from the Spaniards. " This," writes Carver, " is the great mart where all the adjacent tribes, and even those who inhabit the remote branches of the Mississippi, annually assemble about the latter end of May, bringing with them furs to dispose of to the traders."

From the earliest historic times this broad, bluff-fringed plain at the junction of the Wisconsin and Mississippi rivers was widely known as a convenient meeting-place for natives and fur-traders, who tarried here, both spring and autumn, for bartering, merry-making, or purposes of rendez-vous. La Salle and Perrot, and probably an occasional successor, maintained trading stations here or in the immediate vicinity, but it is not known when anything akin to a permanent white settlement was formed. It has generally been assumed that this event occurred in 1781, when Basil Giard, Augustin Ange, and Pierre Antaya first staked their *habitan* claims upon the prairie. But we shall see that in 1773 Pond appears to have found here a white community of considerable commercial importance. Carver does not specifically mention such; but despite the absence of documentary evidence, there would seem no reason to doubt that French stragglers began somewhat early in the eighteenth century to dwell among the natives at the western terminus of the Fox-Wisconsin trade-route, and that thereafter such settlement was as continuous, or nearly so, as that at La Baye.

Ascending the Mississippi to the site of Minneapolis, Carver visited the surrounding country in Minnesota, and wintered with the Sioux of the plains, who told him of the Black Hills, and described as far distant in the west a river they called Oregon, which flowed into the Pacific — the stream later styled Columbia. Carver claimed that with these tribesmen he visited a large sandstone cave not far north of St. Paul, used by his hosts as a council chamber. He pretended that at such a council, held the 1st of May, 1767, he was given by them a formal deed to a large tract of land, including the sites of the present cities of St. Paul and Minneapolis, a considerable outlying territory in Minnesota, and the whole or a portion of the present Wisconsin counties of Pierce, Pepin, Dunn, Clark, Buffalo, Trempealeau, Jackson, Chippewa, Eau Claire, Polk, Barron, Taylor, Price, and Marathon. Soon after the receipt of this enormous grant, the traveler proceeded to Lake Superior by way of the Chippewa and St. Croix rivers. Thence he returned to Boston, which was reached in October, 1768.

Whatever may have been his real business in the West, Carver had nevertheless, if we may rely on his own statement, made a remarkable wilderness journey of some seven thousand miles, the description of which was embraced in a fairly well-written volume of travel, published in London in 1781, a year after his death. Of course Carver himself was incapable of writing such a book. Nothing is known of the facts concerning its publication; but it is quite evident that he kept some rough notes, — possibly like those of Peter Pond, of which a sample will be presented later, — and that these were given proper form by some literary hack in the employ of the publishers. There is no reason, we think, to doubt Carver's veracity in the main, so far as concerns the tour itself, — the story contains undoubted facts relative to the Wisconsin of his day, — but the often-cited part containing descriptions of Indian life and customs is a mere patchwork of selections from the journals of Hennepin, Lahontan, Charlevoix, and Adair.[1] Like the volumes thus stolen from, this met with an immediate and enormous sale in Europe; from that day to this twenty-one editions have been noted, including translations into German, French, and Dutch, and it is one of the most quoted of early American travels. As for his enormous land claim, Carver's children transferred their right in the deed to the Mississippi Land Company of New York (1822), for £50,000 sterling. Elaborately investigated by Congress, the case was finally decided against the petitioners; but notwithstanding, lands in Wisconsin and Minnesota were long after sold under the Carver title by Eastern speculators, and fraudulent deeds of this character are still on record at St. Paul and Prairie du Chien.[2]

Another interesting traveler of that period was

[1] See E. G. Bourne, "The Travels of Jonathan Carver," in *American Historical Review*, vol. xi, pp. 287–302; also, notes in *Wis. Hist. Colls.*, vol. xviii.

[2] See D. S. Durrie, "Captain Jonathan Carver, and Carver's Grant," in *Wis. Hist. Colls.*, vol. vi.

Peter Pond, a native of Connecticut (1740), who
served with credit as a commissioned officer in the
French and Indian War. After some experience
as a sailor to the West Indies, he entered upon the
fur traffic, his first year in the Northwest being
about 1765. As usual with British traders, his
goods were shipped to him from Albany by way of
Schenectady, Niagara, and Lakes Erie and Huron,
to Mackinac.

In September, 1773, Pond crossed Lake Michigan to Green Bay with a small fleet of bateaux,
having in his company nine clerks (or agents)
engaged to head as many branch parties in various
parts of the country around the upper Mississippi.
The journal of his experiences has been preserved
for us [1] — a valuable and picturesque document,
not less interesting because of its extraordinary
orthography and capitalization. Speaking of the
Creole settlement at the mouth of the Fox, he says:
" We went a Short Distans up the River whare is
a small french village and thare Incampt for two
Days. This Land is Exalent. The Inhabitans
Rase fine Corn and Sum Artickels for fammaley
youse in thare Gardens. They Have Sum trad with
y[e] Indans which Pas that way. . . . I ort to have
Menshand that the french at y[e] Villeg whare we
Incampt Rase fine black Cattel & Horses with
Sum swine."

Ascending the Fox, visiting the Winnebago at

<hr>

[1] Published in *Wis. Hist. Colls.*, vol. xviii.

Doty's Island on the way, the party carried over into the Wisconsin, being assisted at the portage by the French trader mentioned by Carver, but whose name our phonetic diarist spells Pinna-shon; the man had deserted from the army, Pond says, to enter the fur-trade. At Prairie du Chien they met " a Larg Number of french and Indans Makeing out thare arrangements for the InSewing winter and sending of thare cannoes to Different Parts." Among the traders assembled at the prai-rie were several from New Orleans, who came in boats rowed by thirty-six oarsmen ; each of these craft being laden with as many as " Sixtey Hog-seats of Wine, Besides Ham, Chese, &c — all to trad with the french and Indans." Pond alludes to the fact that on this " Very Handsum plain " the French and Indians, who rendezvoused there every spring and autumn, played " the Grateist Games," the former billiards and the latter *la crosse*, an aboriginal form of tennis.

After taking part in these animated scenes for ten days, in the course of which he dispatched his clerks to different tributaries of the Mississippi, our diarist set out with two traders for St. Peter's River ; later spending his winter on " the Plains Betwene the Mississippey & the Miseura among the [Sioux] on such food as they made youse of themselves which was Verey darteyaly Cooked." A few years later (1782–83), Pond was among those who formed the North West Company, whose widespread fur-trading operations will subsequently be alluded to.

In 1774, Parliament passed the Quebec Act "for making more effectual provision for the government of that province." This confirmed to the French in Canada, including of course those living in what is now Wisconsin, "the benefit and use of their own laws, usages, and customs," a privilege enjoyed by the people of the present province of Quebec unto our own day. It further contained the important and beneficent but stoutly contested provision that the British king's "new Roman Catholic subjects may profess the worship of their religion according to the rule of the Romish church, so far as the laws of Great Britain permit." This act had met with keen opposition in Parliament, and for various reasons awakened a storm of dissent in the American colonies at a time when English authority was on the verge of being overthrown, and when every untoward incident but helped make matters worse. South of the Great Lakes, the act was, broadly speaking, a dead letter from the start.

As for the little French Canadian settlements to the west of Lake Michigan, so remote were they from centres of population that this formal attempt at the establishment of civil government in the Northwest had small effect upon them. So far as official interference was concerned, they were self-governing. The *voyageurs* and *habitans* were peacefully inclined, save for small neighborhood quarrels, and for the natural tendency of these simple folk to petty litigation. The fur-traders, however, kept the upper hand, and the word of the imperious *bourgeois* was law, while not far away was the garrison at Mackinac, exercising a repressive influence on possible disorder.

Meanwhile La Baye, the metropolis of the country beyond Lake Michigan, was growing slowly. Augustin Langlade died about 1771, leaving Charles the head of the firm and the principal man in the valley of the Fox. Two years later came from Canada Pierre Grignon, and these two families, intermarrying, founded a long line of prosperous fur-traders, whom to-day a goodly proportion of the French Creoles of northeastern Wisconsin are proud to claim as forbears.

And now came the Revolutionary War. The Wisconsin French had loyally supported New France. Under the fleur-de-lis, Charles Langlade and his barbaric followers struck heavy blows against English settlers to the west of the Alleghanies. But with the change in political control, especially after the suppression of Pontiac's conspiracy, liberal treatment from politic English military officials won their hearts and, quite naturally and properly, a majority of those who had been in French military service became firm friends of the newcomers. Dwelling far from the Atlantic slope, they knew little if anything of the cause, nature, or extent of the uprising of the colonists against British power; moreover their sympathies and associations, social, personal, religious, and commercial, were as a matter of course wholly with Canada. There was every reason for taking service under the standard of their new king, and many did so.

We have seen that Charles Langlade rendered important service to the English in the Pontiac uprising. Now a captain in the Indian department, he was particularly efficient as recruiting agent and partisan leader; with him being associated his nephew, Charles Gautier de Verville. Their many friends and relatives in Wisconsin, red and white, were for the most part readily enlisted. Operating under orders from Colonel De Peyster, the commandant at Mackinac, these two men engaged in several important forays against the "Bostonnais," as the Wisconsin Creoles ineptly styled Clark's little army of Virginians then operating in the Illinois. The Menominee were of Langlade's following; on Lake Superior, Jean Baptiste Cadotte represented English interests and secured the fidelity of his relatives the Chippewa; while traders on the upper Mississippi won like support from the Sioux, whose principal chief was the sturdy Wabashaw.

Absorbed in his enterprise (1778) against the Illinois and Wabash forts, seeking to check disastrous British-Indian forays from northwest of the Ohio River against American settlements in Ken-

tucky, George Rogers Clark did not himself penetrate into Wisconsin. But from his headquarters
in Kaskaskia active agents were sent among the
Indians of this region, awakening within those of
southern Wisconsin, farthest removed from Langlade's influence, a wholesome feeling of doubt as to
the outcome of the war. He secured from several
cautious Sauk, Fox, and Winnebago chiefs a promise
of neutrality toward these family hostilities between
the Long Knives and their great white father across
the sea; and the Milwaukee Potawatomi boldly
accepted the proffered American alliance.

Godefroy Linctot, a French trader of considerable importance at Prairie du Chien, also openly
espoused the American cause. At the head of a
picturesque company of four hundred French and
half-breed horsemen, he substantially assisted
Clark in several of the latter's subsequent expeditions in the West. Clark rewarded him with a captain's (later a major's) commission, and made him
Indian agent for the upper Mississippi. As for
Spanish officials at St. Louis, on the Louisiana
side of the Mississippi, Clark obtained from them
friendly sympathy and much substantial aid. Had
the American commander been able to make his
intended foray against Detroit, there is little doubt
that he could easily have rallied to his support a
majority of the French and Indians of southern
Wisconsin, and many from the trans-Mississippi.

In the late autumn of 1779, Samuel Robertson,

master of 'the sloop Felicity, — one of three such
naval vessels maintained by the British on Lake
Michigan, — made a reconnoitring voyage around
the lake, visiting and supplying Indians and traders
at the mouths of several rivers on the east shore,
and at "Millwakey" on the west. At the last-named
port, which was reached the 3d of November, after
exceptionally stormy weather, he found a French
trader whom he calls "Morong," and heard of
another named Fay, at Two Rivers, fifty miles to
the north, also on the lake shore.

Robertson's log was written in somewhat chaotic
English, as note his paragraph in allusion to Milwaukee: [1] —

Mr Gautley gives them [Morong and "a war chef
named Lodegand"] a present 3 bottles of Rum & half carrot of Tobaco, and told them the manner governor Sinclair
[of Mackinac] could wish them to Behave, at which they
seemd weall satisfeyed,   he also give instructions to Mon-
sier St Pier to deliver some strings of Wampum and a
little Keg of rum to the following & a carrot of Tobaco
in governor Sinclairs name; likewise the manour how to
behave; he also gave another small Kegg with some
strings of Wampum with a carrot of Tobaco to Deliver
the indeans at Millwakey which is a mixed Tribe of
different nations.

During the same year, Spain declared war against
Great Britain, and under the leadership of Galvez,
governor-general of Louisiana, captured Natchez,

[1] *Wis. Hist. Colls.*, vol. xi.

Baton Rouge, Mobile, Pensacola, and other English settlements in the South. Galvez was proceeding against the Bahamas and Jamaica when the news of peace arrived, thus putting a stop to his ambitious undertaking.

One of the features of this embroglio with Spain was an expedition against the Spaniards of St. Louis and their American friends in the Illinois, projected by the English commandant at Mackinac. He had been informed by Governor-General Haldimand of Canada that an English fleet and army were to ascend the Mississippi to attack New Orleans and other Spanish settlements, and that a coöperating demonstration from the north would be helpful. Moreover, some of the Mackinac traders operating on Western waters were complaining of injuries received at the hands of Spaniards.

" Seven hundred & fifty men including Traders, servants and Indians," so runs the official report,[1] left Mackinac the 10th of March (1780) and proceeded over the Fox-Wisconsin route to Prairie du Chien, where they were joined by several French traders at the head of bands of Chippewa, Sioux, Menominee, Winnebago, Sauk, and Foxes. A large armed boat, with a crew of thirteen Americans and a valuable cargo of trading goods and provisions, was captured off Turkey River, furnishing the sinews of war for the furtherance of the enterprise. From the neighboring lead mines about the present

[1] *Wis. Hist. Colls.*, vol. xi.

Illinois town of Galena, the warriors brought in
" seventeen Spanish & Rebel Prisoners, & stopp'd
Fifty Tonns of Lead ore," together with additional
provisions. Meanwhile, Langlade assembled at Chicago a considerable party of French and Indians
to make an attack by way of Illinois River, " and
another party [Ottawa] are sent to watch the
Plains between the Wabash and the Mississippi,"
and thus cut off Vincennes.

But despite these elaborate arrangements and
early successes, the demonstration lacked strength.
The savage allies of the English, particularly the
Sauk and Foxes, were but half-hearted; three of
their French leaders — Hesse, Du Charme, and
Calvé, well-known Wisconsin fur-traders — were
accused of bold-faced treachery, no doubt allowing themselves to be tampered with by American
agents; and the Potawatomi of the Milwaukee
neighborhood were doing their best to upset Langlade's plans. In fact, the lead mines and the Illinois
generally, together with most of southern Wisconsin, were now found to be filled with American
sympathizers, both traders and tribesmen, a circumstance well calculated to give pause to French
and Indian allies of England, for seemingly their
chief desire was to be friendly with the victors,
whoever they might be.

Spaniards and Americans had received advance
notice of every movement against them, and were
so well prepared that the assault was easily check-

mated. The principal features were the burning of
outlying cabins at St. Louis, the raiding of traders'
and cattle-men's camps, and the intercepting of
American supply boats on the Mississippi. The
marauders, returning by various routes through
Wisconsin and Illinois, "brought off Forty-three
Scalps, thirty-four prisoners, Blacks and Whites
& killed about 70 Persons. They destroyed several
hundred cattle, but were beat off on their attacks
both sides of the River."

Contemporary Spanish reports of this affair allude
with bitterness to Hesse's conduct, as "the ferocity
of an officer deeply dyed with inhumanity."[1]

As a result of conflict between this expedition
and the American garrison at Cahokia, on the east
side of the Mississippi, a few miles only from St.
Louis, Colonel Clark sent a small detachment to
punish the Indians on Illinois River. This vigorous invasion of native territory, and the usual
wholesome fear of Clark's intentions, so alarmed
the English traders that it was thought desirable
to remove from harm's way their large stock of
furs at Prairie du Chien.

Accordingly there was dispatched from Mackinac in June (1780) a party of twenty Canadians
and thirty-six Foxes and Sioux, in nine large birch
canoes. One of the members of this force was
John Long, a trader who had been operating on

[1] English documents in *Wis. Hist. Colls.*, vol. xi; Spanish, in
vol. xviii.

the north shore of Lake Superior, but who had
spent the winter of 1779–80 with the Chippewa
near Fort Mackinac. To Long's interesting journal [1] we are indebted for our knowledge of the
enterprise. Arriving at Prairie du Chien, " a town
of considerable note, built after the Indian manner," they found Langlade, "the king's interpreter,"
who with the help of several Indians — all of whom
" were rejoiced to see us " — was guarding the bales
of peltries in a log house. Three hundred packs of
the best skins were placed in the canoes, the remaining sixty being burned to prevent their falling
into the hands of the enemy; whereupon the res-
cuers took up their return journey to Mackinac,
which they reached after an absence of eighty
days. " About five days after our departure " from
Prairie du Chien, wrote Long in his journal, " we
were informed that the Americans came to attack
us, but to their extreme mortification we were out
of their reach."

The Spaniards, on their part, soon replied to
the attack on St. Louis by dispatching (January,
1781) a force of sixty-five militiamen, half of them
French, together with the usual savage camp-fol-
lowers, against Fort St. Josephs, four hundred
miles distant to the northeast from St. Louis. The
men had a weary midwinter march across Illinois
and northern Indiana, but succeeded in driving off
the small English garrison, capturing rich spoils

[1] Thwaites, *Early Western Travels*, vol. ii.

from the considerable group of fur-traders collected there, and destroying such other stores of ammunition and goods as they and their Indian allies could not carry away.[1]

[1] See *Wis. Hist. Colls.*, vol. xviii, for a discussion of this curious affair, based on recently-discovered documents. While nominally a Spanish expedition, it appears to have been incited by Americans and the *habitans* of Cahokia, taking advantage of the defection of the neighboring Potawatomi, who were deserting the British interest.

CHAPTER VI

EARLY in the peace negotiations at Paris (1782), it was evident that Spain wished to retain control of both the Gulf of Mexico and the Mississippi River. She sought to restrain the United States from extending as far south as the Gulf, basing her claims on the coastwise conquests of Galvez (1779–81) ; while on the west she aimed at obtaining as the result of her expedition against St. Josephs a large slice of the country lying back of the Alleghanies and abutting on the east bank of the Mississippi. In these bold demands Spain was quietly backed by her neighbor, France. Although having recognized and assisted at American independence, neither of these European powers seemed desirous that the new republic should have much room for growth beyond the Atlantic slope.

Notwithstanding instructions from Congress to act only with the consent of France, the astute American commissioners (Franklin, Adams, and Jay) took alarm at the attitude of our ally and conducted their own negotiations with Great Britain. In the matter of the western boundary, they stoutly held for and ultimately gained the

Mississippi. For the northern, they offered two alternatives — one, a line passing through the middle of the Great Lakes, the other the forty-fifth degree of latitude. This last-named boundary would have allowed Great Britain to retain the northern half of Maine, all of the upper peninsula of Michigan, that portion of southern Michigan stretching north of Otsego Lake, and so much of Wisconsin as lies north of a line drawn due west from Peshtigo Harbor to Hudson, together with all of Lake Superior, the outlet of Lake Michigan, and the northern waters of Lake Huron; whereas to the United States would have been awarded the southern and most fertile portion of Ontario, with the sites of Kingston, Toronto, and London, as well as complete control of Lakes Erie and Ontario. The boundary finally adopted by Great Britain was a better and more natural arrangement for both countries — from Connecticut River westward along the forty-fifth parallel to the St. Lawrence, thence through the middle of the Great Lakes and connecting waters to the Lake of the Woods, whence the line was to run due west to the source of the Mississippi. This latter provision was based upon a geographical error then current on American maps, placing the source of that river much farther north than it was afterwards found to extend, which mistake was later the cause of misunderstanding. With this boundary arranged, the definitive treaty was finally signed on Septemᵬer 3, 1783, preliminary articles of peace having been negotiated ten months before.

In the seventh article of the definitive treaty, it was promised that " His Britannic Majesty shall, with all convenient speed, . . . withdraw all his armies, garrisons, and fleets from the said United States, and from every post, place, and harbor within the same." In the spring of 1784 Washington's representative, Baron Steuben, was sent to Quebec to make arrangements with Governor Haldimand for the transfer of the northern posts, — among them Detroit and Mackinac,[1] — but was met by the polite but firm statement that British military officials had as yet received no orders to turn them over to the Americans. Later, diplomatic assurances were to the effect that these strongholds were being retained until the new federal government had secured from the several states restitution of confiscated Loyalist property. The United States were also accused of placing obstacles in the path of private British claims against American citizens, and of allowing the continued persecution of those who had sided with England in the late war.

Secretary Jefferson reminded the British minister that all that the United States had promised

[1] The posts concerned were: on Lake Champlain, Pointe au Fer and Dutchman's Point; in New York, Niagara, Oswego, and Oswegatchie; on Lake Erie, Fort Erie; on the upper lakes, Detroit and Mackinac.

in the treaty was to recommend the states to
make such restitution, Congress having neither
authority nor power to coerce them. In the course
of these negotiations, Great Britain was charged
with not treating the Americans fairly. She had
declined to enter into a treaty of commerce with
them ; she was crippling American trade with the
West Indies ; and had failed to make compensation for the many negro slaves — thousands in
number, it was claimed — that had been taken
away by the British at the close of the war.

Jefferson pointed out that, through retention of
the posts, the English were continuing their hold
upon territory south of the international boundary
agreed upon; exercising power over persons dwelling within the United States ; even denying navigation rights to American citizens in American
territory ; and " intercepting us entirely from the
commerce of furs with Indian nations to the northward, a commerce which has ever been of great
importance to the United States, not only for its
intrinsic value, but as it was a means of cherishing
peace with those Indians and of superseding the
necessity of that expensive warfare we have been
obliged to carry on with them during the time
those posts have been in other hands."

There was much ground for friction between
the new nation and its parent, and, as usual in
such cases, both were in a measure to blame. But
Great Britain's real reason for the retention of the

posts upon the upper lakes was not difficult to find. Jefferson had hinted at it. The fur-trade of Canada had, for those times, grown into enormous proportions during the twenty years between the downfall of New France and the close of the Revolutionary War. In the far north the great Hudson's Bay Company, whose offices were in London, had for a century been reaping large profits for its privileged coterie of stockholders. Immediately after the surrender of Montreal (1760), the country to the south of the Hudson Bay hinterland, all the way from the Ohio to the Saskatchewan and Great Slave Lake, — a thousand miles beyond Lake Superior, — swarmed with independent British traders, such as Alexander Henry, Peter Pond, and John Long, whose experiences in Wisconsin have already been alluded to. In the employ of these merchant adventurers, Scotchmen to a large extent, whose daring enterprise equaled if it did not surpass that of their French predecessors, were many experienced French traders; while French and half-breed *voyageurs* found under their new masters quite as lucrative positions as in the days of the French régime.

Montreal was the business headquarters of the majority of the independents, from here being forwarded in large bateaux the goods and supplies imported from England and Scotland. Detroit, Mackinac, Sault Ste. Marie, and Grand Portage (near the mouth of Pigeon River, on the north-

west shore of Lake Superior) were the secondary
centres of distribution ; and to these several posts
returned each spring large fleets of bark canoes,
laden with packs of peltries secured in barter from
Indians throughout the vast region between Lake
Huron and the Pacific Ocean.[1]

At least twelve large operators, with considerable companies of retainers, were at work in this
territory at the time of the treaty negotiations in
Paris. These rivals had long carried on a bitter
warfare among themselves, occasionally marked
by wilderness broils and even murder. In the
winter of 1783–84, immediately following the establishment of the international boundary, the majority of the Canadians formed a stock corporation
under the name of the North West Company,
which in 1787 admitted to their union those who
had failed to join the first organization. Thereafter
the Canadian fur-trade was controlled by two
organizations only, the Hudson's Bay and the North
West, the former having its chief operating headquarters at Prince of Wales Fort, and the latter on
Mackinac Island and at Grand Portage. Of the
life led by the " Nor' West " chiefs at Grand Portage, the gateway to the Canadian Northwest, during these palmy days of the fur traffic, Washington
Irving has given us a vivid description in his charming " Astoria."

[1] Consult Frederick J. Turner, " The Character and Influence of
the Fur Trade in Wisconsin," in Wis. Hist. Soc. *Proceedings*, 1889.

Taking into consideration the fact that there still were large tracts of fur-bearing wilderness in the spacious triangle lying between the Ohio and Mississippi rivers and the Great Lakes, and that the important *entrepôts* of Detroit, Mackinac, and Grand Portage lay within this region, it is small wonder that the British government, influenced by powerful business interests, should be loth to surrender the posts upon the upper lakes, controlling as they did both the fur-trade and the Indian tribes. Jefferson was right in maintaining that commerce was a sure road to the affections of the tribesmen. Had the posts been surrendered in 1783, as stipulated, the Indian trade would at once have been prosecuted through American channels, and the United States probably saved a long and exhausting period of frontier wars.

Then, again, it must be remembered that English statesmen, kept informed by spies, were not slow to observe that seeds of disunion were being sown, contemporaneously with the establishment of the American republic. The settlers of Kentucky were restless, and not infrequently rebellious, over Spanish ownership of the fair country to the west of the Mississippi, and particularly at Spain's mastery of the mouth of the Mississippi, the chief highway for such of their products as sought the markets of the world. There was, as well, much discontent at the retention of the fur-trade in British hands. Indeed, at one time some of the

Kentuckians were proposing to organize an expedition to proceed up the Mississippi and over the old Fox-Wisconsin route to raid Fort Mackinac. The West was for several years a hotbed of discontent over apparent federal indifference to its peculiar needs, and for a considerable period there was fear among acute observers that the trans-Alleghany might detach itself from the Union and possibly join either France or Spain. England saw that France was desirous of again possessing the trans-Mississippi, an act accomplished in 1800, and that Spain was too weak to resist. In view of the pressing demands of the Montreal traders and the uncertainty of the political future of the West, it is not surprising that Great Britain welcomed an excuse for keeping firm hold upon the forts and Indians of this region, and planned to resist by armed force any American attempts to dispossess her; and that most British officials in Canada firmly believed that the Northwest might in whole or in part be regained.

It was freely asserted by Northwest frontiersmen, and very likely the charge was true, that the tribesmen of this region were being persistently advised by these Canadian officials that the time was not far distant when their great father in London would regain the land, in which English and Indians, together with their French friends, had dwelt together in loving relationship. Just as the savages of twenty years before had, under Pontiac's eloquence, waxed indignant over being handed over by the French to the British as so many chattels; so now, having come highly to regard the latter, they stoutly objected to being transferred, without permission, to the domination of the savage-hating Long Knives and Bostonnais, whom they thought they had every reason to detest and fear. With a view of placating them, British officers continued to receive the tribal delegations that swarmed upon them at the northern posts. As of old, the visitors were given military commissions, gay uniforms, medals, arms and ammunition, and a profusion of miscellaneous presents — liberality in sad contrast with the method of the economical Americans, who without doubt were somewhat niggardly toward their red wards.

It was and still is believed by many that the British did not stop at prophecy and hospitable present-giving, but actively fomented among their guests dissatisfaction against the land-grabbing and miserly Americans; and, perhaps unofficially, nevertheless effectively, encouraged and indeed actually outfitted murderous native raids against frontier settlements in the Ohio country. Considering the prevalent official opinion in Canada, that the Northwest was soon to be regained, it is quite probable that here and there an unwise officer may have overstepped the bounds of discretion and neutrality. That, however, there was any general policy of this character, or widespread assistance to the warring savages, in their hideous forays, has yet to be proved. No trace of it is to be found in the public documents of the period. Abundance of ground is there for complaint of the political policy of the Georges towards America, in her younger and weaker days. But the English people are of the same stock as ourselves ; the tendency to inhuman practices is not in the blood.

Those Atlantic states which, from the terms of their colonial charters, claimed all territory to the west of them, as far as the Pacific Ocean, were induced to surrender to the federal government their respective claims to lands between the Great Lakes and the rivers Ohio and Mississippi, in order that this area might constitute a national domain from which new states should eventually be formed.[1] As early as September 7, 1783, but four days after the signing of the Treaty of Paris, Washington offered tentative suggestions [2] relative to the formation of a commonwealth north of Ohio River, roughly equivalent to the present State of Ohio. In the following April, the same day that Virginia made cession of her claim, Jefferson drafted a committee report to the Congress of the Confederation, providing for the government of the Western territory

[1] Virginia's cession was made in 1784 ; Connecticut's in 1786 and 1800 ; Massachusetts's in 1785. Territory north of 43° 43′ 12 ″ was acquired from Great Britain under the treaty of 1783.

[2] To James Duane, congressman from New York. Sparks, *Life and Writings of Washington*, vol. viii, p. 477.

and its division into seven states, to be styled Washington, Saratoga, Illinoia, Metropotamia, Chersonesus, Assenisipia, Michigania, and Sylvania — the three last named embracing territory now wholly or in part included in Wisconsin.[1] Congress practically accepted his plan of division in the Ordinance of April 23, 1784, but not these fantastic names, each section being wisely left to choose its own title on entering the Union.

July 13, 1787, Congress adopted another and far better plan, the " Ordinance for the government of the territory of the United States northwest of the river Ohio." This second scheme of government for the Western country is popularly referred to as the " Ordinance of 1787 ; " the district was thereafter known as Northwest Territory — the " Old Northwest " of present-day histories, to distinguish it from the later Northwest, on the Pacific Coast. The ordinance, which has served as a model for all subsequent American territorial government, provided for freedom of religion, inviolability of contracts, a humane treatment of the tribesmen, the permanence of " the not less than three nor more than five " new states into which the Northwest Territory was eventually to be divided, the entire freedom of all portages and waterways, the perpetual " encouragement of schools and the means

[1] Randall, *Life of Jefferson*, vol. i, p. 397. Map in *Wis. Hist. Colls.*, vol. xi, p. 452.

of education," and the freedom of all persons save
fugitive slaves from the original thirteen states. It
was expressly declared that these several liberal
provisions — of which those laying the foundations
of our present popular educational system, and prohibiting slavery in the Northwest, have been the
most admired — " shall be considered as articles
of compact, between the original states and the
people and states in the said territory, and forever
remain unalterable, unless by common consent."
In a later chapter, we shall have occasion to refer
in some detail to the plan of division into states.

At the time of the adoption of this famous ordinance, there already were sparse settlements of
Americans at what is now Cincinnati, at Clarks-
ville (Indiana), and at other points on the banks
of the Ohio. Small hamlets of French and half-
breeds were to be found at Fort Wayne, South
Bend, and Vincennes, within the present Indiana;
at Peoria, Kaskaskia, and Cahokia, in the Illinois
country; at Detroit, Sault Ste. Marie, and on the
island and straits of Mackinac, in Michigan; and
at Green Bay, Prairie du Chien, and La Pointe, in
Wisconsin. A census of these widely separated
communities — between which lay a wilderness of
forest and prairie, lakes, marshes, and rivers, and
among which wandered tribes of semi-nomadic barbarians — would at that time probably have revealed in all the vast Northwest Territory not more
than thirty thousand whites. The following spring

a party of Revolutionary veterans settled on serv-
ice-bounty lands at Marietta, Ohio, and thereafter
the growth of the territory was constant and considerable.

Wisconsin lay within the newly organized Northwest Territory. But owing to British retention of
Mackinac, of which the country between Lake
Michigan and the Mississippi was both a fur-trade
and a military dependency, it was many years
before the territorial government assumed control
of this, the farthest American Northwest. Life ran
on, therefore, in much the same fashion as of old.
British traders, operating from Mackinac, were the
commercial lords of the manor. They were, however, few in number. Their agents, boatmen, and
trappers were the French of the old régime. At
the little riverside hamlets, the *habitan* was still
chiefly in evidence, leisurely working his narrow
field when not absent upon far-away trading expeditions. The transfer of political mastery, from
French to English, had wrought no visible change
in this conservative folk. Americans were unknown here, save by their unwelcome reputation as
a nervous, discontented people, heralds of a relent-
less system of conquest, bent on ruining the forests,
browbeating the Indians, driving sharp bargains,
and in general making the world an uncomfortable
place wherein to live. The annals of these quiet
Wisconsin neighborhoods are few. The nearest
register of marriages, births, baptisms, and deaths

was kept at Mackinac.[1] What of importance we
have to record, up to the time of the actual coming
of the dreaded Americans (1815), is fragmentary.
Arcady furnishes scant material for historians.

We have seen that lead-mining in the Mississippi River hinterland, within what are now Wisconsin, Illinois, Iowa, and Missouri, — one of the
richest lead-bearing regions in the world, — early
became an industry of considerable importance.
The French were continually seeking for beds of
mineral, particularly copper and lead, and closely
questioned the Indians concerning them. While
in a measure superstitious with regard to all ores,
their cupidity soon induced them to betray the
presence of both of those so persistently sought.
The white man had introduced firearms among the
aborigines, and induced them to hunt fur-bearing
animals on a large scale ; thus lead at once assumed
among them a considerable economic value, both
for use as bullets and as an article of profitable
traffic with the traders, the latter coming from long
distances to obtain their supplies of this essential.

So far as we can now ascertain, Nicolet was the
first to teach Northwest tribesmen the use of gunpowder. Radisson and Groseilliers heard of lead
among the Bœuf Sioux, apparently in the neighborhood of Dubuque. The journals of Marquette,
Hennepin, and Lahontan allude to the mineral

[1] The marriage entries are published in *Wis. Hist. Colls.*, vols.
xviii and xix.

wealth of the district — Hennepin's map shows a lead mine in the vicinity of Galena. Joutel (1687) says that "travelers who have been at the upper part of the Mississippi affirm that they have found mines of very good lead there." Perrot, by the aid of natives to whom he taught the rudiments of mining and smelting, obtained lead from a mine about opposite Dubuque. The operations of Le Sueur have been alluded to in a previous chapter. In 1712 Sieur Anthony Crozat was granted a monopoly of trade and mining privileges in Louisiana, and his men worked shafts in southeastern Missouri; so also the representatives of Governor La Mothe Cadillac, who three years later penetrated to these parts. Various prospecting parties sent out under military protection by Philippe François de Renault, "director-general of the mines of the Royal India Company in Illinois," were successfully operating in the district from 1719 to 1723. There exists a report made in 1743 of certain independent lead miners hereabout, who worked at surface diggings and conducted wasteful smelting methods, — "but in spite of the bad system . . . there has been taken out of the La Mothe mine 2500 of these bars in 1741, 2228 in 1742, and these men work only four or five months in the year at most."

The withdrawal of France from the country east of the Mississippi (1763) brought several excellent mines within British boundaries; Jonathan Carver

noted at least one such near Prairie du Sac, on
Wisconsin River. But the bulk of the lead product
of the upper valley of the Mississippi still came
from west of the river, Spain now profiting from
the mines instead of France. St. Geneviève was
long the principal market, but when St. Louis became the commercial centre of the region the traffic
was transferred thither. As early as 1766 the product was shipped to New Orleans in "large boats
of 20 tons, rowed with 20 oars." During the last
quarter of the eighteenth century lead was, next to
peltries, the most important and profitable export
of the country, and served as currency. We are
told that individual lead miners, working for themselves, often took out "thirty dollars per day, for
weeks together."

One of the most interesting characters attracted
to the lead district in its early days was Julien
Dubuque, a trader of remarkable energy and singularly popular among the Indians, whom he employed in considerable numbers as prospectors and
miners. Having made important discoveries in the
neighborhood of the present Iowa city of Dubuque,
he later extended his field to the east of the Mississippi. A full council of Sauk and Fox Indians
at Prairie du Chien granted him (1788) formal
permission "to work lead mines tranquilly and
without prejudice to his labors;" and thereafter,
for many years, he and his agents conducted operations in northwestern Illinois and southwestern

Wisconsin, in diggings wherein Indians were said to have crudely delved for bullet lead, a full century before.[1] Dubuque waxed wealthy from his lead and peltries, and in 1805 formally acknowledged the ownership of a mining tract west of the Mississippi, " twenty-eight or twenty-seven leagues long, and from one to three broad."

British retention of the frontier forts was of course not allowed to pass unnoticed. Diplomatic negotiations for the righting of what the United States government considered a wrong and a serious menace were continued by John Adams, the American agent in London (1785–88), who vainly sought recognition of his country's claims. But under the Congress of the Confederation, the United States were almost as weak as any small South American republic of our own day, and might easily be put off at the behest of fur-trade magnates in London and Montreal. Adams was succeeded by Gouverneur Morris, whose patience was also severely taxed.

Meanwhile, various complications had arisen, tending still further to strain relations between the two countries. Spain was intriguing with the Westerners, chiefly through the secret agency of General James Wilkinson of the American army, with the ostensible view of securing their interest in return

[1] For a general survey of this subject, see Thwaites, "Notes on Early Lead Mining in the Fever (or Galena) River Region," *Wis. Hist. Colls.*, vol. xiii.

for navigation rights upon the Mississippi, but apparently seeking only to alienate them from, and thus to weaken, the Union; at the same time that, with characteristic duplicity, she was secretly urging the jealous Southern tribes to destroy American settlements in Tennessee and Kentucky. On her part, France was forwarding a conspiracy among these same frontiersmen to raise an army of filibusters, under George Rogers Clark, to oust Spain from Louisiana.

The Indians of Northwest Territory, who had complained bitterly of the cession of their country to the Americans, grew restless over the steady irruption of settlers into lands north of the Ohio. By a treaty at Fort Harmar, in 1789, some of the chiefs ceded to the newcomers a considerable strip of territory; other tribesmen, however, denounced this transaction as fraudulent. The recalcitrants precipitated a disastrous border war of five years' duration, in the course of which the British, taking advantage of the situation, erected a new fort within American territory, at Maumee rapids, the site of the present Perrysburg, Ohio, an embarrassing menace to our military department. Cowed at last, but after great expenditure of American lives and treasure, the Indian malcontents consented to a treaty of peace signed at Greenville, August 4, 1795. At this council the American commissioners were able to announce to the tribesmen that a treaty had been concluded in London (November

19, 1794), through the diplomacy of John Jay, by which the northern posts were to be evacuated by the British on the 1st of June, 1796.

Besides this agreement, so essential to the interests of the Northwest, the Jay Treaty made provision for complete freedom of trade between the United States and Great Britain and her colonies, for the free navigation of the Mississippi for both nations, and for a survey of the sources of that river with a view to establishing the international boundary in our Northwest.

The year after the execution of Jay's Treaty, and a month following that of Greenville, there was signed at Madrid (October 27, 1795) a covenant between the United States and Spain, by which Americans were granted by the latter country full rights of navigation upon the great river, and of depositing their products at New Orleans. Thereafter no more was heard either of Spanish intrigues in Kentucky or of Western uneasiness.

In October (1796), American troops first took possession of Mackinac, and with it, of course, the dependency of Wisconsin. The English, however, were still so confident that they would some day win back the country of the upper lakes, that their garrison retired only to St. Joseph's Island, some fifty miles to the northeast, where the year previous had been erected a new fort.

CHAPTER VII

ALTHOUGH the American flag was now displayed above Fort Mackinac, it was to be nineteen years before this emblem of the new sovereignty fluttered to the west of Lake Michigan.

Article 2 of the Jay Treaty of 1794 had provided that

All settlers and traders within the precincts or jurisdiction of the said posts shall continue to enjoy, unmolested, all their property of every kind, and shall be protected therein. They shall be at full liberty to remain there, or to remove with all or any part of their effects; and it shall also be free to them to sell their lands, houses, or effects, or to retain the property thereof, at their discretion; such of them as shall continue to reside within the said boundary lines, shall not be compelled to become citizens of the United States, or to take any oath of allegiance to the government thereof; but shall be at full liberty so to do if they think proper; and they shall make and declare their election within one year after the evacuation aforesaid. And all persons who shall continue there after the expiration of the said year, without having declared their intention of remaining subjects of his Britannic majesty, shall be considered as having elected to become citizens of the United States.

Article 9 stipulated that

British subjects who now hold lands in the territories of the United States, and American citizens who now hold lands in the dominions of his Majesty, shall continue to hold them according to the nature and tenure of their respective estates and titles therein ; and may grant, sell or devise the same to whom they please.

Had the inhabitants of Green Bay been directly asked of which country they would prefer to be citizens, the practically unanimous reply would undoubtedly have been Great Britain. Although under the treaty they became Americans within a year, from having taken no formal steps to remain British subjects, they nevertheless, in their wide isolation from any seat of government, knew little of this arrangement, and continued to consider themselves citizens of Great Britain. British traders, also, still freely operated west and southwest of Mackinac. In fact, for many long years after the treaty, affairs went on in substantially the same fashion as before. The personnel of such trading stations as La Baye, and of the far-scattered trading camps, remained unchanged. To all intents and purposes, Frenchmen, still clinging to Canadian connections and traditions, and in British fur-trade employ, occupied Wisconsin almost as completely as at any period during the two centuries or more of the old régime.

La Baye being a commercial dependency of Mackinac, there was a constant flitting back and forth, in their long bateaux, of fur-trade agents and *voyageurs* between the little settlement on the Fox and the North West Company's *entrepôt* on the island. La Baye's population in 1785 was stated to be fifty-six souls. The Langlades, the Grignons, the Porliers, the Franks, and the Lawes were the principal families, and the others their employees; practically all of them being engaged in the one absorbing enterprise of collecting and selling peltries.

In 1803, nine years after Jay's Treaty, came the first official American notice of the existence of the village, when Governor William Henry Harrison of Indiana Territory (of which Wisconsin was now a part) appointed Charles Reaume as justice of the peace. A bald-headed, pompous, erratic old Frenchman, ever with an eye to the main chance, Reaume drafted all manner of legal and commercial papers; baptized, married, and divorced his neighbors; acted as a primitive civil judge; certified indifferently to either British or American documents, and was general scribe, notary, and civil functionary for almost the entire country west of Lake Michigan. Many amusing stories of his curious court decisions, which recognized no known statutes of the United States, have come down to our own day. Wisconsin became attached to the new Territory of Illinois in 1809. Nevertheless Reaume, a picturesque and useful functionary, evidently quite forgotten by his American superiors to the south, long continued to exercise unquestioned a rude equity in the Fox

River valley through all political changes, even during British military rule in 1814.[1]

Prairie du Chien (or "Prairie des Chiens," as the name frequently appears in contemporary documents), being much farther south than La Baye, was in somewhat closer touch with the seat of American territorial government. Its inhabitants for the most part allowed themselves, through inaction in the matter, to become enrolled as American citizens a year after the signing of the Jay Treaty. At the same time that Reaume received his appointment for the Green Bay district, Henry Monroe Fisher, a prominent American trader at the prairie, received a like commission from the governor of Indiana Territory as justice of the peace, with the additional duties of captain of militia. Fisher, a tall, athletic man of much courage and perseverance, but possessed of a violent temper, was also sub-Indian agent for the Prairie du Chien region, and held firm control over the Sioux, Sauk, Foxes, Winnebago, and Menominee, who resorted in large numbers to his post. Upon the formation of Illinois Territory, Fisher was succeeded both as justice and as sub-Indian agent by John Campbell, an Irishman, whose amusing methods of court procedure much resembled those of Reaume, giving rise to tales that still enliven the early legal annals of the state.

Lieutenant Gorrell reported traders on the site

[1] His papers are preserved by the Wisconsin Historical Society.

of Milwaukee, a considerable Indian village in 1763, operating directly from Mackinac rather than La Baye. In 1779 Captain Robertson found there a trader whom he called " Morong ; " and doubtless the mouth of Milwaukee River was throughout the second half of the eighteenth century more or less regularly visited by men of this type, for it was a favorite native rendezvous. It was long claimed that one Mirandeau, a French blacksmith and trader, erected a log smithy and trading shanty here in 1789; but probably this date is a decade too early. Certain it is that, in 1795, Jacques Vieau, an agent of the North West Company, opened secondary or " jackknife " trading-posts — possibly so called because easily opened or closed at will — on the sites of Kewaunee, Sheboygan, and Manitowoc, and established a permanent post at Milwaukee. He regularly wintered there until 1818, in that year introducing to the scene his son-in-law, Solomon Juneau, first mayor of the later city. To the latter has generally been accorded the honor of being Milwaukee's pioneer; but this is because Juneau was owner of the land on which Milwaukee was platted, in 1833, and none of the newcomers to that settlement had ever heard of Vieau, who many years before retired to Green Bay.[1]

[1] See " Narrative of Andrew Vieau, Sr.," in *Wis. Hist. Colls.*, vol. xi; and Edwin S. Mack, " The Founding of Milwaukee," in Wis. Hist. Soc. *Proceedings*, 1906.

From the earliest historic times there had been a steady stream of travel over the well-worn portage plain, a mile and a half in width, between the Fox and Wisconsin rivers, on the site of the modern city of Portage. No documentary evidence has yet been discovered, indicating that under the French régime any regular transportation agent was established here. But, as previously related, Jonathan Carver found such a person in the autumn of 1766, — a French fur-trader called by him " Pinnisance," who carried bateaux and cargoes from one waterway to the other. This man is identical with the Pennesha Gegare of Grignon's " Recollections," [1] and the Pennensha commended in Gorrell's journal of three years before, as having brought the Sioux to the English interest and helped save Fort Edward Augustus, at Green Bay, in 1763. Pond found " Old Pinnashon" still at work in 1773. Twenty years later we have account of a successor in this enterprise, Laurent Barth, whose forwarding equipment consisted of a horse and a wheeled barge. But after five years of service his evident success attracted a competitor, Jean Ecuyer, who gradually crowded poor Barth to the wall. In his anxiety for further profits, Ecuyer, who had married the daughter of a Winnebago chief, opened a trading-post, as had Pennesha, and soon himself tasted the fruits of competition; for Vieau came out from Milwaukee with a stock of goods and maintained a branch

[1] In *Wis. Hist. Colls.*, vol. iii.

here for several summers, being followed (1801)
by Augustin Grignon and Jacques Porlier of La
Baye. Barth was succeeded as forwarder by François le Roy (1810), who did duty for the British
through the War of 1812–15, — his fees, we learn
from an old bill of lading, being ten dollars for
carrying an empty boat from one river to the other,
and for the cargo fifty cents per hundred weight.
It is no wonder that by the time traders' goods
reached the distant camps of Indian hunters they
were worth almost their weight in gold. In due
course Joseph Rolette, and lastly Pierre Paquette,
were carriers at the portage. In 1829 Fort Winnebago was erected at this strategic point, and a
hybrid settlement sprang up without the walls, the
kernel of the present agricultural and manufacturing city of Portage.

We have seen that La Pointe, on Madelaine Island, in Chequamegon Bay, attained some importance
under the old régime; but it again fell into decay
during the closing years of the French and Indian
War. Alexander Henry revived its old-time fur-
trade in 1765, and the station once more became
the principal peltry market for the Chippewa
country. The island reached the height of its prosperity after Michel Cadotte, son of Jean Baptiste,
established his headquarters here (1800). Taking
unto wife the daughter of the village chief of the
Chippewa, he wielded a strong influence over the
region, as agent first of the North West Company

and later of Astor's American Fur Company. In
1818 came two shrewd Massachusetts brothers,
Lyman Marcus and Truman Abraham Warren.
Marrying Michel's two half-breed daughters, the
young Warrens soon succeeded their father-in-law,
became powerful agents of Astor's interests in the
Northwest, and were the last of the great La Pointe
fur-traders. To-day, the revenues of dreamy little
Madelaine Island are chiefly derived from summer
cottagers from Chicago and St. Louis.

The continuance of the North West Company's
domination from Mackinac aroused constant protest,
both from Americans who wished to enjoy the fruits
of the fur traffic in that quarter, and from federal officials who sought to wean the Indians from
foreign influence. Between 1795 and 1822 experiments were made, establishing among the tribesmen public trading houses, whereat goods were sold
at low prices. But official factors were unable to
give credit, which the improvident savages desired
far more than low prices — it was the very foundation of the Indian trade. Moreover, besides anger-
ing private traders, it was soon discovered that the
wild hunters felt something akin to contempt for a
government that descended to keeping a shop and
haggling over the prices of peltries and cottons.
The fort traders were in time driven from the market, and this plan of courting native favor was
abandoned.

In 1802 Congress ruled that trading licenses

were only to be granted to citizens of the United States, within a territory which included Mackinac but did not extend as far west as Wisconsin. Little attempt was made to enforce this regulation until 1810, and then with small success, save that the North West Company withdrew from the island. In that year a party of independent British traders, interested in Wisconsin stations, determined to run the blockade of Fort Mackinac with Canadian goods consigned to La Baye merchants. In a large bateau, laden with fifty thousand dollars' worth of merchandise, the conspirators succeeded in passing Mackinac Island at night, without arousing the sentry, and successfully landed their cargo at the mouth of the Fox.[1]

The previous year John Jacob Astor of New York, who had been operating from Montreal as an independent trader, and had opened a profitable traffic with China, where prices for furs were high, founded the American Fur Company, which, aided by governmental favor, sought to secure a monopoly of the American fur-trade. Astor's field headquarters were established at Mackinac; but several large traders there, still in the British interest, remained such powerful rivals that in 1811 he purchased their interests and established the South West Company.

The trans-Mississippi province of Louisiana had been ceded by Spain to France in 1800, and three

[1] Neville and Martin, *Historic Green Bay*, pp. 137, 138.

years later sold by France to the United States. It will be remembered that one of the principal objects of the Lewis and Clark exploring expedition of 1804–06, up the Missouri and down the Columbia to the Pacific, was to open to Americans a new fur-trade route. The North West traders were found to be freely trafficking with the natives of the upper Mississippi, of the Missouri from the Mandan villages to the Omaha, and of the vast plains stretching to the Saskatchewan on the north. While American enterprise soon practically dispossessed foreigners from the Missouri itself, the "Nor' Westers" for several years thereafter held the northern plains.

This was the situation when Astor's new company entered the field. His aim was, by a line of posts, to hold the Missouri-Columbia route and dominate the trade to the south thereof, as well as to compete on the Pacific coast with the Nor' West's commercial fleet. For this latter purpose he organized the Pacific Fur Company, in which Canadians freely took stock and employment.

Through the agency of the new company Astor now dispatched two expeditions. One, leaving Montreal in September, 1810, proceeded by sea, around Cape Horn, to the mouth of the Columbia. The other, under Wilson P. Hunt and Ramsay Crooks, two of his most noted lieutenants, departed from Montreal on June 10, 1811, and journeyed up the Great Lakes to Mackinac, thence over the Fox-

Wisconsin route to the Mississippi, then up the Missouri and overland to the Columbia. The innumerable hardships of the two coöperating parties, their final meeting, the building of Astoria at the Columbia's mouth, and the subsequent loss of that outpost to British rivals, as a result of the War of 1812–15, is a thrilling story made familiar in American literature through Irving's " Astoria." [1]

The sagacious Tecumseh's not unnatural revolt, in 1811, against American trespassers on Indian lands in Indiana, involved many isolated bands of Wisconsin Indians, chiefly Chippewa, Winnebago, Potawatomi, Sauk, and Foxes. Not a few chiefs of some renown among our forest warriors participated in the fateful battle of Tippecanoe, on the 7th of November. Again was it stoutly believed by Northwest settlers that Canadian officers had egged the natives on, and armed them, but this charge has never been substantiated. The fact that the savages were largely using English-made arms was doubtless due to the enterprise of irresponsible Canadian traders who were freely circulating through the Indian camps.

The American government had adopted a weak and vacillating tone towards the British, who undoubtedly were overbearing in many ways. A

---

[1] See also Franchère's *Narrative of a Voyage to the Northwest Coast*, and Ross's *Adventures of the First Settlers on the Oregon*, in Thwaites, Early Western Travels (Cleveland, 1904–07), vols. vi and vii respectively.

variety of complications, not necessary here to re-
hearse, had aroused popular clamor on our side of
the water to such an extent that war was inevitable.
By the act of June 18, 1812, hostilities were declared at Washington. A month later Mackinac
was captured by the enemy.

In Wisconsin the principal event of the War of
1812–15 was a rather farcical invasion by British
troops. General William Clark, the famous explorer, and a younger brother of General George
Rogers Clark, was at that time governor of Missouri Territory, and as such military commandant
in the upper valley of the Mississippi. Late in the
autumn of 1813 he dispatched to Prairie du Chien,
to guard the western approach to the Fox-Wisconsin trade route, an expedition consisting of about
a hundred and fifty regulars and militiamen, commanded by Lieutenant Joseph Perkins. Erecting
a stockade here, which he called Fort Shelby, Perkins divided his force between the fort and the
supposedly bullet-proof gunboat that had transported them hither from St. Louis. The garrison
ashore was protected by six pieces of cannon ; the
gunboat, anchored in the middle of the Mississippi,
opposite the stockade, mounted fourteen.

The village of Prairie du Chien itself was divided in interest. The majority of the French
traders and *habitans*, while cautious, appeared to
be pro-British in their sympathies — young Michel
Brisbois and Joseph Rolette openly so. But Nicho-

las Boilvin, who had succeeded Campbell as American Indian agent, managed to secure the support of many of his neighbors, red and white, and was substantially aided by Jacrot, one of the traders.

Meanwhile, Robert Dickson, a prominent Nor' West trader — just now British "agent and superintendent of Western nations," with Chicago and La Baye as his rendezvous — was collecting throughout the winter at Garlic Island, in Lake Winnebago, a considerable body of Indians, largely Winnebago, with the view of aiding a proposed British attack on Fort Shelby in the spring. From his camp spies were frequently dispatched to Prairie du Chien, Milwaukee, and the Illinois country, and news of American movements was also received by him from correspondents in Mackinac and La Baye. By the middle of April Dickson proceeded with his followers to the Fox-Wisconsin portage, and began the task of massing at that rendezvous still another body of Indian allies.

At La Baye, a community wholly British in its sympathies, as might be expected, Captain James Pullman, from Fort Mackinac, was busy organizing a small militia company among the *habitans*, his lieutenants being the traders Louis Grignon and John Lawe. The thirty members of this command, chiefly *voyageurs* in Grignon's employ, were classed in the muster as "almost all old men unfit for service."

War parties depending upon Indian allies were always laggard in their movements. It was June 28 before Colonel Robert McDouall, the Mackinac commandant, could gèt his main expedition started from the island. Under the leadership of Major William McKay, it consisted of a hundred and thirty-six Sioux and Winnebago; some seventy-five *voyageurs* under their *bourgeois*, Joseph Rolette of Prairie du Chien and Thomas G. Anderson, both commissioned as captains, and about twenty of the Michigan Fencibles (*habitan* militia), under Pullman.

In six days the flotilla reached La Baye, where the party were joined by Grignon and Lawe's raw recruits and a hundred savages. At the Fox-Wisconsin portage, Dickson and his Sioux, Winnebago, Menominee, and Chippewa bands joined them, the allied forces now numbering six hundred and fifty, of whom all but a hundred and twenty were Indians, who, McKay afterwards reported, "proved to be perfectly useless."

Upon July 17 McKay's motley crew reached the prairie, to find the expectant Americans apparently well fortified. The outlook seemed dubious to him; nevertheless within half an hour of his arrival he boldly summoned Perkins to " surrender unconditionally, otherwise defend yourself to the last man." The American promptly replied that he accepted the latter alternative.

The siege began at once. A three-pounder can-

non, which McKay had brought with him chiefly
for the purpose of awing his savage allies, was for
three hours employed in firing eighty-six shot. A
skillful artilleryman was in charge, and two thirds
of these hit the gunboat in the river, which replied
vigorously; but, pressed too closely, the vessel finally
ran in behind an island and then escaped down-
stream. It was followed by French and Indians in
canoes, who pestered the fugitive craft as far as the
rapids at Rock Island, where a fortified American
keel-boat was met coming up-stream, and the British
allies were frightened off.

During this episode the Indian camp followers,
bent on loot, plundered the village houses, irre-
spective of the sympathies of their owners, and
kept up a noisy but ineffectual fire on the fort. A
desultory artillery and musketry duel was maintained throughout the 18th and the 19th. At six
in the evening of the latter day McKay's ammunition was running short. He had but six rounds
left for his three-pounder, and was just preparing
to send these into the fort red-hot, with a view to
setting it afire, when to his surprise and very great
relief a white flag was run up on the stockade.

Perkins now offered to surrender, provided the
Indians were prevented from ill-treating the garrison. McKay stipulated to this effect; but while he
was successful in carrying out his promise, the savages were so eager for scalps that supplication,
threats, and constant vigilance on the part of the

British alone saved the incident from culminating in
a massacre. The Americans had lost five killed and
ten wounded on board the boat, and three wounded
in the fort; the allies do not appear to have suffered any casualties. A large stock of ammunition,
provisions, and armaments fell into the hands of
the captors; but so difficult was it to safeguard the
prisoners from the bloodthirsty tribesmen, that
Perkins and his men were given back their arms
and sent down the river to St. Louis. As for the
stockade, it was repaired, and rechristened Fort
McKay.

McKay had intended, after ousting the Americans from Prairie du Chien, to drop down the
Mississippi to the mouth of the Illinois, and by
ascending that stream to attack the American fort
at Peoria. The Americans were so strong at Rock
Island, however, that he abandoned this project
as impracticable. He even considered his position at the prairie as untenable. An attack by a
fleet of American gunboats was momentarily expected; but it never came, for on their part the
authorities at Rock Island and St. Louis had received exaggerated reports concerning the strength
of the invading expedition, and would not make
the venture.

On the 10th of August McKay left for Mackinac, taking with him some of the Indians, fur-
trade militia, and regulars, and leaving Captain
Anderson in command, the latter being afterwards

relieved by Captain Andrew H. Bulger of the regulars. Upon the closing day of December Bulger proclaimed martial law within his jurisdiction. This action was occasioned by the fickle character of the French along the Mississippi, who played fast and loose with him according to varying reports of the progress of the war ; while within the fort the poor commandant was worried by the mutinous conduct of the Fencibles, who grew restive over the dull round of garrison duty. The resident French traders also gave Bulger much annoyance; they fretted under military rule, and Rolette in particular was out of favor at headquarters. The winter was further marked at Fort McKay by many and weary councils with delegations of visiting Indians, who adopted this diplomatic method of preying on the British stores.

Upon the 24th of December (1814), at Ghent, Great Britain and the United States signed a treaty of peace. The news did not reach Bulger until the following 20th of May. On the 22d he formally announced to the Indians, amid much ceremony, the terms of the treaty, and the following day notified Governor Clark of his acceptance of the situation. The latter requested the captain to await the arrival from St. Louis of a detachment of troops to which the post could formally be surrendered. But Bulger understood his late savage allies well enough to know that when they saw the British actually turning over the establishment to the American troops, without lifting a finger to prevent it, the former would be dubbed old women and cowards, and their retreat to Mackinac undoubtedly be marked by plunder and maltreatment. He therefore pulled down his flag on the 24th, and under shelter of a plausible excuse to the Indians beat as hasty a retreat as dignity would allow. At Mackinac he turned over to the American commandant whatever of captured arms and stores remained in his possession — " it being impracticable to send them to Saint Louis," and hastened on to Canada.

Thus ignominiously ended the British régime in Wisconsin, fifty-four years after the arrival of Gorrell, and thirty-two after its nominal surrender to the United States. Henceforth the country between Lake Michigan and the Mississippi River was American territory in fact as well as in name.

CHAPTER VIII

AMERICAN DOMINATION ESTABLISHED

WHILE throughout the United States at large the result of the War of 1812–15 was hailed with rejoicing, very different were the sentiments aroused by this event in Wisconsin, where we have seen that the French régime was still practically in vogue. *Bourgeois*, *habitans*, and half-breeds had freely been employed by the British, who fostered the all-pervading fur-trade, and had at last learned to be liberal and indulgent to their Indian allies. The British departed from our territory with regret, and both Creoles and aborigines were equally reluctant to witness the advent of the " Bostonnais " into their beloved land. It was recognized that Americans were quite out of tune with the easy-going methods of the people who had dominated Wisconsin for upwards of a century and a half; moreover, the newcomers were an agricultural folk, bent on fast narrowing the limits of the hunting grounds. French Canadians felt that their interests were identical with those of the savages, who found that there was no room for them alongside the Anglo-Saxon settler ; hence we find in the familiar correspondence of the time a bitter tone toward the victors, who were regarded as intruders, and covetous disturbers of existing commercial and social relations.

Mackinac and its dependencies were not formally transferred to the Americans until July 18, 1815.[1] Soon after this event, Green Bay — thenceforth " La Baye " was but a reminiscent term among the older French — was visited by its first American official under the new order of public affairs, Colonel John Bowyer, Indian agent. This was a fortunate appointment. A short, stout, elderly man, with French blood in his veins, he had a pleasant yet impressive manner that quite won the hearts of his people, white and red. At about the same time a government trading-post, or " factory," — in accordance with the policy of Indian management already alluded to, — was opened under the charge of Major Matthew Irwin. The very nature of his office, however, aroused the opposition of this old-time fur-trading community, and from the first he was in ill favor with the people.

A year later (August 7, 1816), government having determined to safeguard the American fur-trade in this quarter, four vessels arrived in port, bearing Colonel John Miller and several companies of the Third Infantry. They at once erected " on

[1] When Colonel McDouall, the British commandant at Mackinac, reluctantly retired from that Malta of the Northwest, he built a fort on Drummond Island, at the mouth of River St. Mary's, territory soon thereafter found to belong to the United States.

the west of Fox River, a mile from its mouth,"
Fort Howard, named for General Benjamin Howard, commandant of the West during the war just
concluded, who had died at St. Louis two years previous. Blockhouses of logs, bearing small cannon,
guarded the angles of a timber stockade thirty feet
in height, inclosing barracks and officers' quarters,
while some additional buildings were constructed
just without the walls.

Green Bay was, at this time, described as an attractive waterside settlement, containing from forty-five to forty-eight families, all of them avowedly
British subjects. The prosperous fur-traders who
ruled the village appeared at first to take so hostile an attitude toward the American officials that
Irwin, the principal object of dislike, recommended
their expulsion. This drastic course was, however,
not adopted, for the traders had the support of
their powerful employer, the American Fur Company. The pliant Creoles were finally allowed,
doubtless not without some display of humor, to
take oath to the effect that their aid to the British
during the recent hostilities had been but a necessary yielding to " the tyranny and caprice of the
reigning power and its savage allies." Thus averring, they were tardily converted into American
citizens, quite without reference to the provisions
of Jay's Treaty of twelve years before, which had
been annulled by war.

Upon June 21 of the same year (1816), four

companies of riflemen, under Brigadier-General
Thomas A. Smith, landed at Prairie du Chien
and began the erection of a post on the site of
Fort McKay. This stronghold, also consisting of
squared-log blockhouses connected by a stockade,
and designed to accommodate five companies, was
called Fort Crawford, in honor of William Harris
Crawford, then federal secretary of the treasury.
The public trading house in connection with the
outpost was in charge of John W. Johnson of
Maryland. During the first three years the military authorities were accused of undue harshness
to British sympathizers in the district, such as
Brisbois and Rolette, and there was much friction.
But eventually a kindlier spirit prevailed, as Americans and Creoles became better acquainted with
and more tolerant of each others' peculiarities.
Astor's agents, many of them having large experience with the Canadian French, soon obtained a
firm foothold throughout Wisconsin by adopting
the complacent methods by which Nor' Westers
had won the hearts of these mercurial people.

In a council at St. Louis, upon November 3,
1804, the Sauk and Fox tribes ceded to the United
States, for the paltry annuity of a thousand dollars, fifty million acres of land, comprising in general terms the eastern third of the present State of
Missouri, and the territory lying between Wisconsin River on the north, Fox River of the Illinois
on the east, Illinois River on the southeast, and

Mississippi River on the west. This enormous tract contained not only the rich lead-mining district to which allusion has alre dy been made, but some of the most fertile soil in che Middle West. In the succeeding chapter we shall find that a clause in this treaty, allowing the savages to remain upon the land until it was disposed of to individual settlers, gave excuse for the Sauk uprising of 1832, known as the Black Hawk War.

Owing to the alliance of the savages with England during the late war, this cession of 1804 was, upon May 13, 1816, formally "recognized, established, and confirmed" by the Sauk and Foxes. But the Ottawa, Chippewa, and Potawatomi, who were present at the series of peace councils being held during that summer at St. Louis, stoutly contended that their own rights within this huge grant had been ignored by the Sauk and Foxes. To end this contention, a treaty was concluded with the objectors on August 24, by which, on consideration of a thousand dollars' worth of goods, they relinquished their claims to so much of the tract as lay "south of a due west line from the southern extremity of Lake Michigan to the Mississippi River," — substantially, the Illinois section ; and to them was ceded outright by the United States "all the land contained in the aforesaid cession of the Sacs and Foxes which lies north of" said line, — including that lying in the present Wisconsin. There was, however, exempted for the federal government a lead-mine reservation eight leagues square, " on or near to the Ouisconsin and Mississippi rivers." The Sauk and Foxes, still a proud and highly sensitive people, quite naturally objected to this cavalier treatment, which left them without authority for even a temporary abiding-place east of the Mississippi, save so far as they might find one within this mining reservation. Under these several conventions all prisoners were mutually given up, the tribes being placed on the same footing with the federal government that they occupied before the war.

At the Wisconsin Creole settlements of Green Bay and Prairie du Chien, the presence of American troops brought added interest to life. The former, in particular, was a typical frontier garrison town, with the especial distinction that in the main the military and civil officials were in race and temperament far removed from the people they ruled. Indeed, although courtesies came soon to be exchanged between townsmen and soldiery, several years were to elapse before a spirit of true *camaraderie* prevailed between the inhabitants and the little army of occupation.

During the period of navigation there was, as in the French and British régimes, frequent business, social, and official communication with Mackinac, the principal *entrepôt* of the fur-trade and military headquarters for the upper lakes. Long bateaux propelled by soldiers and *voyageurs* would, in fine weather, make the distance of two hundred and forty miles in five days; but if storms arose, necessitating delays in camp to await calm water, six and even seven might be occupied in the voyage. Such expeditions were usually occasions of much jollity, of which interesting contemporary descriptions have been preserved for us.[1] Somewhat similar boat trips were not infrequent over the Fox-Wisconsin route between Prairie du Chien and Green Bay, consequent upon exchanges of officers or garrisons, or in the conduct of the fur-trade.

But for nearly six months in the year Green Bay was ice-bound and almost isolated: wholly so from Mackinac, and only connected with Prairie du Chien, Chicago, and other southern outposts by overland Indian trails winding deviously through dense forests, across wind-swept prairies, or following closely the banks and beaches of rivers and lakes. The pedestrian mail carrier, — either alone or with an Indian companion, — limited to a burden of sixty pounds, would occupy a month in making the round trip between Green Bay and Chicago, and the hardships and dangers experienced on the way were such as none but men of the toughest fibre could endure.[2] The Eastern mail

[1] See Mrs. H. S. Baird, " Early Days on Mackinac Island," in *Wis. Hist. Colls.*, vol. xiv.

[2] The " Narrative of Alexis Clermont," in *Wis. Hist. Colls.*, vol. xv, although of a somewhat later period, presents a close picture of a wilderness mail carrier's experience any time after the establishment of Fort Howard.

came from Detroit but twice a year, being brought
by a soldier, whose long and weary overland route
was by way of Chicago, around the southern bend
of Lake Michigan.

The country lying between Lake Michigan and
the Mississippi River had under the French and
English been fairly free from disorders. But with
the coming of the Americans, adventurers and
social outcasts began slowly to appear in the district, with the inevitable train of violence. Mur-
ders of whites by Indians came now occasionally to
be reported; and among the enlisted men were not
a few desperate characters, who required the exercise by their officers of severe measures of repres-
sion and punishment.

But apparently the most serious task before the
gay and often very young garrison officials of Fort
Howard was the devising of ways and means to
beguile the tedium of their lives, especially during the severe and protracted winters. Breakfasts,
dinners, balls, and sledging parties were functions
frequently mentioned in the social correspondence
of those days. Among the better class of French
were several young women, the reputation of whose
beauty and talent — the fur-traders of early Wisconsin not infrequently educated their children at
Montreal [1] — has come down to us in the annals of

[1] In 1791 Jacques Porlier was established as a tutor in the
family of Pierre Grignon; but it was not until 1817 that a regular school was opened in Green Bay — the first by M. and Mme.

the picturesque old town. The American families, both official and professional, — for representatives of the bar, of medicine, and of the Church came soon upon the scene, — were not behind them in social graces.

The blanketed Indian was ever present, either lounging about the fur-trade warehouses or acting as domestic servant. In the veins of perhaps most of the Creoles of that day, high and low, coursed more or less aboriginal blood, which brought no stigma. Social distinctions were still sharply drawn, however, between the well-to-do *bourgeois*, who maintained a retinue of clerks and *voyageurs*, and the humble *habitan*, placidly cultivating his narrow field abutting on the riverside.

It is not surprising that in such a varied society, at that period, and under these picturesque conditions, the spirit of romance held high sway; or that when men and women of the early day came, in more prosaic times, to write their memoirs of primitive Green Bay, they invariably dwelt most fondly upon the decades immediately following the advent of American·domination.

It will be remembered that in 1800 the territory now embraced in the State of Wisconsin became a part of Indiana Territory. Nine years later Indi-

Carron, who served but temporarily. Later in the year an English school was taught by Thomas S. Johnson of New York, who experienced much annoyance at the friction between American and Creole children.

ana was reduced to the present limits of that state, all that had been lopped from her domain being set off as Illinois Territory. After another nine years (1818), the State of Illinois was created with its existing boundaries, and all of the old Northwest Territory not included in Illinois, lying westward of Lake Michigan, was added to Michigan Territory. In this manner the future Wisconsin became a part of Michigan, whose governor at the time was Lewis Cass, a man of unusual mental breadth and insight.

By act of the Michigan territorial legislature, approved October 26, 1818, there were established west of Lake Michigan three counties, which included all or part of the present Wisconsin: Brown, being substantially the eastern half of the present state, with Green Bay as its county seat; Crawford, embracing the greater part of the western half, with its seat at Prairie du Chien; and Michillimackinac, which included a part of northern Wisconsin and practically the present upper peninsula of Michigan, and stretched from Lake Huron to the Mississippi, with its seat "at the Borough of Michillimackinac." The following day Governor Cass appointed officials to carry on a civil government within Brown and Crawford counties. As elsewhere in Michigan, each county was given a court of quarter sessions, consisting of a chief justice and two associates, who were judge of probate and justice of the peace respectively.

The amusing, nevertheless popular, Reaume was for a time one of the associates in Brown County, still serving in the last-mentioned capacity. There were also a court commissioner, a clerk, and a sheriff. Many years passed before trained lawyers were appointed to judicial positions, it being considered sufficient that such officials be men of standing in the community; the wise policy of selecting for many of the local offices Frenchmen, who understood the people, was followed from the beginning.

During the first two years justice was administered under the old French law, the *coutume de Paris*, which had been guaranteed to the people of the old Province of Quebec under the Quebec Act of 1774. Substantially, this was the system which Reaume had sought to enforce, so far as his limited stock of legal learning enabled him; when necessary this was supplemented by martial law, administered by the British and American garrisons successively. In 1821, however, Michigan Territory introduced its own code, a radical change which at first wrought considerable confusion and no little amusement, particularly at Green Bay, where the then chief justice was Jacques Porlier, who, while able to read English, could not speak it.

In January, 1823, Congress established a circuit court for the three counties, a term of which was to be held in each county during the year. Heretofore, cases of capital crime or civil cases

involving over a thousand dollars, as well as writs
of error, mandamus, etc., had necessarily to be
tried before the supreme court of the Territory at
Detroit, which involved long and costly journeys.
The new court had concurrent civil and criminal
jurisdiction with the supreme bench, but most
cases might still, by writ of error, be carried up
to Detroit. The first session of the circuit court
was opened at Mackinac in July, under the administration of James Duane Doty, a young man
twenty-three years of age, who in February preceding had been appointed "additional judge of
the United States for the Michigan Territory," his
district extending between the Straits of Mackinac
and the sources of the Mississippi. In later years
Doty, who possessed talent and unusual dignity,
became one of the most conspicuous political leaders
in Wisconsin Territory.

Green Bay was first visited by the court in October, 1824. The prosecuting attorney was Henry
S. Baird of that settlement, a young Irishman who
was the first to practice law west of Lake Michigan, and soon rose to prominence in the new country. If not the most important, certainly the most
interesting business coming before the court at
this time was the attempted regulation of marriages between French and Indians. Heretofore,
these had usually been common-law unions; but
now no less than thirty-six offenders were formally indicted and notified that they must be married

according to either civil or church law, or stand
trial for punishment. This action of the new bench,
in declaring mutual-consent marriages invalid, and
their offspring illegitimate, aroused fierce indignation among the Creoles, and gave rise to protracted
litigation in the courts of Wisconsin. Later decisions generally upheld the common-law agreements
of the old régime.

American occupation was disturbing to the Creoles in another particular. Heretofore, Indian title
having been acquired by them through either consent or purchase at an early day, the settlers at
Green Bay and Prairie du Chien occupied their
fields " much in the manner of an Indian village,
the lands being alternately in common, and improved in detached parts as each should please,
and this by the common consent of the villagers."
As a rule the holdings were, as upon the lower
St. Lawrence and elsewhere in New France, narrow strips running far back from the river, which
was the common highway. This system of partition
brought the houses of the *habitans* close together
upon the waterside, for purposes of sociability as
well as for common access to the one avenue of
intercommunication.

Exact boundaries were of small account in these
primitive French-Canadian villages, and Wisconsin
Creoles had characteristically failed to obtain definite title to their plots. But now a business-like
people had come into possession of the country;

settlers were arriving, who sought absolute locations, and the federal government determined to ascertain and record the limits of the old French claims. No other method appearing, it was decided to accept as proof of title undisputed evidence of " individual and exclusive " occupancy by present claimants " between the 1st day of July, 1796, and the 3d day of March, 1807." [1]

A commission was therefore established in the summer of 1820, with headquarters at Detroit, and Isaac Lee, a surveyor, appointed agent for the taking of testimony.[2] Reaching Green Bay on August 24, Lee created considerable commotion by announcing his purpose, and bidding the people prepare their testimony against his return from Prairie du Chien, at which place he arrived October 2. Twenty-two days sufficed for discovering which of the Prairie du Chien claimants were, under the rules of the commission, entitled to their houses and fields. The Prairie had suffered much, he

[1] In opening the first circuit court at Mackinac, in July, 1823, Judge Doty stated at length the qualifications of grand jurors, in the course of which he defined freeholders to be all " Those persons who were in the possession of land in the Michigan Territory in the year 1796, at the time of the surrender of the Posts in this country. . . . It is understood to have been the intention of the Treaty, to secure to these people such quantities or tracts of land as they occupied and cultivated at that time, and to give them a freehold estate therein." — Doty's MS. Docket Book, in Wisconsin Historical Library.

[2] See reports and testimony in detail, in *American State Papers : Public Lands*, vol. iv, pp. 851–879.

found, from the lawlessness of bodies of American troops who from time to time had been stationed there, and who had occasionally and somewhat capriciously evicted many of the inhabitants. Concerning these, Lee declared that "docility, habitual hospitality, cheerful submission to the requisitions of any Government which may be set over them, are their universal characteristics."

The agent thereupon hurried back to the same task at Green Bay, where, however, he found himself ice-bound for the winter. This experience had the advantage of bettering his acquaintance with the simple, kindly folk of that quarter, and enlisting in their behalf his most cordial sympathy. Several claims had necessarily to be set aside because proof of continuous occupancy as far back as 1796 was lacking; but throughout the report it is plainly to be seen that both agent and commissioners were impressed with the possibility of injustice even to those whom they felt compelled to deny. Not a little litigation ensued, and it was several years before the burning question of French claims in Wisconsin became merely a matter of history.

At this period, the Chippewa occupied the northern third of the present Wisconsin, with about six hundred hunters, whose trade was chiefly reached from Lake Superior by the Ontonagon, Montreal, Bad, and Bois Brulé rivers. Such of the Sioux as were visited by Wisconsin traders from Prairie du

Chien were located on the west bank of the Mississippi, and toward its source, but frequently ranged into Wisconsin as far as the falls of the Black, Red Cedar, and St. Croix. The Sauk and Foxes were to be found for the most part in the lead district. The Menominee, with four hundred hunters, were on the Fox and generally throughout northeastern Wisconsin, Black River being their western boundary, while the country of the Chippewa penned them in upon the north; Green Bay was their chief *entrepôt*. Milwaukee was the most important rendezvous of the Potawatomi, who extended along the entire west shore of Lake Michigan and numbered two hundred hunters. The Winnebago sought peltries around Lake Winnebago, up the Fox River to its source, on the Wisconsin up to Stevens Point, about the headwaters of Rock River, in the region of the Madison lakes, and northwest to Black River, where they often overlapped the Menominee grounds; there were also a few of them on the Mississippi, above the mouth of the Wisconsin.

Until about 1830 the fur-traffic with these several tribes continued to be the dominating commercial interest in Wisconsin. The American Fur Company, now in full control of this section, had introduced many improvements; but although officered by some of the most acute business men of their generation, they were to the last obliged to accommodate themselves to the easy-going methods of the Creole and mixed-blood employees, who were essential intermediaries in dealing with the aborigines.

Mackinac remained the chief *entrepôt*, but important warehouse agencies were maintained at Green Bay, La Pointe, and Prairie du Chien. These were generally in the hands of semi-independent traders, like Porlier and Grignon at Green Bay, and Rolette at the Prairie, whose operations were widespread. Their ultimate profits, however, were slight, for Astor's establishment contrived through its fixed charges and percentages to absorb the lion's share. Subsidiary trading-posts — either wintering places or still smaller "jackknife" fur-gathering stations — were to be found, about the year 1820, on the Menominee, Peshtigo, Oconto, and Wolf rivers, on Lakes Flambeau, Chetac, Court Oreilles, Nemakagon, and Tomahawk, and at many other important native rendezvous, such as Oshkosh, Milwaukee, Sheboygan, Manitowoc, Two Rivers, and Portage. Indeed, very many of the present-day cities and villages of the state owe their origin, first to old Indian camps upon their sites, next to the fur-traders (French, British, or American) who assembled thereat, and finally to the agricultural settlers or to the pioneer ferrymen or tavern-keepers who, in the initial days of Americanization, established themselves in the neighborhood of these little commercial centres.

In their primitive condition the tribesmen laboriously made for themselves clothing, ornaments, weapons, implements, and utensils. Their food was in large measure obtained by hunting, fishing, and rudely cultivating the soil, although at times they were forced to resort to the usually plentiful supply of fruits, nuts, and edible roots. Indian corn (maize) was the principal crop; but they also raised beans, pumpkins, watermelons, and sunflower seeds — and in some states (but not ours), tobacco and sweet potatoes. In Wisconsin the marshes furnished large crops of wild rice (or oats), which when boiled or parched made an excellent substitute for maize.

The introduction of the fur-trade by Europeans wrought a serious change in the life and manners of the Indians. They were induced to abandon much of their agriculture and most of their useful village arts. Becoming hunters, they thus took a backward step in the long and painful road toward civilization. Heretofore they had needed furs only for raiment, sleeping mats, and tepee coverings; now, peltries were eagerly sought by the stranger, who would exchange for them weapons, cloth, iron kettles and tools, ornaments, and other marvelous objects of European manufacture, generally far better and more efficient than those which they had been wont to fashion for themselves.

Thus the Indians soon lost the arts of making clothing out of skins, kettles from clay, weapons from stone and copper, and beads (used for both ornament and currency) from clam-shells. They were not slow to discover that when they hunted, their labor was far more productive than of old. Comparatively slight effort on their part now enabled them to purchase from the white traders whatever they desired.   Moreover, the latter brought intoxicating liquors, heretofore unknown to our savages, but for which they soon acquired an inordinate greed, of which advantage was taken by charging prices therefor that brought enormous profits to the dealers. Aside from this new vice, the general result was disastrous to the improvident aborigines, for in considerable measure they ceased to be self-supporting. They soon came to depend on the fur-traders for most of the essentials of life ; and so general was the credit system among them, the summer's supplies being bought on the strength of the following winter's hunt, that tribesmen were practically always heavily in debt to the traders, which rendered it advisable for them to stand by their creditors whenever two rival nations were contesting the field. In the end, these conditions materially assisted in the undoing of the Indian.

The goods used in the forest traffic of the American Fur Company were of much the same character as those brought into the wilderness by the earliest French — coarse cloths, blankets, and shawls of brilliant hues, cheap jewelry, beads of many colors and sizes, ribbons and garterings, gay handkerchiefs, sleigh and hawk's bells, jews'-harps, hand mirrors, combs, hatchets, scalping knives, scissors, kettles, hoes, firearms and gunpowder, tobacco, pitch for mending bark canoes, and the ever-present intoxicant; which latter masqueraded under many euphemisms, ranging in degree between "fire-water" and "the white father's milk." Brought to Mackinac, at first by canoes and bateaux and later by sailing vessels, — after 1821, by occasional steamers, — the cargoes were there divided and distributed to the several larger agencies, whence the bales ultimately found their way to the farthest trading "shanties." It is estimated that "in 1820 between $60,000 and $75,000 worth of goods was brought annually to Wisconsin for the Indian trade."[1] This doubtless was the heyday of the traffic, which thenceforth, as American agricultural settlement slowly developed, and lead-mining came to be an important industry, began gradually to dwindle, both actually and relatively.

[1] F. J. Turner, "The Indian Trade in Wisconsin," in *Johns Hopkins University Studies*, vol. ix, p. 606.

CHAPTER IX

LEAD-MINING AND INDIAN WARS

It will be remembered that in 1804 the Sauk and Fox claimants of the large lead-bearing region in Illinois, Wisconsin, and Missouri ceded that tract to the United States ; but by a clause in the treaty they were permitted to occupy their old camping-places until such time as the land was disposed of by the federal government to actual settlers. Although this sale was in 1816 confirmed by these two tribes, the Chippewa, Ottawa, and Potawatomi now advanced a claim to joint ownership with them in the grant. To the three protestants was thereupon ceded by the United States — quite ignoring the Sauk and Foxes — all that portion lying north of the latitude of the southernmost bend of Lake Michigan, with the exception of a large lead-mine reservation abutting on the Wisconsin and Mississippi rivers.

We have also seen that French, Spanish, and British miners, chiefly connected with the fur-trade, had in turn taken much ore from the country. Americans, as well, conducted desultory operations within the district during the Revolutionary War, and thereafter. Indeed, access to the lead mines

was from the earliest times of the white conquest
eagerly sought, for neither military nor fur-hunt-
ing enterprises could exist without material for
bullets.

In 1809 the first shot tower in the region was
erected at Herculaneum, Missouri. Two years following, Indian Agent Boilvin, at Prairie du Chien,
reported that thrifty Sauk and Fox Indians on the
east side of the Mississippi River, below that hamlet, and Iowa tribesmen on the west side, had
" mostly abandoned the chase, except to furnish
themselves with meat, and turned their attention
to the manufacture of lead." In 1810 they had in
their rude furnaces smelted 400,000 pounds of
metal, which they exchanged for goods, partly with
venturesome Americans, but mostly with Canadian
traders, who were continually inciting them to opposition against the former. He suggests that the
federal government would be wise to introduce
among them a blacksmith and civilized tools, and
thereby counteract Canadian influence. A few
years later a St. Louis lead-dealer bought at one
time from Indians in the district around the present Galena, Illinois, seventy tons of metal. As for
ousting the Canadians, this long proved impossible.
Up to 1819, several American traders who had
sought to compete with them among the Sauk and
Fox miners, paid the penalty of their lives. It was
believed by the Indians, and in this opinion they were
amply justified by events, that if American cupid-

ity were aroused by the richness of the deposit, the latter would, under the treaty of 1804, promptly attempt to dispossess the natives.

By 1819, American control over the trans-Lake Michigan country had become firmly established. Thenceforth we hear little of the Canadian traders, and American miners were now freely operating in the lead district, independently or in conjunction with Indians. In June and July of that year, Major Thomas Forsyth, Indian agent for the Sauk and Foxes, made a voyage from St. Louis to the Falls of St. Anthony, and reported upon " the number, situation, and quality of all lead mines between Apple Creek and Prairie du Chien." Contractors for army and Indian supplies were at this time frequently passing the mines, on their way between St. Louis and Prairie du Chien, and Green Bay and Mississippi points, and both Indian and white miners found ready customers for their lead.

Leases of lead lands in Missouri had been granted by the federal government as early as 1807, but until 1822 mining in Wisconsin and Illinois was intermittent, individual, and without system. In the latter year a thrifty Kentuckian, Colonel James Johnson, secured a lease of a part of the present site of Galena, and under strong military protection, with competent implements and miners, aided by negro slaves, began operations on a scale heretofore unknown in the lead country.

Johnson's success at once attracted a horde of
squatters and prospectors from Missouri, Kentucky,
and Tennessee, while many came from southern
Illinois. Few of the newcomers paid much attention to governmental regulations. Such as secured
leases suffered from encroachments, and the consequent disputes were disastrous to many. In 1823
there were thirteen lessees who had established a
considerable mining colony, but unlicensed plants
could be numbered by the score. So unsatisfactory
was the leasing system, and so slight the resultant
revenue, that in 1846 Congress abolished it and
thereafter the lands were sold in open market.

Upon the 1st of July, 1825, about a hundred
persons were reported to be employed in mining in
the Galena district. By August of the next year,
this population had increased to 453. It was estimated that in Missouri, however, where the mines
were privately owned and prospectors sharply ordered off, two thousand men were thus engaged, —
"miners, teamsters, and laborers of every kind
(including slaves)." In 1827 the name Galena was
applied to the principal settlement. Two years
later the heaviest immigration began, reaching
well up into the present Wisconsin; and from that
time forward the lead region lying north and south
of the Illinois-Wisconsin boundary was the centre
of a great industry, which soon came quite to
overshadow the now declining fur-traffic of earlier
days.

The rush of prospectors and speculators into the lead-mining country of Illinois and Wisconsin was accompanied by scenes and conditions similar in character to those obtaining in the later silver and gold-mining camps of California, the Rocky Mountains, the Black Hills, and Alaska. Dozens of the old Indian trails reaching northward from central Illinois were soon converted into highways for Concord coaches and lumber-wagon expresses. Men poured into the district on foot and by Mississippi River boat, on horseback and by team, from all sections of the East and West. New England, New York, the Middle and Southern states, and Europe were freely represented ; Cornishmen, omnipresent in mining operations, began to arrive as early as 1827. In a few months prospectors were picking holes all over southwestern Wisconsin, and soon isolated log shanties and stockades for protection against possible assaults of resident Indians were familiar objects in the landscape. Men worth their thousands bivouacked along the roads and native foot-trails, alongside of well-armed vagabonds of every grade. A traveler of that day [1] tells us that " to come upon a couple of rough fellows sitting on a log or stone, playing old sledge for each other's last dollar, was no uncommon experience."

The Sauk and Foxes and occasional Winnebago, who through several generations had, in their

[1] " Narrative of Morgan L. Martin " in *Wis. Hist. Colls.*, vol. xi, p. 398.

crude fashion, done a good share of the mining and
smelting in the district, were now rudely pushed
aside by the army of new arrivals whom they could
not withstand. Native shafts were boldly appropriated by armed whites, who came to stay ; and sink-
holes that the former could no longer operate with
their rude tools were reopened and found to be
exceptionally rich. Mushroom towns sprang up all
over the district; the "diggings" were fitted out
with modern appliances ; smelting furnaces were
erected at convenient points ; deep-worn native
paths became ore roads. The aboriginal miner
was quickly crushed beneath the wheels of civilization.

The Indians of Wisconsin, Minnesota, Iowa,
and Illinois — the Chippewa, Sauk, Foxes, Menominee, Iowa, Sioux, Winnebago, and a portion
of the Ottawa and Potawatomi — had long engaged spasmodically in intertribal warfare. The
United States government felt that if a stop were
not put to these disturbances, they might "extend
to the other tribes, and involve the Indians upon
the Missouri, the Mississippi, and the Lakes in
general hostilities." By a treaty concluded at
Prairie du Chien on August 19, 1825, it was agreed
between the respective chiefs that "There shall be
a firm and perpetual peace between the Sioux and
Chippewas ; between the Sioux and the confederated tribes of Sacs and Foxes ; and between the
Ioways and the Sioux ; " and definite boundaries

were established between their hunting ranges. The participating chiefs nevertheless took umbrage at the American commissioners, William Clark and Lewis Cass, whom they accused of cold formality and of parsimony, for failing liberally to ply them with "milk" and presents, after the fashion of their old-time British father; moreover, they were not allowed to ratify the new treaty by a savage carousal. The result was that the tribesmen returned home with their natural dislike of the unsympathetic Americans much intensified.

The succeeding winter was marked by various disorders. Predatory expeditions were reported between Chippewa and Sioux; while both Sioux and Winnebago were growing offensive in their attitude toward American settlers and miners, and some of the few French traders remaining in the region were busy circulating among the forest barbarians rumors that another war was imminent between England and the United States. On their part, the Winnebago were irritated because two of their warriors were imprisoned at Fort Crawford for some petty offenses. During the summer of 1826 there was much uneasiness among the whites on both sides of the upper Mississippi, and the garrison of Prairie du Chien was expecting a native attack.

In the midst of these alarming rumors and actual disturbances, the federal war department ordered that Fort Crawford be abandoned, its garrison being

dispatched to Fort Snelling, which had been built
six years previous in the neighborhood of the present St. Paul, some two hundred miles farther up the
Mississippi. This withdrawal was upon the request
of the commandant, Colonel Josiah Snelling, who
had experienced some personal difficulties with the
people of Prairie du Chien. Retirement in the face
of native threats was quite naturally construed by
the neighboring Winnebago as a confession of weakness. During the following winter, apparently convinced that another British-American conflict was
impending, young Winnebago hot-heads stirred
themselves into a warlike spirit, and British sympathizers were in the ascendant.

Among our North American Indians, while in
the wild stage, no young man might be accepted
among the tribesmen as a warrior, and thus a full-
fledged member of society, until he had taken at
least one scalp; which accounts for the eagerness
with which Indian youth always welcomed the suggestion of war. The elders, who had long since won
their eagle feathers, — one being worn for each scalp
taken, — and with these acquired some degree of
wise caution, were apt to advise a waiting policy.
The young, scoffing such counsel, were almost inevitably the first disturbers of peace in the long and
bloody story of frontier warfare, generally carrying the conservatives with them when the enemy
attempted reprisal.

Several young Winnebago bucks were, in March,

1827, hunting upon Yellow River, twelve miles north of Prairie du Chien, on the Iowa side of the Mississippi. Coming across the log cabin of one Methode, a civilized half-breed from Prairie du Chien, who with his family was making maple sugar, the hot-bloods could not resist their passion for scalps, and killed the man, his wife, and five children.

While popular excitement over this event was at its height in Prairie du Chien, a Sioux contingent from west of the Mississippi arrived at the village of Red Bird, a petty Winnebago chief whose camp was pitched on Black River, near the present village of Trempealeau. The visitors brought a story, which quite likely they knew to be false, that the two Winnebago prisoners carried from Fort Crawford to Fort Snelling had been executed by white soldiers. The effect of this malicious tale was to drive Red Bird and his little band of warriors into a vengeful frenzy. To the quiet satisfaction of the American-hating Sioux, the villagers set out to take at least four white scalps in retaliation, for the tribal code of reprisal demanded that for each scalp taken from their people two must be obtained from the enemy.

There were not lacking other incentives as well. The continued inhospitality of the Indian agent at Prairie du Chien, who closely calculated his expenses, irritated them, and they conjured up contrasting pictures of British generosity. They bit-

terly resented, too, being driven from the lead-mine
region, and the often brutal treatment awarded
them by American miners. These and a hundred
other annoyances, some petty and others serious,
combined to arouse native animosity and thus
kindle the flame of the incipient uprising.

Just at this time there were being propelled up
the Mississippi two keel-boats laden with provisions dispatched from St. Louis to Fort Snelling.
Red Bird's followers boarded the craft, as was customary in those waters, and with a semblance of
friendliness, a subterfuge of which the Indian was
master, sold venison and native trinkets to the crew.
It was noticed by the savages that the boatmen
were practically unarmed, but the former lacked
the nerve to attack. All along the west bank, as far
as the fort, the Sioux made no attempt to hide their
disaffection, but they also failed to open active hostilities, and allowed the cargoes to reach their
destination.

Red Bird, with Wekau and two others of his
fighting men, now turned their canoes down river
to Prairie du Chien, where they hoped for better
fortune: apparently forgetting that its peaceful
Creole settlers were firm friends of the aborigines
and had given them no cause of complaint. It was
the 26th of June, and many of the men were
absent in their fields or upon fishing excursions.
The Winnebago contented themselves with bullying
some of the women, and then set out for the farm

of Registre Gagnier, two miles south of the village. Gagnier was an honest, hard-working fellow, son of a negro woman and a French *voyageur*, noted for his friendliness to Indians. With him were his white wife, two children, and a serving-man named Lipcap. Red Bird had long been Gagnier's friend, hence they were met by cordial greetings. The four agents of death calmly sat for hours enjoying the mulatto's hospitality, and then, seizing a favorable moment, Red Bird and Wekau killed Lipcap and Gagnier, and scalped the latter's infant girl of eighteen months. After a desperate struggle, Madame Gagnier escaped to the village with her ten-year-old boy. The hue-and-cry being now raised, the murderers promptly escaped. The scalped child was brought back to the settlement, where she survived her brutal treatment, grew to womanhood, and was the mother of a large family.

When the fugitives, skulking along the bush-grown shores of the Mississippi, arrived at the mouth of the Bad Axe, forty miles north of Prairie du Chien, they there found a hunting camp of nearly forty of Red Bird's warriors. Although but three of the required scalps had thus far been obtained, the feat was celebrated in a protracted drunken debauch. In the afternoon of the third day there hove into sight upon the Mississippi the foremost of the two plank-armored keel-boats already mentioned, now returning to St. Louis. The boatmen had all the way from Fort Snelling been jeered and threatened by Sioux along the west bank, but had been unharmed. When the Winnebago at the Bad Axe showed fight, the crew of the forward boat in a spirit of bravado ran their craft close in toward shore. This was the signal for a heavy fusillade from the drunken natives, some of whom boarded the vessel and ran her on a sandbar. After a spasmodic rifle duel lasting for three hours, dusk set in, and the boatmen, although obliged to remain under cover, now adroitly managed to free their craft from the bar, and she was soon borne off by the swift current. Nearly seven hundred bullets had pierced the boat through and through, yet the casualties were slight — on board, two killed outright, and two mortally and two slightly wounded; of the savages, seven were killed and fourteen wounded. The rear keel passed the camp at midnight, and was fired on, but escaped unhurt.

The news of this fierce engagement was promptly disseminated from Prairie du Chien, and a widespread frontier war confidently expected. Militiamen and volunteers came pouring into the village from the neighboring lead-mine country, which in the general panic soon lost half of its white population. The settlers strengthened the old fort, which soon was reoccupied by a small battalion from Fort Snelling. A full regiment came from Jefferson Barracks, near St. Louis, under General Henry Atkinson. Early in August, Major William Whistler of Fort Howard proceeded up Fox River with a portion of his command. Whistler's progress was delayed by his presence at a council held at Grand Butte des Morts with the Winnebago, Chippewa, and Menominee, regarding lands granted by them to certain New York Indians, concerning which transaction we shall hear later. At this council, concluded August 11, Whistler notified the Winnebago that their security as a tribe wholly lay in surrendering Red Bird and Wekau as murderers of the Gagnier family. The headmen were given to understand that were this done nothing further would be said concerning the keel-boat fight.

Whistler reached the Fox-Wisconsin portage on September 1, while Atkinson was with some difficulty advancing up the swift-flowing Wisconsin with the intention of effecting a junction with him at this, the heart of the Winnebago country. Immediately on his arrival, Whistler was notified by an Indian runner that at three o'clock in the afternoon of the following day the two culprits, who were voluntarily surrendering themselves to save their tribe from threatened destruction, would appear at military headquarters. At the hour agreed on, the troops were on dress parade, and with full martial honors received the murderers, who advanced singing their mournful death-songs. Wekau was a rather miserable specimen of his tribe; but the young Red Bird, a tall, manly fellow, acted with exquisite dignity, and appeared clothed in the picturesque regalia of a chief.

In judging the motives and conduct of Red Bird, justice demands that we do so strictly according to the view-point of his own race, however mistaken we of ours may consider it. Abiding by the stern ethics of his people, he had in the scalp-taking acted impersonally as the supposed avenger of his tribe. His methods undoubtedly were cruel and treacherous, but they accorded strictly with the rules of warfare in which he and countless generations of his forbears had carefully been trained, and which they deemed eminently proper — for in war the end and not the means concerned them. In the eyes of his fellows he was now as popular a hero as any leader of a forlorn hope. He suffered no qualms of conscience. The same lofty purpose that actuated him in his vicarious vengeance led him freely to offer himself as a tribal sacrifice when this alone seemed necessary to prevent the destruction of his clansmen by the all-conquering Americans ; and he compelled the cowardly and reluctant Wekau to join him. This was the spirit in which Whistler and his men, as frontier soldiers familiar with the savage point of view, regarded the surrender — the spirit that gives point and meaning to perhaps the most striking picture in Wisconsin history, next to the landfall of Nicolet in 1634.

Upon being imprisoned at Prairie du Chien, the chief was relieved of the necessity of wearing irons, and given much freedom. Opportunities were abundant for his escape, and sympathetic soldiers

sometimes seemed to place these in his way; yet
Red Bird was too proud to break his promise to remain and stand for trial for his life. A few months
later he died in prison, of an epidemic then raging
in the village.

The murderers of Methode were tried and condemned to death, but received pardon from President Adams, upon the Winnebago renouncing their
claim to the coveted lead mines. The following
year (1828), Fort Winnebago was erected at the
Portage, with especial reference to keeping that
tribe in order.

During and succeeding the Revolutionary War,
the Stockbridge and Brothertown [1] tribes, by this
time Christianized and well-advanced towards civilization, moved from New England to western
New York, in the neighborhood of the Oneida and
Munsee. But soon after 1810 there arose among
the four tribes a strong desire to seek homes in the
still farther West. White persons interested in the
Stockbridge, in particular, expressed solicitude that
these converts be permanently removed from the
evil influences radiating from fast-growing settlements; and land speculators were eager that the Indian title in that part of New York be extinguished
as rapidly as possible, consequently they were not
slow to foster the movement.

Among the friends of the Stockbridge was Dr.

[1] The Brothertown consisted of remnants of various New England tribes, who had settled near the Stockbridge.

Jedediah Morse, a Presbyterian divine, and father of the inventor of the electric telegraph. In 1820, Morse was sent into the Northwest by the War Department as a special agent to select lands for the four tribes. Among other places, he visited the Fox River valley, and on July 9 delivered in Green Bay probably the first Protestant sermon ever heard there. Morse selected this valley as the most eligible site, the principal native owners of the chosen land being the Menominee and the Winnebago.

At that time there was resident among the Oneida an erratic quarter-breed named Eleazer Williams, who during the War of 1812–15 had served the Americans as a spy among his relatives, the Canadian Indians, but who was now an Episcopal missionary. Possessed of considerable natural ability, and of attractive manners, an Iroquois-English translator, and the author of several minor religious works, Williams had won a rather wide reputation among persons interested in Indian ethnology, languages, history, and missions; he was frequently referred to as an authority on these subjects. He had also acquired an ascendency over certain of his own people, although by some of them instinctively mistrusted — and rightly so, for while in some respects an interesting and unusual character, he lacked sincerity, was self-seeking and vainglorious, and perversely untruthful. Always a *poseur*, we now find him assuming leadership in this new phase of native emigration, which he eagerly supported from motives of personal ambition; for it appears that he dreamed of a revived but Christianized Iroquois confederacy in the West, with himself as its dictator.

In 1821, Williams, then about thirty-three years of age, led to Green Bay a large and enthusiastic delegation of New York chiefs and headmen interested in the project, their conveyance being the first steamer to appear upon Lake Michigan. This novel craft bore the picturesque name, borrowed from the Indians, of Walk-in-the-Water.[1] The long tour of these native pioneers was financed by the missionary bodies of the Episcopal and Presbyterian churches and the New York Land Company — the last-named representing the speculators who wished access to the territory now occupied by the several tribes. In August a treaty was concluded with the reluctant Menominee and Winnebago, by which was ceded to these New York Indians, for five hundred dollars in cash and fifteen hundred dollars' worth of goods, a strip some four miles in width, crossing Fox River at right angles, with Little Chute as the centre.

This grant satisfied none save Williams. The two Wisconsin tribes quickly repented the bargain, and the New Yorkers deemed it a paltry exchange for their present homes. As for the missionary, he was

[1] Constructed in 1818, the first steamer on Lake Erie; lost in a storm, near Buffalo, in November, 1821.

loudly condemned by all. Another council was therefore held by him at Green Bay, in September and October of the following year (1822). From this conference the Winnebago withdrew in disgust; but the Menominee, yielding to Williams's specious arguments and easy promises, finally agreed to accept the New York tribesmen as joint owners with themselves of all Menominee lands — then embracing almost a half of the present Wisconsin. But within a twelvemonth the Menominee came bitterly to regret their complacency, and there followed ten years of confusion and wordy discussion. Congress had several times to interfere in an attempt to quiet the contest.

Williams and the little band of Oneida who clung to his counsels immediately took up their residence on Fox River, not far above Green Bay. Gradually thereafter, chiefly in 1832, a considerable number of the New York tribesmen moved to Wisconsin, — the Stockbridge and Brothertown settling to the east of Lake Winnebago, in the present Calumet County, and in due course becoming citizens; the Oneida and Munsee establishing themselves upon Duck Creek, near the mouth of the Lower Fox, and upon the Oneida reservation near Green Bay, but not until recent years (1890–93) did they take their lands in severalty and assume citizenship.

The migration had throughout been managed so badly and awakened such general discontent

among both whites and reds, and his own character had been exhibited in so unfavorable a light,
that Williams's political dreams were necessarily
at an end ; probably they could not, in any event,
have been realized. For over twenty years he came
and went among the Oneida as a missionary,
although most discriminating persons discredited
him as crafty and unscrupulous. Suddenly, in
1849, when in his sixty-first year, the man posed
in public as Louis XVII, hereditary sovereign of
France; he had, however, privately made assertions
to that effect as early as 1838.

There seems no reason to doubt that after Louis
XVI and his queen, Marie Antoinette, were executed in Paris (1793), their son of eight years, the
dauphin, died two years later (June 8, 1795) of
ill-treatment and neglect in his cell in the tower of
the Temple. Sufficient mystery, however, attached
to the death of young Louis XVII to warrant the
growth of myth, and during several political up-
heavals of France there arose in various parts of
Europe more than two dozen impostors, who sev-
erally claimed to be the " lost dauphin." The
theory advanced in each case was, that Bourbon
adherents had spirited the young prince from his
prison and substituted a child of meaner clay —
the little fugitive, with mind weakened by confinement and bad usage, being thenceforth reared
among peasant surroundings. Although these
various pretenders have each in his turn been dis-

credited by competent publicists and historians, nevertheless there still exist many Frenchmen who appear seriously to believe that the pretensions of descendants of at least one of these claimants are just, and worthy of their earnest adherence.[1]

The novelty of Williams's assertions created far more popular attention in the United States of his day than could similar royalist pretensions in our more sophisticated times. Embellished with much sensational detail, they were in effect that as the veritable dauphin, then mentally weak but later outgrowing this defect, he had been brought to America and given to a somewhat prominent and very worthy Indian family of the St. Regis tribe of Canada, to rear as their own child. Further, that when, in 1841, the young Prince de Joinville, third son of Louis Philippe, King of the French, was traveling in Canada and the United States, he visited Williams's home on Fox River, and proposed that the latter " abdicate the crown of France in favor of Louis Philippe " in return for a splendid establishment either in France or America — a proposition promptly rejected by the Wisconsin Bourbon, who " though in poverty and in exile, would not sacrifice his honor."

[1] Referring to Naundorff, who died at Delft, Holland, August 10, 1845, claiming to be Charles-Louis de Bourbon, duke of Normandy. There is a considerable literature on the subject, and the claims of the family are persistently maintained, their organ being a monthly magazine, *Revue Historique de la Question Louis XVII*, established at Paris in January, 1905.

Despite his somewhat theatrical fondness for mystery, the facts regarding Williams's lineage and career were well known to many. His indignant Indian relatives repudiated his pretensions and showed their falsity. The color and texture of his skin indisputably proved his aboriginal blood. He was three years younger than the real dauphin would have been. His reputation for veracity had long since departed. Nevertheless his features bore some resemblance to those of the Bourbons, and this was helpful to his deception. The American pretender was seriously discussed in thousands of homes in this country, and even in Europe attracted some attention. He died in 1858, his last years marked by neglect and by only slight attempts at self-exploitation. Occasionally, and with an air of serious acceptance, irresponsible writers still use the fantastic tale, in order to lend "color" to Wisconsin annals.[1]

On Rock River, in Illinois, near its junction with the Mississippi, there was a considerable Sauk village, inhabited by a large band of active sympathizers with the British, and under the domination of Black Sparrow Hawk (commonly called Black Hawk), an ambitious, restless, and somewhat demagogic headman of the tribe.[2] Although himself

---

[1] The standard authority on this subject is William W. Wight, "Eleazer Williams: his forerunners, himself," in *Parkman Club Papers*, vol. i.

[2] He was not a chief (an hereditary office), as is commonly assumed — simply a popular leader.

"touching the quill" at both the treaty of 1804 and that with the Sauk and Foxes in May, 1816, he afterwards denied the authority of the tribal chiefs to sign away the common lands, thereby ignoring his own earlier assent.

When, in 1816, the federal government treated separately therefor with the Ottawa, Chippewa, and Potawatomi, and it was found that the lower Rock River was south of the prescribed boundary line, the majority of the Sauk and Foxes on that stream, under the Fox head-chief Keokuk, discreetly moved to the west of the Mississippi. But Black Hawk's "British band," as they were called, — two hundred of them had fought under Tecumseh, — continued to hold the old village site, where he himself was born and where was the great cemetery of the tribe; quite ignoring the fact that their tribal rights in the territory were no longer recognized by the United States, even for the temporary abode provided in 1804.

White squatters, coveting land far beyond the frontier of legal entries, still some sixty miles eastward, began to annoy the Hawk as early as 1823, burning his lodges while he was absent on the hunt, destroying his crops, insulting his women, and now and then actually beating him and his people. Persistently advised by the tribal chiefs to abandon his town to the on-rushing tide of settlement, he nevertheless obstinately held his ground. In the spring of 1830, affairs had reached a crisis.

When the British band returned from their winter's hunt they found their cemetery plowed over, for several squatters had now preëmpted the village site, the cemetery, and the extensive aboriginal planting grounds; yet a belt of forty miles of Indian lands still lay unsurveyed between this and the western line of regular settlement.

The indignant Hawk now took his band overland by the great Sauk trail, south of Lake Michigan, to consult with his friend the British military agent at Malden, in Canada, not far from Detroit. He was there advised that the spirit of the treaty of 1804 had clearly been violated, and that if he persisted in repelling the squatters the government's sense of fair play would surely support him; but the British official evidently had not carefully studied the trend of our Indian diplomacy. Thus fortified, Black Hawk returned to his village in the spring of 1831, his people in a starving condition, only to find white intruders more numerous and offensive than ever. He thereupon indiscreetly threatened them with force if they did not at once depart. This was construed as being a " bloody menace," and the Illinois militia were promptly called out by Governor John Reynolds in a flaming proclamation, to " repel the invasion of the British band." On June 25, the Hawk cowered before a demonstration made at his village by some seven hundred militiamen and regulars, and fled to the west of the Mississippi, humbly promising never to return without the express permission of the federal government.

Black Hawk, now a man of some fifty-four years, a somewhat remarkable organizer and military tactician, and for one of his race broad-minded and humane, was nevertheless too easily led by the advice of others. He was now beset by young Pota-watomi hot-bloods from northeastern Illinois and along the western shore of Lake Michigan, scalp-hunters from the Winnebago along the upper Rock River, and emissaries from the Ottawa and Chip-pewa, all of whom. urged him to return and fight for his rights. Particularly was he influenced by a Winnebago soothsayer named White Cloud, who throughout was his evil genius. No crop had been raised, and the winter in Iowa was unusually harsh, so that by early spring the British band were men-aced by famine.

Driven to desperation, and relying on these prof-fers of intertribal assistance, the Hawk crossed the Mississippi at Yellow Banks, April 6, 1832, with five hundred warriors, mostly Sauk, accompanied by all their women, children, and domestic equip-ment. Their intention was to raise a crop at the Winnebago village at Prophet's Town, on Rock River, and then if practicable the bucks would take the war-path in the autumn.

But the news of the "invasion" spread like wildfire through the Illinois and Wisconsin settle-ments. Another fiery proclamation from Spring-

field summoned the people to arms, the United
States was also called on for troops, those settlers
who did not fly the country threw up log forts,
and everywhere was aroused intense excitement
and feverish preparation for bloody strife.

In an incredibly short time, three hundred regulars and eighteen hundred horse and foot volunteers were on the march.[1] The startled Hawk sent
back a defiant message, and retreated up Rock
River, making a brief stand at Stillman's Creek.
Here, finding that the promised assistance from
other tribes was not forthcoming, he attempted to
surrender on stipulation that he be allowed peacefully to withdraw to the west of the Mississippi.
But his messengers, on approaching with their
white flag the camp of a party of twenty-five hundred half-drunken Illinois cavalry militia, were
brutally slain. Accompanied by a mere handful of
braves, the enraged Sauk leader now ambushed
and easily routed this large and boisterous party,
whose members displayed rank cowardice; in their
mad retreat they spread broadcast through the
settlements a report that Black Hawk was backed
by two thousand bloodthirsty warriors, bent on
a campaign of universal slaughter. This greatly

[1] Abraham Lincoln was the captain of a militia company. Jefferson Davis was a lieutenant of regulars, nominally stationed at
Prairie du Chien, but he appears to have been absent on detached
duty throughout the greater part of the war; after its close, he
escorted the captured Black Hawk from Prairie du Chien to Jefferson Barracks. Zachary Taylor was also an officer of regulars.

increased popular consternation throughout the West. The name of the deluded Black Hawk became everywhere coupled with stories of savage cruelty, and served as a household bugaboo. Meanwhile, so great was the alarm that the Illinois militia, originally hot to take the field, now, on flimsy excuses, promptly disbanded.

Black Hawk himself was much encouraged by his easy victory at Stillman's Creek, and, laden with spoils from the militia camp, removed his women and children about seventy miles northeastward, to the neighborhood of Lake Koshkonong, near the headwaters of Rock River, a Wisconsin district girt about by great marshes and not then easily accessible to white troops. Thence descending with his braves to northern Illinois, where he had spasmodic help from small bands of young Winnebago and Potawatomi, the Hawk and his friends engaged in irregular hostilities along the Illinois-Wisconsin border, and made life miserable for the settlers and miners. In these various forays, with which, however, the Sauk headman was not always connected, fully two hundred whites and nearly as many Indians lost their lives. At the besieged blockhouse forts (particularly Plum River, in northern Illinois) there were numerous instances of romantic heroism on the part of the settlers, men and women alike; and several of the open fights, like one on the Peckatonica River, are still famous in local annals.

Three weeks after the Stillman's Creek affair, a reorganized army of 3200 Illinois militia was mobilized, being reinforced by regulars under General Atkinson and a battalion of two hundred mounted rangers from the lead region, enlisted by Major Henry Dodge, then commandant of Michigan militia west of Lake Michigan, and in later years governor of Wisconsin Territory. The entire army now in the field numbered about 4000 effective men. Dodge's rangers, gathered from the mines and fields, were a free-and-easy set of fellows, destitute of uniforms, but imbued with the spirit of adventure and the customary frontiersmen's intense hatred of the Indians whom they had ruthlessly displaced. While disciplined to the extent of obeying orders whenever sent into the teeth of danger, these Rough Riders of 1832 swung through the country with small regard for the rules of the manual, and presented a striking contrast to the habits and appearance of the regulars.

As the new army slowly but steadily moved up Rock River, Black Hawk retired toward his Lake Koshkonong base. The pursuit becoming too warm, however, he retreated hastily across country, with women and children and all the paraphernalia of the British band, to the Wisconsin River in the neighborhood of Prairie du Sac; on his way crossing the site of the present Madison, where he was caught up with by his pursuers, now more swift in their movements. On reaching the rugged bluffs overlooking the Wisconsin, he sought again to surrender; but there chanced to be no interpreter among the whites, and the unfortunate suppliant was misunderstood. The battle of Wisconsin Heights followed (July 21), without appreciable loss on either side. Here the Sauk leader displayed much skill in covering the flight of his people across the broad, island-strewn river.

A portion of the fugitives, chiefly women and children, escaped on a raft down the Wisconsin, but near Prairie du Chien were mercilessly fired upon by a detachment from the garrison of Fort Crawford, and fifteen killed.[1] The remainder, led by Black Hawk and some Winnebago guides, pushed across through a rough, forbidding country, to the junction of the Bad Axe with the Mississippi, losing many along the way, who died of wounds and starvation. The now sadly depleted and almost famished crew reached the Mississippi on the first of August, and attempted to cross the river to the habitat of the Sioux, fondly hoping that their troubles would then be over. But only two or three canoes were obtainable, and the work was not only slow but, owing to the swift current, accompanied by some loss of life.

In the afternoon the movement was detected

---

[1] A French and Menominee Indian militia contingent from Green Bay now appeared on the scene, but its sole service was to slaughter most of the non-combatants who escaped from the raft.

by the crew of the Warrior, a government supply
steamer carrying a detachment of soldiers from Fort
Crawford. A third time the Hawk sought to surrender, but his white signal was fired at, under
pretense that it was a savage ruse, and round after
round of canister swept the wretched camp. The
next day (August 2) the troops, who had been delayed for three days in crossing Wisconsin River,
were close upon their heels, and arrived on the
heights overlooking the beach. The Warrior thereupon renewed its attack, and caught between two
galling fires the poor savages soon succumbed.
Black Hawk fled inland to seek an asylum at the
Dells of the Wisconsin with his false friends, the
Winnebago, who had guided the white army along
his path; fifty of his people remained on the east
bank and were taken prisoners by the troops; some
three hundred miserable starvelings, largely non-
combatants, reached the west shore through the hail
of metal, only to be waylaid by Sioux, dispatched by
army officials to intercept them, and half of their
number were slain. Of the band of a thousand Sauk
who had entered Illinois in April, not much over a
hundred and fifty lived to tell of the Black Hawk
War, one of the most discreditable punitive expeditions in the long and checkered history of American
relations with the aborigines.

As for the indiscreet but honest Black Hawk, in
many ways one of the most interesting of North American Indians, he was promptly surrendered (Au-

gust 27) by the Winnebago to the Indian agency at Prairie du Chien. Imprisoned first at Jefferson Barracks and then at Fortress Monroe, exhibited to throngs of curiosity-seeking people in the Eastern States, and obliged to sign articles of perpetual peace, he was finally turned over for safe-keeping to his hated and hating rival, the Fox chief Keokuk. In 1834 his autobiography was published — a book probably authentic for the most part, but the stilted style is no doubt that of his white editor.

Dying in 1838 (October 3) upon a small reservation in Iowa, Black Hawk's grave was rifled by a traveling physician, who utilized the bones for exhibition purposes. Two years later the skeleton was, on the demand of indignant sympathizers, surrendered to the State of Iowa; but in 1853 the box containing it was destroyed by a fire at Iowa City, then the capital of that commonwealth.

With all his faults, and these were chiefly racial, Black Hawk was preëminently a patriot. A year before his death, he made a speech to a party of whites who were making of him a holiday hero, and thus forcibly defended his motives : " Rock River was a beautiful country. I liked my town, my cornfields, and the home of my people. I fought for them." No poet could have penned for him a more touching epitaph.

CHAPTER X

ESTABLISHMENT OF WISCONSIN TERRITORY

MUCH space was given to the Black Hawk War in the periodical press of the day. It had been many years since an Indian uprising had startled the country, and its novelty and picturesqueness attracted general attention. Not only many of the Western papers, but several of the Eastern, had soldier correspondents, who, when nothing of moment was occurring in camp or on the march, sent to their respective journals descriptions of the fertile and interesting region through which the army was passing. The alternating groves, prairies, hills, lakes, and streams appealed strongly to the imagination of the writers, and their enthusiasm often expressed itself in amusingly florid terms. Not only during the war, but closely following it, there were also published several books and pamphlets giving accounts of this newly-discovered paradise. The westward movement being then popular in the Eastern and Middle States, these publications were eagerly read, with the immediate consequence that a strong migratory tide was set flowing toward southern and eastern Wisconsin and northern Illinois.

The quelling of the discontented aborigines had at last made settlement therein safe, and large cessions of land were for meagre sums promptly secured from the now pliant tribes. On July 29, 1829, the united Chippewa, Ottawa, and Potawatomi agreed at Prairie du Chien to cede their possessions, given to them by the treaty of 1816, lying between Rock and Wisconsin rivers; also a tract from Grosse Pointe, near Chicago, westward to Rock River, but with hunting rights reserved until these lands should be sold to settlers. The Menominee, in a treaty held September 3, 1832, at Cedar Point, on Fox River, ceded four million acres on Wolf River and 184,320 acres along the Wisconsin. Twelve days later, at Rock Island, the Winnebago agreed to vacate their extensive planting, hunting, and fishing grounds south and east of the Wisconsin and of the Fox River of Green Bay. Six days after that, the Sauk formally relinquished all claims they might have to holdings east of the Mississippi. At a further treaty with the Chippewa, Ottawa, and Potawatomi, concluded at Chicago on September 26, 1833, these tribes ceded "all their land along the western shore of Lake Michigan, and between this lake and the land ceded to the United States by the Winnebago nation," just referred to, "bounded on the north by the country ceded by the Menominees, and on the south by the country ceded at the treaty of Prairie du Chien, made on the 29th July, 1829, supposed to contain five million acres." The effect of these several conventions was to quiet aboriginal title to all remaining lands in Illinois, and to all of that portion of the future Wisconsin lying south and east of both the Wisconsin and the Fox.

North and west of these streams was still for the most part Indian country, but was ceded to the United States in a series of treaties, chiefly with the Chippewa and Menominee, between October 4, 1842, and February 11, 1856. By the last-named convention, all Indian title to Wisconsin lands was finally quieted, save for a few small reservations to certain tribes.[1]

With peace restored, and millions of fertile acres thus newly opened to the use of white men, federal land offices were in 1834 opened at Mineral Point and Green Bay, another being established at Milwaukee two years later. The lead-mine district again attracted miners and speculators, Fox River valley suddenly entered on a larger and busier life, and small agricultural communities sprang up at many sites in southern and eastern

---

[1] In the report of the Commissioner of Indian Affairs for 1904 their population is given as follows: —

Green Bay school	1804
La Pointe agency	5275
Oneida agency	2058
Wittenberg school	1386
Total in Wisconsin	10,523

This count does not include the civilized Brothertown and Stockbridge, chiefly resident in Calumet County.

Wisconsin, that in our day are occupied by cities and villages. By the year 1836 nearly eleven thousand whites were living within the borders of the nascent commonwealth. Up to December 1 of that year it was reported that 878,014 acres had been sold therein to settlers and speculators — two thirds to the latter class, who were now overrunning the Western country. This was a remarkable record, when it is considered that previous to 1834 no public lands had been disposed of within the limits of Wisconsin, save that Congress had confirmed the private French claims at Green Bay and Prairie du Chien.

The country lying between Lake Michigan and the Mississippi River, north of the Illinois line, remained until 1836 a portion of Michigan Territory. But so far removed were these fast-growing settlements from the seat of government at Detroit, that much inconvenience was experienced in the administration of civil government. As early as 1824, James Duane Doty, federal circuit judge at Green Bay, and political leader in the Fox River valley, — a man of good education and fine manners, — began an agitation for a new territory, for which he proposed the name " Chippewau." Congress failed to act upon this proposition, but three years later he was again at work in behalf of his project. This time he suggested, in recognition of its principal river, the name " Wiskonsin," such being Doty's phonetic rendering, always persisted

in by him, of the French spelling, "Ouisconsin,"[1]
itself an attempt to phoneticize the aboriginal
name. In 1829, Henry Dodge, one of the leading
spirits in the lead-mine region, and later Doty's
political rival, forcefully presented to Michigan's
territorial delegate in Congress the "claims the
people have on the National Legislature for a division of the Territory."

Meanwhile Doty continued active in the matter, and succeeded in inducing the Committee on
Territories, in the federal House of Representatives, to introduce (January 6, 1830) a "Bill establishing the Territory of Huron," which was to
be bounded on the south by the states of Illinois
and Missouri, westwardly by the Missouri and
White Earth rivers, northwardly by the international boundary, and eastwardly by a line running
practically through the middle of Lake Michigan,

[1] In the oldest French documents it is spelled "Misconsing,"
"Ouisconching," "Ouiskensing," etc., but in time this crystallized
into "Ouisconsin." The meaning of the aboriginal word, thus va-
riously rendered, is now unknown. Popular writers declare that it
signifies "gathering of the waters," or "meeting of the waters,"
having reference, possibly, to the occasional mingling of the divergent streams over the low-lying watershed at Fox-Wisconsin
portage; but there is no warrant for this. In order to preserve the
sound in English it became necessary, on the arrival of Americans, to modify the French spelling. At first it was locally
rendered "Wiskonsan" (which is closely phonetic), then "Wiskonsin;" but Congress seemed to prefer the hard c, and this was
retained in place of k, despite the protest of Governor Doty and
many Territorial newspaper editors. Thus the official spelling
became "Wisconsin."

the Straits of Mackinac (south of Mackinac and Bois Blanc islands), and River St. Mary's. This would have given to the proposed new territory all of the present upper peninsula of Michigan and a wide tract to the west of the Mississippi.

It is possible that the scheme for the Territory of Huron might have been adopted, had not there now developed a somewhat bitter and wordy rivalry between the two centres of population in the country west of Lake Michigan, — the rapidly-developing and somewhat radical industrial region of the lead mines, and the conservative agricultural and commercial valley of the Fox. Should the territorial capital be established at the old and staid fur-trading and garrison town of Green Bay, the seat of Brown County? or at the new log-cabined village of Mineral Point (first settled in 1827–28), metropolis of the lead mines and seat of Iowa County, which in 1829 had been formed out of that portion of Crawford situated to the south of Wisconsin River? This contest appears to have dulled the interest of Congress; moreover, Michigan vigorously protested that the proposed division " would have the effect to impair her future importance as a state."

Another bill to create a new territory out of western Michigan passed the House in 1831, but, largely because of the local quarrel, failed in the Senate. The following year, still another was reported in the House, this measure reviving the name " Wisconsin," but the project was laid over among the unfinished business of the session. In February, 1834, a similar proposition was reported in the Senate; the attempt, however, once more proved futile. In June following, all of the trans-Mississippi country that had been mentioned in the Huron bill was, "for administrative purposes," attached to Michigan Territory, which still further emphasized the importance of dividing the latter. The agitation for division now received assistance from the movement of the people of Michigan to form a state government; it came to be admitted upon the peninsula that the bounds of the territory were far too extensive for the proposed commonwealth.

There still remained the difficulty of establishing a boundary between the would-be Territory of Wisconsin and the projected State of Michigan. This being finally arranged, the former was erected by Congress under a bill approved April 20, 1836, to take effect "from and after the third day of July next." Wisconsin Territory was given the same boundaries as the present state, so far as Michigan and Illinois were concerned; but to the south and west its limits ran far beyond the state's present bounds — including as it did all the lands lying north of the State of Missouri and between the Mississippi River on the east and the Missouri and White Earth on the west. This trans-Mississippi region was the same as had, "for adminis-

trative purposes," been annexed in 1834 to the
Territory of Michigan.

It was provided in the act that the laws of Michigan Territory should prevail until Wisconsin could
form her own code, that the first legislative assembly (consisting of a council and a house of representatives) was to hold its opening session at such
time and place as the governor might appoint, and
that the governor and assembly should locate and
establish the seat of government. Twenty thousand
dollars were appropriated by the United States for
aiding in the erection of public buildings at the
selected capital, and five thousand were given toward
a territorial library; the governor was directed to
hold a general election for the assembly, and a
census was ordered to be taken previous to this
election. The governor, to be appointed by the
President of the United States, was also made superintendent of Indian affairs and commander-in-chief
of the militia, his annual salary being fixed at
$2500. There was also provided by the enabling
act a supreme court consisting of a chief justice and
two associates, and the customary district and probate courts and justices of the peace. The scale of
living expenses upon the then national frontier
may be appreciated when one reads in the act
of establishment that the supreme court judges
were to receive $1800 per year. Three hundred
and fifty dollars were allowed by Congress for the
expenses of the first legislative session, including

printing and other incidentals ; but the cost actually
incurred aggregated over twenty-five thousand dollars, then thought to be an exorbitant expenditure.

Meanwhile, the political affairs of Michigan were
much confused. Presuming that statehood would
readily be granted by Congress, a state constitution
had been adopted and ratified during 1835, and in
October of that year an election for state officers
was held. Although as yet unauthorized by the
federal power, the machinery of state government
was now in full operation, save for the judicial
branch, which was not organized until the Fourth of
July, 1836. Provision had been made for the peninsula; but the country west of Lake Michigan, then
containing the counties of Brown, Milwaukee, Iowa,
Crawford, Dubuque, and Des Moines, was "no
man's land" so far as the new state government
was concerned. The inhabitants thereof, together
with a small minority in Michigan proper, were
nevertheless persisting in their rights as citizens
of Michigan Territory.

John Scott Horner had, in September, 1835,
a month before the state election, been appointed
by President Jackson as secretary and acting
governor of Michigan Territory. The coming to
Detroit of this young and apparently tactless
Virginian, quite unfamiliar with Western men and
affairs, was regarded as an intrusion and aroused a
spirit of opposition; so that the unfortunate official

was subjected to neglect, and more than once to
actual insult.

It had been arranged by Horner's predecessor
that the territorial legislative council should hold
a session at Green Bay, commencing the 1st of
January, 1836, chiefly for the benefit of the western part of the territory. But in November Horner
issued a proclamation announcing that " for divers
good causes and considerations " the date would be
shifted to the first of the previous December. This
occasioned much annoyance, for so slow were the
mails that few if any of the western members-elect
received notice of the change in time to attend the
December meeting, which therefore was not held ;
neither did Horner himself report for duty. A
quorum assembled on New Year's day, but still
without the executive, whose presence was essential
to the transaction of business, and the session ended
on the 15th. Little had been done beyond voting a
caustic arraignment of the absentee, renewed bickering over the location of the proposed territorial
capital of Wisconsin, and the adoption of a report
declaring that the people of Michigan Territory
west of Lake Michigan had been ruled " rather as
a distant colony than as an integral portion of the
same government."

In the preceding October Stevens T. Mason had
been elected governor of the State of Michigan, and
with him was chosen a full state ticket. Horner was
thus left in an anomalous position. President Jack-

son eased the situation for his appointee by promising him the secretaryship of Wisconsin Territory, for which it was by this time seen that Congress would soon make provision. In the spring of 1836 the Winnebago were making considerable disturbance around Fort Winnebago, because their annuities were not being paid, and they were in a famished condition. Horner, who had now removed to the west of the lake, was directed to proceed to the scene of trouble and pacify them, which he did by distributing to the malcontents a large part of the food stores in the fort.

Dodge, now well known because of his part in the Black Hawk War, had on May 6 been appointed by President Jackson as first governor of the new territory. Of fine physique but somewhat pompous manner, at times amazingly obstinate in disposition, and obviously deficient in early education, he nevertheless was a creditable official and a man of action; as an Indian fighter he had exhibited a dash and bravery that appealed strongly to the populace, who overestimated his other qualities. Dodge and Secretary Horner, who had been appointed the same day, took the oath of office at Mineral Point, by this time the largest town in Wisconsin, upon the Fourth of July. The ceremony was the principal feature of a noisy celebration of the national holiday by the miners of the district, many of whom had served under Dodge and idolized him. Later in the summer, the President appointed Charles Dunn as chief justice, and William C. Frazer and David Irvin as associate justices of the supreme court, and William W. Chapman as federal district attorney. Henry S. Baird, the pioneer lawyer of Wisconsin, was appointed by the governor as attorney-general.

As for Michigan, vexatious delays attended her statehood bill, chiefly owing to boundary disputes with Ohio, Indiana, and the incipient Wisconsin, all of them growing out of conditions imposed by the Ordinance of 1787, which we shall presently discuss. But the commonwealth was finally admitted to the Union by virtue of a bill approved January 26, 1837, being given the territorial limits which she possesses to-day.

The first legislative assembly of Wisconsin Territory was convened on October 25, 1836, in a story-and-a-half frame building built for the purpose, at Belmont, a freshly-platted town in the present county of Lafayette,[1] and then in the heart of the lead-mine district. There were thirty-nine members, thirteen in the council and twenty-six in the house of representatives. That part of the territory in which the original title had thus far been ac-

---

[1] Now a decayed hamlet of meagre proportions, called Leslie. The name Belmont was in 1867 removed to a new town, three miles to the southeast. The building in which the legislative session was held, together with the neighboring dwelling built for Chief Justice Dunn, and the office of the Belmont *Express*, were still in existence in 1908. See Wisconsin Historical Society *Proceedings* for 1906, pp. 48–53.

quired by purchase — south and east of Wisconsin and Fox rivers — was subdivided into convenient counties; three banks were established, — at Dubuque, Mineral Point, and Milwaukee, — all of which, together with a Green Bay bank incorporated by Michigan the year before, ultimately failed and wrought widespread financial disaster among depositors. But the discussion awakening the deepest interest in the legislature was, as usual in new territories and states, the location of the capital.

Among the older towns, Green Bay and Mineral Point were still the chief contestants for this honor, it being supposed that prosperity would quickly follow in the wake of such prominence. But the young village of Milwaukee, then three years old and ambitiously representing commerce on the Great Lakes, had appeared in the lists. Other claimants were Racine, Koshkonong, Fond du Lac, Madison, City of the Second Lake, City of the Four Lakes, Peru, Wisconsin City, Portage, Helena, Belmont, Mineral Point, Platteville, Cassville, and Belleview; while Dubuque also had adherents, for it will be remembered that what is now Iowa was then a part of Wisconsin. Many of these were town sites existing only on paper and in the brains of real estate speculators; among whom Governor Mason of Michigan and Judge Doty, themselves proprietors of several rival sites (including Madison), were particularly prominent.

Thus distributing their interests, this pair had from the first a decided advantage over the field, for, losing on one contest, they could contentedly shift their votes to another, and thereby prolong the fight. Doty, who astutely managed the speculation, was as well the best-informed man of his day relative to the topography and resources of Wisconsin. He had known the country intimately since 1820, when with Governor Cass and Indian Agent Henry R. Schoolcraft he made an expedition to Lake Superior and the sources of the Mississippi; and since his appointment as federal judge, his long and somewhat circuitous horseback tours between the court towns of Green Bay and Prairie du Chien had given him a rare opportunity to become intimate with the interior. The legislative discussion, which at times closely approached a wrangle, continued throughout the first month of the session, and long hung on the question as to which of the three extreme centres of population should be preferred. Green Bay, situated in the northeast corner of the territory, was closely connected with the stream of immigration coming westward by the Great Lakes, had an interesting history associated with the fur-trade and the French régime, and was already taking on a somewhat aristocratic social tone. Mineral Point, in the southwest, was the larger settlement, and the seat of important industrial interests. Milwaukee, young and hopeful, was on the eastern edge of the territory, and by no means certain of ultimately outgrowing Kenosha and other lakeshore rivals.

Of his several "paper towns," Doty's favorite was Madison, then a virgin forest situated along a narrow, mile-wide isthmus between Third and Fourth lakes,[1] and as yet not even surveyed. On November 24, Madison (named from James Madison, fourth president of the United States) was victorious. The story was long current that city lots therein were freely distributed by the tenacious Doty among members and their friends. But aside from such possible considerations, the argument for Madison was deemed conclusive, because it was in the nature of a compromise between the conflicting interests of Green Bay and the mining country; and being situated midway between settlements on Lake Michigan and the Mississippi, it was hoped that the proposed new town would assist in developing the still wild interior. Moreover, Doty convinced members that the site was exceptionally beautiful and healthful. It was stipulated in the act of establishment that until a public building could be erected at the new capital, the legislature was to meet at Burlington (now in Iowa).

In February following (1837), the ground still

[1] The present Indian names of the Four Lakes at Madison were first applied to them by legislative action in 1855. The Winnebago name for the series was Taychoperah (Four Lakes), and white pioneers called them by their numbers, from south to north: First (now Kegonsa), Second (Waubesa), Third (Monona), and Fourth (Mendota).

thickly mantled with snow, the town site of Madison was roughly platted by a pioneer surveyor — the capitol park in the centre, with streets radiating therefrom after the manner of Washington, and these patriotically named from the signers of the federal Constitution. In March, Eben Peck, keeper of a boarding-house at Blue Mound mine, some thirty miles westward, sent out two Frenchmen to put up for him a log house within the projected city, under whose roof he proposed to open a tavern for the accommodation of workmen who were to be sent out to erect the capitol. Upon April 15, Roseline, his wife, arrived with their two-year-old boy, to take possession of the premises in advance of her husband's coming. Thus a woman and her infant boy were the first permanent white settlers of Madison, and its first building was a boarding-house.

It was the 10th of June before Building-Commissioner Augustus A. Bird arrived from Milwaukee with thirty-six mechanics and laborers, after a dreary and toilsome overland journey of ten days, through rain and mud. There were then no roads in the territory, save in the lead region for the transportation of ore by ox-teams, and these had been developed from the old and well-defined Indian trails which interlaced the country, traces of which can still be seen in some portions of the state. Bird brought with him sawmill machinery and other heavy materials from the East, unloaded for his use upon the steamboat dock in Milwaukee. His were the first wagons wheeled across the prairies and through the oak groves (or "oak openings," as they were then called) of southeastern Wisconsin. Following a native trail from Lake Michigan to the Four Lakes, which in many places was by his little caravan worked into quagmires, the rivers were swum by his horses, and wagons and freight were taken over in Indian canoes.

The capitol was but slowly built, for logs must needs be cut upon the neighboring lake shores and worked into timber at the official sawmill, and quarries had also to be opened, the stone being brought across Fourth Lake upon rafts. In April, 1838, the building commissioner, encompassed by disappointments, turned the work over to a contractor. Their sadly-tangled construction accounts afterwards became a fruitful source of litigation and legislative claims, extending throughout the territorial period.

In November the legislative assembly first met at Madison. But as only fifty boarders could be accommodated in the place, a recess was taken until January 26, 1839, when the situation was somewhat improved. But the statehouse was still far from complete, and for several sessions Madison, which for various reasons grew but slowly in those early days, proved an inconvenient and ill-provided meeting-place for the legislature of the young territory.

CHAPTER XI

THE financial depression of 1837 somewhat checked Western immigration, and Wisconsin business men, with here and there a comparatively wealthy farmer, were seriously affected. But as a rule the capital chiefly needed by pioneers of that period was muscle, pluck, and brain, and it was not long before the movement toward the new territory was resumed with gathered strength.

The earliest American settlers of the Old Northwest had, if from New England, New York, or Pennsylvania, floated down the Ohio River in flatboats, keels, and barges; or if from Virginia and the Carolinas, they trudged on foot or came on horseback, over Boone's famous Wilderness Road, through Cumberland Gap. But Wisconsin's agricultural pioneers for the most part came by more northern paths. These varied according to individuals and circumstances. For example, Whitehall, New York, was for some time the port for Vermont families. Reaching that town by stage or farm wagon, burdened with household goods, farming implements, and seeds, and not infrequently live stock, the emigrants took boat on the Northern Canal to

Troy, where they met others from northern New England and various parts of New York. The Erie Canal was followed to Buffalo, whence a steamboat took the pilgrims to Detroit, then the chief distributing centre for Indiana, Illinois, and Wisconsin.

From Detroit, sailing craft and steamers carried the settlers to Green Bay, Milwaukee, Chicago, or St. Josephs. But frequently all space on board was taken, even to mattresses spread on deck and dining-saloon floor. In such case, a canvas-topped lumber wagon, or a rakish, roomy vehicle popularly styled " prairie schooner," was thereafter the conveyance into the still farther West, sometimes carrying the party all the long way from Detroit to Wisconsin. Occasionally, after crossing Michigan peninsula for a hundred and eighty miles, another vessel might be found at St. Josephs, and if not overcrowded this could be taken to Chicago, Milwaukee, or other lake ports. Thousands came, of course, from the Middle States; others moved on from the older communities of the Northwest (in Ohio, Indiana, and Illinois), dissatisfied with present locations and hoping for better openings in the still newer land; and not a few, even thus early, hailed from the Old World. But whatever their origin or their earlier paths, ultimately they must reach the distributing points of Detroit, Chicago, Milwaukee, or Green Bay, where they formed caravans proceeding into the interior, — all save such settlers and prospectors as came to the lead region from Missouri and the border states, by way of the Mississippi and Ohio, or by overland stage from southern Illinois.

The majority of these pioneers, who obtained lands on easy conditions from the federal government, under the homestead laws of the period, were accustomed to toiling with their hands and to the simplicity of extremely frugal homes; well-to-do folk seldom cared to "rough it" on the frontier. However, the many privations and hardships of Western pioneering, concerning which so much has truthfully been written, meant far less to the average frontiersmen than it might to us, from our present point of view. In practice they took to them kindly, as being not unlike their previous experiences in the outlying sections of the East, in the days before railways. Perhaps to most of them it meant little more than the necessity for still further simplicity; for in the new West, so recently a wilderness, each household, despite the *camaraderie* of backwoods settlements, was in large measure absolutely dependent on itself for material things — tools, implements, clothing, and food. There was, also, to those who loved nature, — and most healthful people have something of the gypsy within them, — much of quiet joy in the untrammeled life of virgin lands. Taking life seriously, as a rule, the intellects of most frontiersmen were quickened by the new conditions and requirements, and to their children they left a heritage of brawn and sober purpose.

From prehistoric times, rivers have been the chief highways of the continental interior. For this reason, French Canadians almost invariably settled upon their banks. But in developing the Northwestern wilderness, the American backwoodsman was seeking good farm lands; ease of intercommunication being with him a secondary consideration. The majority of them had perforce, therefore, to live inland. Not seldom the Wisconsin settler, when at last he had " broken " the prairie with his heavy oxplow, or had chopped and burned out a " clearing " in the dense forest, and begun to study his environment, found himself a hundred miles or more from even a primitive gristmill, possibly upwards of thirty from a post-office or " store," these two conveniences usually being combined. An Indian trail, or a blazed bridle-path, was perhaps the only connection with his base of supplies and his market. Happy the man whose log hut lay along such a trail; then he might occasionally be called on " to put up " some gossipy mail carrier for the night,[1] to entertain a circuit preacher, or be visited by a government official plodding on his lonely tour.

If coming in the summer, the traveler made his way by boat, or on foot, or on horseback ; his win-

[1] Four mail routes were established in Wisconsin by the federal government in 1832, sixteen in 1836, and fifteen in 1838.

ter conveyance, however, was apt to be a "French train" (a long narrow box-sled, drawn by two horses tandem). If located where the trail crossed a river or a small lake, the settler might turn ferryman, perhaps also "keep tavern," for the accommodation of these chance travelers, who would almost always leave for such service a few shillings of ready money. Frequently, however, the backwoodsman was closely hemmed in by gloomy woodlands, or amidst broad prairies stretching to the horizon, quite far removed from any track leading to civilization, save the path he had himself broken on his arrival. Then would he see his neighbors only when log houses were "raised" by the combined effort of the far-scattered settlement, or at "bees" for quilting, harvesting, corn-husking, cider-making, wood-chopping, and the like.

With the growth of settlement, the numerous Indian trails were gradually broadened and straightened into wagon roads, and other highways were added as necessity required. Apparently, the first real road to be opened in Wisconsin was laid out in 1824 along the east side of the Fox, from Green Bay to Kaukauna, doubtless being paid for by private subscription. In 1834 we find Michigan Territory establishing a public road from Milwaukee to the Mississippi, by way of Platte Mounds. The following year, provision was made for another from Blue Mounds to the northern boundary of Illinois, in the direction of Chicago; also one from

Milwaukee to Lake Winnebago, at Calumet village. By 1840, Green Bay, the Lake Michigan towns, and the interior settlements of Janesville, Beloit, and Madison, were connected with each other and with the lead mines of the southwest. The system had extended by 1848 to about a dozen principal highways, although doubtless most of them were in wretched condition during wet weather. Previous to 1843 there were no roads north and west of the Fox-Wisconsin rivers; in that year, however, one was commenced from Prairie du Chien to Chequamegon Bay, by way of the Black and Chippewa rivers.

During the territorial period, Congress appropriated $67,000 for military roads within our borders. The principal one extended from Green Bay, via the east shore of Lake Winnebago, to Forts Winnebago and Crawford. Others were from Fort Howard by way of Milwaukee and Racine to the Illinois boundary, reaching out toward Chicago; from Milwaukee westward, via Madison, to a point on the Mississippi River opposite Dubuque; from Racine, via Janesville, to Sinapee, on the Mississippi; from Sauk Harbor on Lake Michigan to Wisconsin River; from Fond du Lac, via Fox Lake, to the Wisconsin; from Sheboygan, by way of Fond du Lac, to Fox River in the neighborhood of Green Lake; and from Southport (now Kenosha), by way of Geneva, to Beloit. Many of these, however, had little work done upon them. The first plank road of record was built in 1846 between Lisbon and Milwaukee ; but the following year sixteen companies were chartered for the construction of highways thus surfaced, and others followed rapidly.

Most settlers brought with them from their Eastern homes a small stock of the frontier staples, salt pork and flour, supposedly sufficient to tide them over until the first crop could be garnered. In due course this supply became exhausted, and then difficulty was encountered in the effort to replenish it, for usually more time than anticipated was required before the family became self-sustaining. But although there were instances of some suffering from this cause, the rivers, lakes, and woods commonly abounded with fish and game of many kinds, and the average frontiersman was of necessity half hunter, half farmer.

We have seen that among the French Creoles of Wisconsin several were educated in Montreal. It is of record that as early as 1791 a tutor was employed in a Green Bay family, although the " first regular school " was not opened there until 1817. Garrison schools were inaugurated at Forts Crawford (1817), Howard (1824), and Winnebago (1835) for children of both officers and settlers. There were, also, church schools for white and Indian youth alike, chief among them the Episcopal mission at Green Bay (commencing 1825). At the time of the organization of the territory in

1836, there were within the limits of the present state a population, as already noted, of some eleven thousand whites, supporting "eight small private schools, and two hundred and seventy-five pupils attending them." These were located at Green Bay, Portage, Prairie du Chien, Mineral Point (1830), Platteville (1833), Milwaukee (autumn of 1835), Kenosha (December, 1835), and Sheboygan (winter of 1836–37). The school at Madison was not opened until March 1, 1838. Not until the following year were school taxes levied in Wisconsin. Up to that time popular education was on a subscription basis ; indeed, in many communities public funds had, even after this date, to be supplemented by private aid.

At the first session of the legislature, in Belmont (1836), an act was passed for the establishment at that village of " Wisconsin University." The following year, the " Wisconsin University of Green Bay " was likewise provided for, on paper ; and a few months later (January 5, 1838), an act organizing the " University of the Territory of Wisconsin " was approved by the governor, but nothing further was done about it until ten years afterward, when Wisconsin had become a state. Normal instruction, apart from that given departmentally in the state university, was deferred to a much later date (1865).

A newspaper appeared in Green Bay before the organization of the territory. The first number of the "Intelligencer" (semi-monthly), the "first newspaper published between Lake Michigan and the Pacific Ocean," was dated December 11, 1833. Of world or national news there was little, and that obtainable chiefly from "A gentleman just arrived from the East," but occasionally the small doings of the village and of Fox River valley were recorded, and the "poet's column" seldom lacked contributors. Neither was the "Intelligencer" lacking in the usual self-assertion of enterprise, for it headed its meagre news columns with this refrain, having reference to the pedestrian mail carrier from Chicago : —

> "Three times a week, without any fail,
> At four o'clock we look for the mail,
> Brought with dispatch on an Indian trail."

Milwaukee's first public journal was the "Advertiser," established in July, 1836. The Belmont "Gazette" followed in October of the same year; but when Belmont ceased to be the capital, the types and press were removed to Mineral Point, to print the "Miners' Free Press," which appeared the next June (1837). The "Wisconsin Enquirer" began service in Madison in November, 1838.

From the fall of New France in 1763, the Catholic Church appears to have practically abandoned what is now Wisconsin; indeed, services at Green Bay must have been quite irregular after the opening of the Fox Wars and the burning of St. Francis Xavier mission in 1688. We know that the Jesuit

Father Jean Baptiste Chardon was at La Baye in 1721, and it is probable that occasional missionary tours were undertaken hither by Mackinac priests, who kept the nearest registry of baptisms, marriages, and deaths. In 1823 the Church renewed its work at Green Bay; La Pointe Indian mission reopened in 1835, and Milwaukee diocese was erected in 1844.

It will be remembered that the first Protestant sermon in Wisconsin, of record, was preached in 1820 by Rev. Jedediah Morse, a Presbyterian divine; but it was sixteen years later before his denomination formally entered the territory. The Episcopalians opened a church at Green Bay in 1825, contemporaneous with their Indian mission school. The Congregationalists, then doing mission work in conjunction with the Presbyterians, built a church and school in 1827 or 1828, for the Stockbridge mission at Statesburg, near South Kaukauna; and another for the La Pointe Indians in 1833. A Methodist preacher appeared in the lead mines as early as 1828, and four years subsequently similar work was established by that denomination at Kaukauna. The Baptists appear to have begun their labors in Wisconsin in 1839.

With all these evangelizing agencies actively at work among them, the early settlers of the territory seldom lacked the comforts of religion; but so sparse was the settlement and so slender the financial resources of the parishioners, that the

early ministry, largely itinerant, was ill provided
for and often subject to genuine hardships. Its
members deserve to rank among the most useful
and daring of the pioneer class. Churches as well
as schools were among the earliest institutions in
each community; a study of town and county
annals reveals the fact that everywhere they followed speedily in the wake of the first arrivals.
Thus Wisconsin soon took a firm stand in the
cause of secular and religious education.

We have spoken of the industrial "bees," whereat
would gather men, women, and children, often living many miles apart, intent on assisting each other
with work that if carried on unaided might to many
families seem a dreary and in some instances impossible burden. These gatherings, eagerly anticipated by the countryside, were occasions of much
boisterous jollity, and through the familiar meeting
of young folk the source also of much frontier romance. The humors of the day were often uncouth.
There was a deal of horseplay, hard drinking, and
profanity, and occasionally a personal encounter
during the heat of discussion; but an undercurrent
of good-nature was generally observable. Dances,
singing classes, and spelling contests were favorite
amusements, in both village and rural life. The
spasmodic visits of the circuit preacher, and occasional summer camp-meetings and "protracted
meetings," were also welcome breaks in the tedium of farm labor.

The majority of the territorial pioneers of Wisconsin were of course farmers, next in number being mechanics and village storekeepers. But there were also many professional men, and men of affairs, generally young and ambitious, who had flocked to the new territory from the East, seeking fame or wealth or both — just as enterprising young college men of the present generation find openings in the Dakotas, Oklahoma, Oregon, and Washington. This type was chiefly to be found at Green Bay, Milwaukee, Madison, Prairie du Chien, and in the lead region. Green Bay, in particular, was the home of an exceptionally brilliant coterie, who from the first assisted in shaping public opinion and in organizing meritorious enterprises James Duane Doty, his cousin Morgan L. Martin, Henry S. Baird, Ebenezer Childs, and William Dickinson are examples of this class; the first three conspicuous in law and politics, the other two in trade and manufactures.

Of prominent Milwaukeeans we have space to mention but a few types, — Alexander Mitchell, the first and greatest Wisconsin banker; Byron Kilbourn and George H. Walker, who aided in developing business interests in the metropolis; Increase A. Lapham, famous in several sciences, and originator of the federal Weather Bureau; and Rufus King, Philo White, and John S. Fillmore, journalists of repute.

Men of prominence throughout the territory came

to be familiar figures on the streets of the capital, not only from their presence during legislative sessions, but because in summer-time it was a favorite tarrying-place for overland travelers between the lead mines and Milwaukee and Green Bay. In time the village itself soon attracted skillful lawyers to her bar, and the Madison newspapers were edited with unusual ability. Among territorial editors at the seat of government, whose names are deserving of permanent record, were W. W. Wyman, S. D. Carpenter, H. A. Tenney, Benjamin Holt, Beriah Brown, George Hyer, Josiah A. Noonan, and Julius T. Clark. As already noted, the university, which in our day employs many teachers and writers of national reputation, did not exist in territorial times.

The lead region was particularly favored with men who achieved success in several fields of action. The vigorous and ambitious Dodge — miner, soldier, and politician — was perhaps most widely known. Thomas P. Burnett, Charles Dunn, Mortimer M. Jackson, and Moses M. Strong were lawyers who acquired a considerable reputation. Among the miners, John H. Rountree and William Stephen Hamilton (son of the famous Alexander Hamilton) were men of education, mental breadth, and enterprise, who strongly influenced the early life and career of the district.

Prairie du Chien, relatively a far less important community at present than formerly, was the home of several such men as Hercules S. Dousman and Alfred Brunson, types of pioneers highly efficient in their respective spheres of business and the pulpit.

As the political and educational centre of the state, Madison may still be considered as in some respects its most cosmopolitan city. But in territorial times it was notable each winter, during the legislative session, as the gathering-place of prominent men and women from all parts of Wisconsin, who came as legislators, lobbyists, or spectators, and were often accompanied by their families. Transportation arrangements being necessarily primitive, visitors often tarried throughout the season, filling the crude hotels to overflowing, but amid the general social gayety, heeding little the many discomforts. A reminiscent pioneer has left to us this genial picture of early Madison under such conditions : —

With the session came crowds of people. The public houses were literally crammed — shake-downs were looked upon as a luxury, and lucky was the guest considered whose good fortune it was to rest his weary limbs on a straw or hay mattress.

We had then no theatres or any places of amusement, and the long winter evenings were spent in playing various games of cards, checkers, and backgammon. Dancing was also much in vogue. Colonel James Maxwell, member of council from Rock and Walworth, was very gay, and discoursed sweet music on the flute, and Ben. C.

Eastman, one of the clerks, was an expert violinist. They two furnished the music for many a French four, cotillon, Virginia reel, and jig, that took place on the puncheon floors of the old log cabins forming the Madison House [the tavern erected by Eben Peck]. . . . Want of ceremony, fine dress, classic music, and other evidences of present society life, never deterred us from enjoying ourselves those long winter evenings.

" Personal journalism " of the most acrimonious type was then much in vogue, and party spirit ran high. Quarrels between the territorial governor and the legislature were not infrequent. The political pessimist might have found in the Madison newspapers of the day much to confirm his forebodings. Nevertheless, the legislation was on the whole commendable. The country was rapidly filling up with a robust population from the Eastern states and an increasing contingent of foreign-born, and this necessitated new apportionments after each census. These usually gave rise to displays of partisan sharp practice. New counties had to be carved out, either from freshly-ceded Indian lands in the northern and central portions, or by subdivisions of organized counties. The statutory laws, originally borrowed from Michigan, required remolding to accord with local conditions. Ever present, much affecting all political action, was the ambition for statehood at as early a date as Congress could be induced to admit Wisconsin to the Union.

An event occurred during the session of 1841–42

that gained for the territory an unfortunate notoriety. Dodge had early in October been removed
from the governorship by President Tyler, who in
his place appointed Doty. Less tactful than his old
rival, Doty promptly drew on himself the dislike of
the legislature by asserting in his opening message
that no territorial law was effective until expressly
approved by Congress. Despite his undoubted legal
acumen, the executive was worsted in the wordy
dispute that followed, and strained relations were
the result.

The governor had nominated one Baker as sheriff
of Grant County, but there was a strong disposition in the council to table the nomination. Doty's
action was upheld by his neighbor, Charles C. P.
Arndt of Brown County, and opposed, among others,
by James R. Vineyard of Grant. On February 11,
a personal altercation arose between the two, result-
ing in the former striking the latter, who thereupon
shot and killed his assailant. Vineyard was at once
expelled from the council; but upon being tried for
manslaughter was acquitted. Charles Dickens, the
English novelist, was then making his first tour of
the United States, and with customary exaggeration
cited this tragedy in " American Notes " as typical
of public life in the West. The affair remains to
this day the most painful incident in the legislative
records of Wisconsin.

It was not usual for Western pioneers, nerved
by personal ambition and aglow with expectations,

seriously to concern themselves with the reformation of society. Among the hordes of immigrants who annually poured into the promised lands of the Mississippi valley were, however, a few well-meaning people much concerned with questions of social betterment. In the year 1843, the people of Southport became interested in the theories of the French socialist Charles Fourier, then being advocated by Horace Greeley in the New York "Tribune." An association was formed, called "The Wisconsin Phalanx," and in May and June, 1844, a settlement made in the valley of Ceresco, now included in the city of Ripon. About a hundred and fifty persons, a few of them men and women of some ability, and nearly all industrious folk, eventually joined the community, which soon erected substantial buildings. The members ate in common, but each family lived in its own compartment. Labor was voluntary, in common fields and shops, but directed by officials of the phalanx, and each person received dividends in proportion to his value as a worker. Business and social meetings were held in the evenings: on Tuesday evening a literary and debating club met; on Wednesday a singing school; and on Thursday there was dancing. Religious belief was free, and there were other personal privileges, such as the liberty to maintain a horse and carriage "by paying to the association the actual cost of keeping." All children must attend school, and "devote a portion of time each day to some branch of industry ; " but parents might make other provisions for this than the phalanx school.

Had members been content with ordinary rewards for labor, the phalanx might have lasted. Their farming profits were rather above the average ; at less expense they were better fed and clothed than their neighbors ; and they had many social enjoyments denied to others. But the strong and willing were yoked to the weak and slothful ; individual abilities were not given full play ; men around them were acquiring fortunes in land speculation and other enterprises, from which they were debarred. Dissatisfaction arose, and grew to such an extent that after seven years the phalanx began to melt away. The land was eventually sold at greatly increased value, with a considerable profit to each, and the Fourierites went out into the world again, each man to battle for himself.[1]

Two other coöperative industrial communities were established in territorial Wisconsin. A party of thirty Englishmen, mostly married, were led hither in 1843 by Thomas Hunt, a follower of Robert Owen. Buying a farm in Spring Lake, at North Prairie, in Waukesha County, they sought to put in practice Owenite principles. After three dismal years the projectors, none of them accustomed to farm labor, abandoned the plan and melted into the population about them. In the same year, several

[1] See S. M. Pedrick, " The Wisconsin Phalanx at Ceresco," in Wis. Hist. Soc. *Proceedings*, 1902.

London mechanics organized the Utilitarian Association of United Interests, and in 1845 sixteen of them left for America, settling upon two hundred acres near Mukwonago. Much of this land was undrained, and malaria claimed several victims. Crops were poor, for the men were not versed in agricultural methods ; prices were low ; the coöperative plan did not satisfy them in practice ; and at the end of three years they also were " starved out." Selling their farm at a fair price, the members settled in Milwaukee, where, following their respective trades, they again prospered.

Another communistic enterprise in Wisconsin Territory was of a far different type from these. In 1843 there dwelt in Racine County, at the pretty little village of Burlington, a lawyer from New York State, named James Jesse Strang. Erratic, half-educated, and possessed of an almost insane passion for notoriety, he nevertheless was keen-witted and a fluent public speaker. One of his followers described him in later years as " small and spare, with a thin hatchet face, and reddish hair, but one of the most fascinating orators imaginable." At first we hear of him as an active political worker, a temperance agitator, and the editor of a country newspaper.

In January, 1844, Strang visited the large Mormon colony at Nauvoo, Illinois, was baptized by Joseph Smith, became an elder in the church, and was regarded as so valuable an acquisition to the

Latter Day Saints that the Wisconsin missionary field was assigned to his charge. In June following, the Smiths were slain by a mob at Nauvoo, and, although but a fresh convert, Strang claimed the right to succeed Joseph. His pretensions were backed by documents alleged to have been written by the " martyr," but these the " twelve apostles " at Nauvoo denounced as vulgar forgeries.

Driven from Illinois by his fellow religionists, Strang established a communistic Mormon colony on White River, near Burlington, and called it Voree. In a vigorous proclamation, abounding in caustic references to his enemies, he declared that the Angel of the Lord had revealed to him this location as the City of Promise, and had "cut off " the "Brighamites" at Nauvoo. By April, 1845, adherents began to arrive ; for no matter how strange may be a religious cult, followers will soon be attracted to it. President Strang's "visions" were regularly reported in his monthly newspaper organ, the Voree "Herald," and missionaries were dispatched by him to form "primitive Mormon" groups in Ohio, New York, and other Eastern and Central states, where they often had sharp encounters with Brigham Young's representatives. It was claimed in the autumn of 1846 that " from one to two thousand people " were settled at Voree " in plain houses, in board shanties, in tents, and sometimes many of them in the open air."

Strang, claiming to be divinely inspired, was in

this so-called community a dictator in all things, temporal as well as spiritual. From time to time he pretended to unearth sets of brazen tablets, bearing rudely-etched hieroglyphics supposed to be the Holy Law, which "under angelic guidance" he translated into a jargon fashioned in Biblical phrase. In this and other more or less hackneyed devices he displayed much ingenuity in duping his growing company of fanatics.

In May, 1847, a branch of Voree was founded on Big Beaver Island, in a lonely archipelago near the outlet of Lake Michigan. Despite the opposition of neighboring fishermen, who had squatted on the islands and did not relish this invasion of their realm by Strang's "saints," the colony grew rapidly, and soon became headquarters for the sect; Voree being thenceforth allowed to stagnate. Within two or three years two thousand devotees had gathered in the new colony, having built neat houses, roads, a dock, a large tabernacle of logs, and a steam sawmill.

The island is in the midst of a region still famous for its fish, the forests of the archipelago gave promise of great value, the soil was fertile, and access from the mainland difficult. Strang thought this isolated place an ideal location for his little commonwealth, whose city he called after himself, "St. James." Doubtless it would have been, had not the Gentile fishermen made his life a burden. These rude folk, heavily armed and often under the influence of liquor, invaded and broke up the meetings of the elect, debauched their women, fiercely warned new arrivals to leave before they could land at the dock, and spread reports that the sectarians were but freebooters who robbed the mails and sheltered counterfeiters.

In 1850 the colony was, as a result of "revelations," reorganized as a "kingdom." There was a "royal press," from which issued the "Northern Islander," for Strang understood fully the power of printer's ink; foreign ambassadors were appointed; and the leader was formally crowned (July 8) "king, apostle, seer, revelator, and translator." The community system was abandoned, tithes were now collected, and polygamy established — Strang's allowance being five wives; tea, coffee, and tobacco were prohibited, and schools and debating clubs opened. Creature comforts there were, in abundance; the colonists exhibited a certain thrift, and some of the elements of civilization prevailed; but they were a rough, illiterate, sensual people, easily influenced by a suave, intellectual fellow like Strang.

The enemies of the "king" were not confined to the warring Gentile fishermen. With the growth of power, he had become harsh and absolute in his tone, thus arousing opposition in his own ranks. The malcontents did not hesitate to carry malicious tales of misdeeds to the mainland authorities, and soon newspapers in such lakeshore cities as Buffalo,

Cleveland, and Detroit contained long and sensational reports of doings in the Kingdom of St. James. In May, 1851, Strang and a few of the chief apostles were arrested and taken on board a government steamer to Detroit, where they were tried for a long list of misdemeanors — among others, squatting on government land. Strang conducted the defense with remarkable ability and eloquence, and secured a release in the face of violent popular prejudice against him.

Two years later, now returning for a time into political life, and of course controlling a large vote, he was elected to the legislature, where his seat was unsuccessfully contested on the ground that he was an enemy to public welfare; again he skillfully downed his opponents and proved a useful and tactful member. In 1855, however, like many another crowned head, he was assassinated by some of his own subjects. Not being immediately killed by the two bullets fired at him, he was taken on a stretcher to Voree by a small party of his followers. There, until death, he was carefully attended by his first and lawful wife, who had declined to follow him during his polygamous career on Beaver Island. Dying on July 9, Strang was buried at Voree (now Spring Prairie), which soon thereafter was abandoned by the Mormons. As for St. James, the riotous fishermen promptly demolished the city with axe and torch, and its deluded inhabitants were driven forth to seek homes elsewhere. A few of them still dwell upon the islands off Green Bay and along the rugged shores of Door Peninsula.[1]

[1] See H. E. Legler, " A Moses of the Mormons," in Parkman Club *Papers*, vol. ii.

CHAPTER XII

IT will be remembered that the old Northwest Territory embraced all the lands between the Ohio and Mississippi rivers and the Great Lakes. The Ordinance of 1787 provided for the ultimate division of the territory into five states : three south of " an east and west line drawn through the southerly bend or extreme of Lake Michigan," and two north of it. Had this east and west line been strictly adhered to, Ohio, Indiana, and Illinois would have had no footing whatever upon the Great Lakes. Upon one pretext or another, each of them, fortunately, was able to induce Congress to violate this provision and grant lake harbors to the southern tier of states.

When Michigan, the fourth state of the Old Northwest, was being formed, much dissatisfaction was expressed in the peninsula that Ohio had been given Maumee Bay and the site of Toledo, and a clamor arose for Michigan's " ancient rights " to the east and west line of the ordinance as a southern boundary. It had always tacitly been understood that the fifth state, when formed, should have all of the land west of Lake Michigan and the River

St. Mary's. But before Wisconsin Territory was organized, Congress awarded to Michigan the upper peninsula as recompense for having lost Maumee Bay to Ohio, and a narrow strip abutting on Lake Michigan to Indiana. This arrangement was at the time unpopular in Michigan, whose people bitterly lamented the exchange; but ultimately it proved a boon to that state, for the copper and iron mines of the upper peninsula came to be among her richest possessions. While benefiting Michigan, however, the transaction materially lessened Wisconsin's potential share of the Northwest Territory.

The strip that Illinois had been granted (1818) along Lake Michigan, north of the east and west line, was sixty-one miles wide. Upon this splendid tract of 8500 square miles of agricultural and lead-mining lands are to-day planted the cities of Chicago, Evanston, Waukegan, Freeport, Rockford, Dixon, Elgin, and Galena, and between them is a populous and progressive rural district. All of this prosperous territory would now be within the limits of Wisconsin, had the letter of the ordinance been observed.

Trouble over the Wisconsin-Michigan boundary began in March, 1836, when the bill for Wisconsin Territory was reported to the House of Representatives. An attempt was then made to regain for Wisconsin the greater part of Michigan's upper peninsula, but it was defeated, and what is sub-

stantially the present boundary was provided for;
but the description read that the line was to proceed up Montreal River, from Lake Superior to
Lake Vieux Desert; thence down certain head-
streams of the Menominee to the main channel of
that river, and thence to Green Bay. A map of the
region, used in the congressional committees, showed
such a natural boundary extending from Lake Superior to Green Bay. But later, federal surveyors,
in seeking to run the interstate line, established
that there was no continuous waterway as depicted
upon the old map, and that Lake Vieux Desert
was far from being, as erroneously supposed by
the cartographer, the common source of the Montreal and Menominee. It is, in fact, the headwaters of Wisconsin River, and isolated from the
two other streams. There was much haggling over
this discovery, and subsequently over the compro-
mises reached by the boundary surveyors. In February, 1842, Governor Doty declared it an "impracticable line," and urged the legislature to take
advantage of the situation to claim the upper peninsula, which "belongs to the fifth state to be formed
in Northwest Territory."

Governor Dodge was responsible for inaugurat-
ing the contention over the loss of territory to Illinois. In December, 1838, he secured the adoption
by the legislature of a vigorous memorial to Congress on the subject — a paper promptly pigeon-
holed at Washington by the Senate judiciary com-

mittee. Thirteen months after this, resolutions were
again adopted by the Wisconsin legislature, calling
the attention of Congress to the fact that "a large
and valuable tract of country is now held by the
State of Illinois, contrary to the manifest right and
consent of the people of this territory."

These resolutions created an uproar on both sides
of the line. In Illinois, curiously enough, popular
sentiment in the fourteen northern counties interested seemed strongly in favor of Wisconsin's
claim; but in Wisconsin itself public sentiment
was generally against them. A public meeting at
Green Bay "viewed the resolutions of the legislature
with concern and regret," and that body was asked
to rescind them. The reason for this opposition in
Wisconsin will be evident, when it is explained that
the fervor aroused by the two governors and other
politicians at Madison over these boundary contentions was known to be in large measure induced by
a desire to hurry Wisconsin into statehood; the
large population south of the line being deemed
necessary to pad the census, as an inducement to
Congress to favor this project. Most people in the
territory, however, were as yet unprepared to accept statehood, with its attendant increase of taxes
and responsibility.

On taking office in 1841, Doty renewed the attack
both on Michigan and Illinois with even greater
bitterness, were that possible. He ordered out of
the disputed tract to the south certain Illinois land

commissioners. Popular referendums were at his request held in the northern counties of that state, to pass upon the question of jurisdiction, in which elections Wisconsin carried the day. In June, 1842, he officially informed the governor of Illinois that the latter's commonwealth was "exercising an accidental and temporary jurisdiction" over a body of people who should be citizens of Wisconsin.

In December, 1843, Doty again called the attention of the legislature to both the Illinois and the Michigan boundary questions, once more standing stoutly for "the birthright of the State," the "ancient limits of Wisconsin." Under his inspiration a strongly-worded report was prepared by a select Senate committee, who suggested that while there was little hope of getting other states to "surrender any rights of territory," once acquired, Congress should be requested to give Wisconsin, for the loss of territory, some recompense, such as Michigan had obtained for cessions on her southern border. This compensation, the committee thought, should come in the form of congressional appropriations for the construction of certain internal improvements within the territory, such as a railroad between Lake Michigan and the Mississippi, the improvement of the old Fox-Wisconsin waterway for the passage of large vessels between the Great Lakes and the Great River, a canal between the Fox and Rock rivers, and harbors at various ports on Lake Michigan. Should Congress not grant these reasonable suggestions, the committee urge that Wisconsin take the attitude of " a state out of the Union, and possess, exercise, and enjoy all the rights, privileges, and powers of the sovereign, independent State of Wisconsin, and if difficulties must ensue, we could appeal with confidence to the Great Umpire of nations to adjust them." There was an accompanying appeal to Congress " to do justice while yet it is not too late," for the people of Wisconsin " will show to the world that they lack neither the disposition nor the ability to protect themselves."

This belligerent state paper, to which small attention appears to have been paid by the territorial press, aroused in the legislature an acrimonious debate, in which favorable speeches were mingled with others making scoffing allusion to the committee report as a " declaration of war against Great Britain, Illinois, Michigan, and the United States." Finally adopted by a close vote, the memorial reached Congress in March, 1844. It is perhaps needless to add that that body paid no attention to the interesting communication ; and Wisconsin, for all the war talk of her state-rights politicans, regained none of the territory that had been taken from her. Indeed, in 1848, when Wisconsin became a state, Congress took from her, to give to Minnesota, the country between St. Croix River and the upper Mississippi, a vast and wealthy tract in which are now situated Duluth and much of the cities of Minneapolis and St. Paul.

From the first the people of the territory, in common with their fellow citizens of several neighboring states and territories, were much concerned in seeking federal aid for internal improvements. This quest was pursued by Wisconsin with a somewhat feverish persistence that gives point to the futile "demands" made upon Congress in connection with the boundary dispute. But the Democratic party, dominant at the time of Wisconsin's entrance upon the scene as a territory, was opposed to appropriations for this purpose; and even the Whigs, who gained power in 1840, were in this respect illiberal towards Wisconsin, the result being that during the entire territorial period there was obtained but a small fraction of the improvements sought.

As early as 1836 there was a popular agitation in favor of a federal canal to connect Milwaukee and Rock rivers, with the design of thus furnishing continuous navigation between Lake Michigan and the Mississippi. Despairing, however, of obtaining a congressional appropriation therefor, a number of prominent citizens secured from the legislature (1838) a charter for the Milwaukee and Rock River Canal Company. The territory was promptly solicited for the loan of its credit to float the enterprise. This request was ultimately refused, after a protracted fight, partly because of jealousy manifested by the promoters of the Fox-Wisconsin enterprise, but chiefly because the people at large had an almost morbid fear of incurring any manner of territorial debt.

Congress, however, voted a land grant in assistance of the project (1838), with the stipulation that the territory was to conduct sales therefrom and use the income in completing the canal. In accepting this gift, the territory unwittingly became in effect a partner in the undertaking, a condition of affairs leading to much popular discontent and legislative bickering, and ultimate disaster to the canal (1844), upon which some fifty-seven thousand dollars had been expended, chiefly in improvements to Milwaukee River. The territory fell heir to some of the canal bonds, which it repudiated, although later the state itself paid them. When Wisconsin entered the Union, the federal government claimed that she still was owing upwards of a hundred thousand dollars to the canal fund, and withheld this sum from the net proceeds due the state from the sale of public lands within her bounds.[1] As to whether or not this canal, had it been completed as designed, would have proved a valuable asset of the commonwealth, is still an open question in Wisconsin history.

Suggestions for the improvement of the Fox and Wisconsin rivers, especially for a canal connecting

[1] See W. R. Smith, *History of Wisconsin*, vol. iii; M. B. Hammond, "Financial History of Wisconsin Territory," in Wis. Hist. Soc. *Proceedings*, 1893; and R. V. Phelan, "Financial History of Wisconsin," in Univ. of Wis. *Bulletins*, No. 193.

them at Portage, had frequently been made during the French régime, as well as in the English and the early American. A definite project therefor began in 1839 to be actively pushed in the territorial legislature. Seven years later, Congress made a grant of land in its aid. In 1848 the improvement was placed by the legislature in the hands of a board of public works, and by 1851 the long-desired canal at Portage united the two divergent waterways. The latter year, a contract for bettering the navigation of the Fox was awarded to Morgan L. Martin, who later organized the Fox and Wisconsin Improvement Company. This corporation, although the victim of political wrangling, for party tactics and sectional jealousies then entered into almost every walk of life, was aided by increased land grants from Congress.

In time, however, since the work assumed larger porportions than anticipated, Eastern capital was invited to assist in the growing enterprise. This alliance led, along a stormy path which we need not here follow, to financial complications, bankruptcy, and foreclosure; and in 1872 the federal government purchased the works.

First and last, millions of dollars were spent by individual capitalists and the nation upon this time-honored project. Indeed, until about 1875 a disposition to battle for appropriations for this purpose was a cardinal qualification required of candidates for Congress in northern and central Wisconsin.

Nothing now remains to show for the lavish expenditure save an admirable water-power system on the lower Fox, a still shallow and weedy channel on the upper Fox above Berlin, and on the Wisconsin below Portage a few shabby remnants of wing dams vainly designed to control its shifting sands. Except at unusually high stages of water, navigation over this once great fur-trade route between Green Bay and Prairie du Chien is now possible only to row boats and light-draught pleasure launches, and sometimes even these meet with difficulties on the Wisconsin. In short, the route was practicable only so long as its use was confined to canoes, bateaux, barges, and timber rafts — both rivers were of immense importance in the heyday of Wisconsin lumbering, — but no engineering skill has been able to adapt it, throughout, to deep-draught vessels of the present time.

Although the inhabitants west of Lake Michigan came under American domination in 1816, we have seen that, although they were citizens of Michigan, because of their great distance from Detroit the machinery of local government was tardily established among them. Taxes were not collected anywhere within the district before 1820–21, and then only in Crawford County, which seems to have been a more pliant member of Michigan Territory than was Brown County; in the Fox River valley, Michigan statutes were frequently ignored, and relations with the Detroit government were more or less strained. Local assessments appear to have been made from time to time in Green Bay, but apparently no regular tax was levied until after 1833. It was, indeed, not until the organization of Wisconsin Territory that all of the region included within its bounds came under the operations of a well-regulated system of administration.

The tax-gatherer is nowhere a welcome visitor. In a sparsely-settled community like this, that had long existed with but few forms of government, and where little convertible wealth had as yet accumulated, schemes for obtaining public revenue were necessarily unpopular. Plans for taxation were keenly criticised by our pioneers, and every public expenditure found its opponents. Even the school taxes of 1838–40 created much dissatisfaction, and for a time they necessarily were made optional with the community. The expenses of the annual legislative session aroused special antagonism. It was pointed out in 1844 that whereas the whole assessment of the territory was but eight million dollars, the meeting of the legislature alone cost eighty thousand, or one per cent of the valuation. The Grant County "Herald" indignantly expostulated (September 14, 1844) that this meant, "We shall be compelled to pay nearly two per cent of a tax on all our property assessed!" Despite the fact that at one time (1842) Congress liquidated the territorial debt of forty-five thousand dollars, it still had upon entering the Union a new debt of nearly thirteen thousand, the greater part of it, however, being the unpaid bonds of the unfortunate Milwaukee and Rock River Canal.

Even before the coming of American troops to Green Bay, the great pine, hard wood, and mixed forests of the northern two-thirds of Wisconsin began to play some part in the economic development of the region; in time lumbering (chiefly of white pine) came to be Wisconsin's foremost industry, and so remained until quite recent years. No less than seven large rivers, with their many tributaries, drained the enormous "pineries," enabling logs to be floated to far-distant markets, and occasionally furnishing power for sawmills. Six clearly-defined lumbering districts were thereby established, — the shore of Green Bay, Wolf River, Wisconsin River, Black River, Chippewa and Red Cedar, and the Wisconsin branch of the St. Croix.

So far as is now known, the first sawmill in the state was built in 1809, near De Pere. No other appears to have been established in the Green Bay district until twenty years later, on Pensaukee River, but important lumbering operations are not recorded before 1834. The Wolf River district was not operated in until 1835. It would seem that soldiers were cutting logs on the Wisconsin, for the building of Fort Winnebago (Portage), in 1826; and on the same river three years later, for Fort Crawford (Prairie du Chien). Black River was very early entered upon by loggers, a mill being built at Black River Falls in 1819; but because of Indian opposition the industry was abandoned until 1839. Logging operations were commenced on various branches of the Chippewa as early as 1822, but disastrous freshets and aboriginal hostility compelled a retreat of the lumbermen; a successful mill was finally erected in 1828 on the site of the present Menomonie. In the height of the Wisconsin lumber industry (about 1876) a billion and a half feet of pine was annually marketed, some eighteen thousand men being employed in the various stages of production, — cutting, rafting, river-driving, and manufacturing timber and shingles. To-day by far the greater part of our original forests has been cut over. The principal Wisconsin operators, who have amassed large fortunes in this once enormous industry, are now similarly exploiting the woods of Southern and far Northwestern states; while the commonwealth, now that its supply of pine, once supposedly exhaustless, has been seriously depleted, is for the benefit of future generations energetically planning to reforest some of the great areas of gaunt and neglected " cut-over " lands.

During the first half of the nineteenth century, " wildcat " financial methods were in vogue throughout the Middle West. Together with her sister commonwealths, Wisconsin had much unfortunate experience with banks and bankers of this disreputable sort. The Bank of Wisconsin, at

Green Bay, opened in 1834, was the first institution of its kind west of Lake Michigan; it was followed two years later by banks at Mineral Point and Milwaukee, and the year after that by another at Prairie du Chien. The financial panic of 1837, combined with reckless management by their officers, brought these banks into serious trouble. The Prairie du Chien institution was of short duration; the Green Bay and Milwaukee banks had their charters annulled by the legislature (1839) because of irregularity, and that at Mineral Point failed (1841) with heavy loss, its charter being thereafter promptly repealed.

Nominally there were now no banks in the territory. But, patterning by the example of Illinois, there had been organized two insurance corporations, one at Green Bay (1838) and the other at Milwaukee (1839), which, although not styled banks, performed all their functions. Their charters contained stipulations to the effect that "nothing herein contained shall give banking privileges;" nevertheless the recitation of powers, adroitly phrased, included all that any legitimate bank could wish to do. This plain violation of the intent of the legislature led that body to proceed to extraordinary length in seeking to prevent further corporations of any sort from like transgressions. No plank-road, mining and smelting, navigation and transportation, or even church society could be incorporated until a clause had been inserted in its charter to the effect that "nothing herein contained shall be construed as in any way giving to the said company any banking privileges whatever or any right to issue any certificate of deposit, or other evidence of debt to circulate as money."

Despite its irregularity in doing a business not intended by the legislature, the Wisconsin Marine and Fire Insurance Company of Milwaukee soon came to be an important factor in the betterment of banking methods in the West. The corporation was, almost from the first, largely managed by its secretary, Alexander Mitchell, a young but eminently skillful Scotch banker from Aberdeen. In the general scarcity of reputable currency, its certificates of deposit, invariably paid on presentation, came into wide circulation, and "Mitchell's bank," as it was popularly called, did a thriving business in assisting colonists to take up government land. Its manager's reputation became as wide as the nation, and although at one time he had in circulation a million and a half dollars' worth of paper, the integrity of which rested simply on his promise to pay, the Milwaukee company was the only financial concern in the Northwest that stood the pressure of the times and maintained itself without a flaw.

The legislature, beset by Mitchell's rivals, frequently sought to check him in his prosperous although technically illegal career. In 1845 his charter was annulled; but as that document gave

the company existence until 1868, the latter persisted in transacting business, and when enjoined
in Milwaukee made arrangements to pay notes in
Chicago, St. Louis, Detroit, and elsewhere. For
years, amidst this persecution, Mitchell was necessarily legislative lobbyist as well as banker, and
successful in both pursuits. In 1852 a general
banking act was passed ; whereupon, simply adding the word " Bank " to its former title, the company opened the first regular bank in Milwaukee,
under the new law. Years of wildcat experiences
were still before the people of the West, but
throughout this protracted financial storm Mitchell's institution, Scotch-like in integrity and persistence, stood like a rock.

President Tyler removed Governor Doty in the
autumn of 1844, and appointed in his place (September 16) Nathaniel P. Tallmadge, who served
but for eight months, being succeeded by Dodge,
who, as the nominee of Polk, occupied the executive
office until Wisconsin entered the Union. The
agitation for statehood was at once renewed on
Dodge's resumption of office. The census of the
territory now revealed a population of a hundred
and fifty-five thousand, and popular opinion, for
several years averse to taking on the costs and
responsibilities of state government, seemed at last
inclined to view the project with favor. By order
of the legislature a vote on this question was taken
on the first Tuesday of April, 1846, — the franchise

being restricted to "every white male inhabitant above the age of twenty-one years, who shall have resided in the territory for six months." The result was about six to one in the affirmative (ayes 12,334, nays 2487). Meanwhile, a bill enabling Wisconsin to become a state was introduced in Congress, January 9, by Morgan L. Martin, the territorial delegate. Passing Congress, it was approved by the President on August 10.

Governor Dodge issued on the first of August a proclamation calling a constitutional convention, which held its session at Madison between October 5 and December 16. In this body some pugnacious members desired to place in the constitution a proviso that Wisconsin would accept statehood only on the condition that she be "restored to her ancient boundaries." But this bit of bluster failed of passage, as did another proposition to establish a new state along the south shore of Lake Superior, to be named after that body of water; the settlers who were now creeping into the extreme northern littoral had the same objection to being connected with far-distant Madison, separated from them by a wide and almost untrodden wilderness, that the earlier Wisconsin people had against being governed from Detroit. The constitution, for the most part an exceptionally able document, was rejected by the people (April 5, 1847), upon a vote of ayes 14,119, nays 20,231. The Democrats opposed the articles on the rights of married women and exemptions from forced sale ; while the Whigs disliked the restrictions that, with a caution born of intense popular distrust, had been placed upon banking and bank circulation.[1]

The second constitutional convention assembled in Madison on December 15. The territory now boasted of a population of 210,456, and the desire for statehood had become all but universal. The new constitution, carefully avoiding the rocks upon which its predecessor had been wrecked, was adopted by the people on March 13, 1848 (ayes 16,799, nays 6384). On the eighth of May a state election was held, Nelson Dewey, the Democratic candidate, being elected by a majority of 5089 in a total vote of 33,987. Three weeks later (May 29), President Polk approved a new act of Congress, based upon the accepted constitution, whereby Wisconsin was at last admitted to the sisterhood of states.

[1] Banks of issue were prohibited, also the circulation of any bank-note of a less denomination than twenty dollars.

CHAPTER XIII

IN his opening message to the legislature (June 8, 1848), Governor Dewey offered congratulations upon the "favorable auspices under which the State of Wisconsin has taken her position among the families of states. With a population numbering nearly one quarter of a million, and rapidly increasing, free from the incubus of a state debt, and rich in the return yielded as the reward of labor in all the branches of industrial pursuits, our state occupies an enviable position abroad, that is highly gratifying to the pride of our people."

A commonwealth just entering the Union nearly always receives a large accession of new settlers, as the result of prominence given to the new state in the contemporary public press. Accordingly, Wisconsin at once attracted the customary rush of ambitious young Americans seeking an opening in the West. But the most marked feature of her growth during the first decade of statehood was a considerable influx of German immigrants. For two hundred years after the coming of Nicolet, Wisconsin had been French to the core. There followed twelve territorial years (1836–48) during which the American element, having pushed aside the mild-mannered and unprogressive *habitans* and *voyageurs*, was aggressively dominant; but now Wisconsin was to become better known for her Germans than for her native-born.

Several causes contributed to this strong Teutonic migration toward Wisconsin. The political uprising of 1830 in Germany had been followed by reaction, causing thousands to turn their eyes to America as a land of liberty and opportunity. As early as 1832 there was on foot in Rhenish Bavaria a project to purchase a large tract of land in the United States " to be settled by Germans and to be called a new Germany." Three years later there were organized for this purpose several societies, largely composed of political suspects and refugees, chiefly men trained for the learned professions. Numerous books and pamphlets were published in Germany, in advocacy of this scheme, several of whose authors named Wisconsin as the most desirable region attainable. Eventually the plan was abandoned by the majority as impracticable, although it was spasmodically broached thereafter, even as late as 1878.

Throughout this agitation, the attention of many thousands of discontented Germans had become centred on Wisconsin as a land of promise. So much was written and printed on the subject that the characteristics of the territory were familiar to them in a general way. The larger movement for a

German-American state had failed ; but individual agitators began to arrive here by 1846, and almost to a man sent highly favorable reports to their compatriots at home, many of which accounts, the product of men accustomed to literary expression, were printed and very freely distributed among a people eager to receive them. Knowledge of these publications no doubt prompted Governor Dewey's reference to the fact that Wisconsin " occupies an enviable position abroad."

The German-American pioneers who thus heralded this new American commonwealth found here physical features appealing strongly to them because similar in many respects to those sturdy surroundings amid which they had themselves been reared ; and the political possibilities of Wisconsin also kindled the imaginations of men who were fleeing their own land in order to secure personal liberty. In their books, pamphlets, and newspaper letters they laid emphasis on the excellent climate — with extremes of temperature modified by proximity to the Great Lakes, less enervating than that of Michigan, and " comparatively free from the fevers that infest the South." The unbroken hard wood and evergreen forests in the northern half of the state, and the tract of heavy timber along the eastern border, inspired them with admiration. Unlike Illinois, Michigan, and Indiana, that had encumbered themselves with liabilities for internal improvements, Wiscon-

sin was practically out of debt. Potential water-
power was everywhere evident upon the maps, and
promised to be an important asset to the people of
the state. The mineral regions on Lake Superior
and along the Mississippi appealed strongly to
many classes of German laborers. Well-wooded
public lands were sold to emigrants at low prices;
tree-loving Germans, in settling Wisconsin, always
sought forests near the main routes of travel, —
first in the eastern counties, and then spreading
into the denser woods of the north, which they
soon converted into a productive and prosperous
region. But perhaps the most influential factor in
inducing foreign immigration was the clause in the
new state's constitution, allowing an alien to vote
after a year's residence, thus giving him an early
chance of winning political power.

The year of Wisconsin's entrance upon the dignity of statehood was that of the great political,
economic, and social upheaval in Germany known
as the Revolution of 1848. This gave rise at once
to a strong tide of migration hither. It was particularly gratifying to the emigrants of those days
to find their predilections regarding Wisconsin
confirmed at the landing. " In New York," writes
a German settler of 1848, " every hotel-keeper and
railroad agent, every one who was approached for
advice, directed men to Wisconsin." Later disturbances in the fatherland, in which religious interference and the steady growth of militarism had

become additional incentives to popular discontent, materially aided this movement to our state. Although reaching its maximum in numbers by 1854, it continued with noticeable strength until near the close of the nineteenth century, and brought to the state immigrants from nearly every important district in Germany. To-day, perhaps a third of the two millions of Wisconsin people are either German-born or the children of such.

In due time the Germans were followed in large numbers by other European nationalities, particularly Scandinavians (chiefly Norwegians), Irish, natives of Great Britain, Canadians, Bohemians, Poles, Dutch, Belgians, and Swiss. By 1890 Wisconsin was surpassed only by Pennsylvania in the variety and solidarity of its groups of foreign-born folk. There are still many portions of the state where some single nationality occupies blocks of contiguous townships, controlling within the district all political, educational, and religious affairs; and in such neighborhoods the English language is but occasionally spoken. But, ordinarily, our citizens of European birth are quick to adopt English speech and American customs, and freely enter upon the privileges and duties of citizenship. It is a matter for congratulation that the immigrant often brings from the Old World fruits of civilization that are of value to the New; in casting off the old political relations, he does not thereby free himself from the experiences, culture, and patriotic sentiments binding him to his forbears. Wisconsin will always be deeply indebted to this strong infusion of foreign blood for much that is creditable in its career as a state.

The first Norwegian settler to appear in Wisconsin seems to have been Ole Nattestad, who reared a home near Beloit in 1838. He was soon joined by others, until now this element of Wisconsin's population is second only to the German. Strongest in Dane County, Norwegians are nevertheless to be found in large groups in every western and northern county, and in several of the eastern. There are large neighborhoods of Swedes in the northwestern part of the state, but they number far less than those who come from the sister land. Danes are found in considerable bodies in Adams, Milwaukee, Racine, and Waushara counties. Finlanders are numerous in Douglas County. On Washington Island, in the waters of Green Bay, is a large colony of Icelandic fishermen.

Poles are widespread, although chiefly massed in Milwaukeé, Manitowoc, and Portage counties. In Kewaunee County, Bohemians form three sevenths of the population, and are also to be found grouped in other districts. Belgians are strongest in Brown and Door counties. The Dutch are also particularly numerous in the northeast. German Swiss have prosperous colonies in Green, Fond du Lac, Winnebago, Buffalo, and Pierce counties. Italians are a later accession than most of the other nationalities; they have considerable communities in Vernon and Florence counties, but recent arrivals are much scattered. Russians of the several types are chiefly found in Milwaukee, but neighborhoods of Russian Jews are beginning to appear in most of our cities. In addition to French Creoles in the old fur-trading centres of the Fox and Wisconsin valleys, direct descendants of the population of the old régime, there are modern French Canadian settlements in several northern counties — attracted thither, no doubt, by service for the lumber companies.

Cornishmen early settled in the lead region, which also contains several important English groups. The Welsh are planted on Wisconsin soil in several large neighborhoods, chiefly in Winnebago, Columbia, Dodge, Sauk, and Racine counties. The Irish, formerly strong in southeast Wisconsin, have in most places given way before the German wave, and are now widely distributed, although often living in small colonies. Scotch are found in large numbers, particularly in the eastern and northern counties.

The importance of early lead-mining operations, in opening to civilization the southwestern corner of Wisconsin, has been pointed out. We shall see that this industry did much to hasten the development of the entire southern tier of counties, as well as that of the state at large. From the first, the people of the mining district had been closely connected, socially and commercially, with the South. Men from neighboring slave states had been the chief operators, and were frequently accompanied by their black servants; their principal transportation route was the Mississippi, and their chief markets St. Louis and New Orleans, steamers bringing back to them Southern products in return for ore. Cincinnati, Pittsburg, and other Ohio River ports furnished markets for a fair share of the output. Small shipments of lead ore had also been made to the East by way of the Fox-Wisconsin route as early as 1822, and continued at intervals for at least twenty years, forming one of the strongest arguments for the federal improvement of those rivers. Most observers supposed, however, that the Mississippi must forever continue to be the main artery of trade for the lead region.

But a great change was coming. After the completion of the Erie Canal (1826), Eastern merchants slowly became convinced of the superiority of that waterway and the Great Lakes as a Western trade route, over the Mississippi River and the long gulf and sea voyage to New York. In 1836 a company was formed for a combined wagon and steamboat transport between Chicago and Galena, the principal *entrepôt* of the mines. By this means cargoes of lead ore were shipped to Eastern markets; and from Chicago, on the return trips, were transported lumber, shingles, and Eastern goods destined to the mines.

How early Wisconsin miners sought connection with the lakes by overland wagon routes is not known, but lead shipments " from the rapids of Rock River " were recorded in Racine in 1836 ; and in 1838 the " Milwaukee Sentinel " declares it " a common thing to see oxen laden with lead from Grant and La Fayette counties appear at the wharves after a journey of eight or ten days," the distance traveled, by road, being from a hundred and twenty-five to two hundred miles.

In 1839–40 a phenomenally low stage of water prevailed in the Mississippi, creating a stagnant condition in the lead trade, and leading to loud demands, not only for the improvement of the great river, but for better and shorter routes to the East. Specifically, it was pointed out that there were needed both railways and canals between the Mississippi and Lake Michigan. The Milwaukee and Rock River Canal, previously alluded to, was one of the desired connecting links ; another was the important waterway opened in 1851 between Lake Michigan and Illinois River, the route followed by the wagon express of 1836. Meanwhile the wagon routes between the mines and Lake Michigan ports — one ran out from Milwaukee by way of Madison, and along the watershed separating Wisconsin River drainage from that of south-flowing streams, while another stretched westward from Racine, via Janesville — were becoming well worn in the service of the now desperate operators.

In 1847 a Milwaukee paper says, " The lead schooners are constantly arriving here from the mineral region. These singular teams drawn by six, eight, or more yoke of oxen, excite some curiosity in those who are not used to such sights at the East. They sleep under the canopy of heaven, with the camp fires and the primitive meals of a military encampment, pitching tents with the first dusk of evening and rising with the early dawn." The roads followed by these pioneer ore carriers furnished to agricultural settlers tempting paths from the lake shore into the interior, and were an important element in the development of the southern counties.

By this time Wisconsin was growing larger crops than her population could consume, and farmers had joined the miners in clamoring for an improved outlet to Eastern markets. Flour and pork, together with lead, were regularly shipped from Milwaukee to Buffalo, these three Wisconsin products appearing thenceforth in market quotations from that distributing centre.[1] The Great Lakes and the Erie Canal furnished a through water route from Lake Michigan to the Atlantic seaboard, that could transport freight at less than half the expense of the Mississippi River and Gulf route, and enabled shippers to " get the proceeds of their sales at least three months sooner than by the way of New

[1] See O. G. Libby, " Significance of the Lead and Shot Trade in Early Wisconsin History," in *Wis. Hist. Colls.*, vol. xiii.

Orleans." But while this benefited the lead miners,
and correspondingly depressed lower Mississippi
River traffic,[1] the cost of overland hauling was
so great — thirty-one cents per hundred pounds of
lead, between the Mississippi and Milwaukee —
that only farmers in eastern Wisconsin could afford
to send their crops to the Milwaukee and Racine
docks. In the interior, agriculture was declining
for want of a cheap and adequate road to market.
The " Grant County Herald " (April 8, 1843) declared that "the positive result of this state of
things, if continued, will be the gradual depopu-
lation of the western part of the territory." For
reasons soon to be explained, even the mines in
that district were now losing workmen, who migrated in considerable numbers to the Lake Superior copper fields or joined the restless throng then
pressing westward on the long trail to Oregon.

[1] In *De Bow's Review*, vol. xii (1852), p. 38, a Southern writer,
bewailing the diversions of the channels of Western trade from
southward to eastward, says: "All the lead from the upper Mississippi now goes east by the way of Milwaukee. But the most
recent and astonishing change in the course of the northwestern
trade is to behold, as a friend tells us, the number of steamers
that now descend the upper Mississippi, loaded to the guards with
produce, as far as the mouth of the Illinois River, and then turn
up that stream with their cargoes, to be shipped to New York via
Chicago. The Illinois canal has not only swept the whole produce
along the line of the Illinois River to the East, but it is drawing
the products from the upper Mississippi through the same channel, thus depriving not only New Orleans, but St. Louis, of a rich
portion of their former trade."

It had early been evident to at least a few clearsighted Wisconsin men, that while canals might serve for certain classes of freight, a railroad would be a quicker and more efficient route between the Mississippi and Lake Michigan. A project for such construction was first broached in a memorial to Congress adopted by the Michigan territorial legislature at its Green Bay session in January, 1836, in which was emphasized " the immense saving that might [thereby] be made in transporting lead " to New York.

In early railway agitation in Wisconsin, prospective benefit to the lead trade furnished the principal argument for such enterprises. But after 1845, the fast-developing agricultural interests received chief consideration ; it being estimated in 1846 that the farm products (chiefly wheat) to be moved by the proposed road between the great river and the great lake, would probably yield a traffic revenue five times that obtainable from shipments of lead, which could contribute only twelve per cent of the total.

Not only was there a relative falling off in the Mississippi River lead trade, but after 1847 came a steady decline in the actual output. New Orleans had practically lost this trade by 1857, and in St. Louis the shipments of that year were less than half those of the previous decade. Many reasons contributed to this rapid decadence of lead-mining in Wisconsin and Illinois : the tariff of 1846 had reduced the value of the ore; the old shallow diggings had been worked out, and now there were required expensive mining methods and large capital, together with a more intimate knowledge of the geology of the region than was then obtainable; California gold mines and Lake Superior copper deposits were attracting the miners; we have seen that transportation difficulties were coming to be a large factor in the problem; and the discovery in the Rocky Mountains and Black Hills of silver, with accompanying lead, tended to accentuate the virtual neglect of the Wisconsin-Illinois field. During the past few years, however, the district has been successfully reopened for the extensive mining of zinc.

The project of Asa Whitney, a New York merchant, to construct a government railway from Wisconsin to the mouth of Columbia River, and thereby reach out for the trade of the Pacific, was in 1845 much talked of throughout the country. His prospecting journey through Wisconsin in that year attracted much attention, because a proposed road between Milwaukee and Prairie du Chien was considered to be the initial step in his ambitious scheme. Whitney's plans failed; the country was not yet ready for them, but they did much to stimulate public imagination, and in Wisconsin were of direct assistance in calling marked attention to the local project.

Railway charters had been granted by the legislature quite early in the history of the territory: in December, 1836, to the La Fontaine and Dubuque and Belmont companies; in 1838 to the Root River; in 1839 to the Pekatonica and Mississippi; and in 1840 to the Michigan and Rock River — none of these corporations progressed beyond the paper stage. In 1847, four companies were chartered; but only one of these, the Milwaukee and Waukesha, became active.[1] A year later its name was changed to the Milwaukee and Mississippi, the progenitor of the present far-stretching Chicago, Milwaukee, and St. Paul system. In 1851, that company laid the first rails in Wisconsin, and amid great popular rejoicing ran a train from Milwaukee to Waukesha, a distance of twenty miles. Three years later this pioneer railway reached Madison, and in 1857 touched the Mississippi at Prairie du Chien, just twenty-one years after the first suggestion of the project for rail connection between that river and Lake Michigan.

Meanwhile, other companies were pushing into the state. The Chicago and Northwestern, now one of the largest systems in the United States, reached Janesville from the southeast in 1855 and Fond du Lac in 1858. Other and shorter lines were now constructed in various parts of Wisconsin, these

[1] See B. H. Meyer, "History of Early Railroad Legislation in Wisconsin," in *Wis. Hist. Colls.*, vol. xiv.

being for the most part absorbed, extended, and ramified by the two larger companies.

In June, 1856, Congress made two large land grants for the construction of railways in Wisconsin: one in aid of a line to extend from either Madison or Columbus, via Portage and St. Croix River, to the Lake Superior town of Bayfield; the other to endow a line from Fond du Lac to some point on the Michigan-Wisconsin boundary. The prospective companies were to be given "every alternate section of land designated by odd numbers for six sections in width, on each side of said roads respectively."

At the succeeding session of the legislature, the existing railroad companies engaged in a mad scramble for these rich prizes. But with a show of impartiality, the lawmakers declined to allow them the lands, and chartered two new companies pledged to construct the lines: the Lake Superior grant being given to the so-called La Crosse and Milwaukee (charged with being merely a tool of the Chicago, Milwaukee, and St. Paul), and the Fond du Lac grant to the Wisconsin and Superior (supposed to be dominated by the Chicago and Northwestern). Indeed, it was not long before these popular suspicions received apparent confirmation by the " absorption " of the grantee corporations by the two companies respectively named. Later, legal complications arose, calling into question the rightful ownership of the grants.

Among the people at large, grave suspicions were entertained that these legislative railway "deals," particularly that of the La Crosse and Milwaukee, had been accompanied by wholesale corruption. In 1858, a special joint legislative committee reported that "the managers of the La Crosse and Milwaukee Railroad Company have been guilty of numerous and unparalleled acts of mismanagement, gross violations of duty, fraud, and plunder; " that a majority of the legislature of 1856 had been bribed; that of the seventeen senators voting for the grant, thirteen had each received from $10,000 to $20,000 in either stock or bonds, at par; that fifty-eight of the sixty-two complacent assembly-men had each been recipients of from $5000 to $10,000 in the same paper; that Governor Bashford had, for his signature approving the act, been "propitiated " by $50,000 in bonds; that each of three other state officers had accepted $10,000 in similar securities; and that even the private secretary of the governor had contrived to secure from the conspirators a like $5000.

The popular excitement engendered by this document at once reached fever heat, and the state received a great deal of undesirable advertising in the newspapers of the country. Several of the alleged beneficiaries promptly denied that they had taken bribes. Governor Bashford, now out of office, quietly removed into the Far West, and was commonly credited with having disposed of the greater part of his bonds for cash, — more fortunate in this than those who retained their paper, for the La Crosse and Milwaukee company soon went into liquidation, and its bonds and stock were worthless.

CHAPTER XIV

THE dozen years just previous to the War of
Secession were, particularly in the Western states,
a period of great political, financial, and social
unrest. The trans-Alleghany was in a formative
stage, not yet having "found itself." Speculation
ran high; the gambling spirit begat gambling
morals; political passions beat fiercely; never in
our history as a people have the "tricks of the
politicians" been more questionable than they then
were; personal vituperation served as argument;
newspaper offices were the seats of partisan cabals,
which seldom paused to consider the means of
accomplishing desired ends; it was commonly accepted as "good politics" that the "ins" might
properly "feather their nests" at the expense of
the public. Both the civic and the business atmosphere sadly needed clearing.

In the year 1856 there arose in Wisconsin a
cause celèbre, an outgrowth of the bitter political
dissensions of the time, and involving principles of
the highest importance to the welfare of popular
government. During the second term of Governor
Dewey (1850–51), the secretary of state was Wil-

liam A. Barstow, a prominent Democrat from
Waukesha County. Energetic, almost fiercely ag-
gressive, of fine physique, possessed of some of the
qualities of leadership, and cultivating the arts of
popularity, Barstow had a large and enthusiastic
factional following. His party being divided on
issues arising in connection with the fight over the
first constitution, those not of the Barstow wing
were intense haters of those who were. Charges of
corruption were freely laid at his door, and he was
called hard names in the anti-Barstow newspapers,
for this was the heyday of " personal journalism "
in Wisconsin.

Out of this condition of affairs there was coined
an expressive phrase that long held in the political
slang of the commonwealth. State printing contracts, supposed to be awarded to the lowest bidder,
were always eagerly sought by rival Madison newspaper offices. More or less popular suspicion existed, that " deals " were associated with the bien-
nial letting, which was in the hands of the secretary
of state, the state treasurer, and the attorney-general, acting as commissioners of public printing.
During Barstow's secretaryship, such a contest was
on. Before the opening of bids, a confidential letter
was made public,[1] in which one of the Madison
publishers, an intimate friend of the administration,
writing to his absent partner, declared that he had
made arrangements for inside knowledge of the

[1] *Wisconsin Democrat* (Madison), October 5, 1850.

bidding; adding, " We must get a good bid . . . even if we have to buy up *Barstow and the balance*," by " balance " obviously meaning the other printing commissioners. Whether or not Barstow was misjudged by his indiscreet friend is now immaterial; but thereafter his following were by the jeering opposition derisively known as " Barstow and the balance." On retiring from the secretaryship, Barstow still remained the powerful leader of his faction, and the storm centre of the political weather map in Wisconsin.

We have seen that by this time railway companies were yearly importuning the legislature for charters. Previous to 1853 there had been no indication of corruption on the part of railway lobbyists; but the methods of a group of speculators interested in the proposed Rock River Valley Union enterprise were such as quite generally to scandalize the state. The lobbyists rented a club-house, called by them " Monks' Hall," situated but a square distant from the capitol, and here legislators were entertained upon what was in those simple times thought to be a scale of splendor. This band of conspirators were fond of facetiously alluding to themselves as " The monks of Monks' Hall," but their popular designation was " The Forty Thieves," another political term long outliving in Wisconsin the cause of its original bestowal; and in this unholy company many considered that "Barstow and the balance " were duly enrolled. At this distance, and taking into account the virulent character of the partisanship of the period, it is practically impossible to pass safe judgment upon the foundation for these widely-spread accusations.

In November (1853) Barstow was elected governor, having polled a plurality of 8519 votes, his opponents being Edward D. Holton, Republican, and Henry S. Baird, Whig. He was bitterly assailed throughout his term, being charged with allowing his official staff to mismanage the school funds of the state and make ill-secured loans therefrom to personal friends. Certainly, he lost ground, and when running for reëlection in 1855 failed to draw his full party strength; moreover, the new Republican party, born in Wisconsin the previous year,[1] and represented in this election by Coles Bashford of Winnebago County, was making great gains in popular favor. The vote was so close that from the middle of November to the middle of December the result was unknown, because of a needed recount, and there was much suppressed excitement.

On December 15 the state board of canvassers

---

[1] It would appear to be established that the first formal meeting to organize the party was held at Ripon, February 28, 1854. At a subsequent meeting in that village, Alvan E. Bovay, a resident Whig, suggested the name "Republican." Michigan was the first, however, to perfect a state organization, doing so at a meeting in Jackson, July 6. Wisconsin, which had conceived and named the party, held its state convention at Madison a week later (July 13). See F. A. Flower, *History of the Republican Party*.

— the same officials who composed the printing commission, and all of them Barstow's colleagues — announced that Barstow had received 36,355 votes and Bashford 36,198, a majority for the former of 157. Bashford's supporters at once claimed forgeries of supplemental county returns and general unfairness, and a contest was at once prepared for.

Barstow took the oath for his second term, on January 7, 1856, amid the usual civic and military display, and remained in possession of the executive chamber. Meanwhile, Bashford was quietly sworn in by Chief Justice Whiton, at the chamber of the state supreme court, and promptly brought into that court an information in the nature of *quo warranto* to oust the incumbent governor and establish his own claim to the election. This being the first time in the history of the United States that a state court had been called upon to decide as to whether a governor had been properly elected, the case at once attracted general attention.

The court consisted of Chief Justice Whiton and Associate Justices Smith and Orsamus Cole. The lawyers engaged upon both sides were men of considerable distinction at the Wisconsin bar: Bashford's counsel being Timothy O. Howe, Edward G. Ryan, James H. Knowlton, and Alexander W. Randall, while for Barstow appeared Jonathan E. Arnold, Harlow S. Orton, and Matthew H. Carpenter. Barstow's counsel questioned the jurisdiction of the court, claiming that to allow one of the

three coördinate branches of government to decide
upon the eligibility of another would be to elevate
the judiciary above the people, thus enabling only
the creatures of the court to hold office. After a
fierce contest, lasting several weeks, the court held
that its jurisdiction was undoubted. Throughout,
Bashford's cause was handled with great skill, his
counsel winning on nearly every motion; until, on
March 8, Barstow and his representatives indignantly withdrew from the case, declaring that the
court was actuated by political prejudices.

Nevertheless, the court proceeded with its in-
quiry into the facts, the result of the investigation
being to establish gross irregularities in the work
of the board of canvassers. A reëxamination of the
returns developed that Bashford had been elected
by 1009 plurality, and on March 24 he was declared
to be the rightful governor.

Foreseeing the result, Barstow, who all along
had declared that he would not " give up his
office alive," had three days before this sent in
his resignation to the legislature, and the lieutenant-governor, Arthur McArthur, whose election
was unquestioned, assumed office as the supposedly legal successor under the constitution. McArthur took a stubborn attitude, asserting that he
would, in the face of all hazards, hold his chair
throughout the remainder of the term. The court
ruled, however, that as Barstow's title was worthless, McArthur could not succeed to it, — a view

of the case that apparently the Barstow faction had not anticipated, for the announcement threw them into much confusion.

The decision had been rendered on March 24 (Monday). Bashford announced that on the following morning he would take possession of the governor's office. Particularly in and around Madison, popular interest in the trial had developed to the stage of intense excitement that promised trouble. Bodies of armed men, siding with either the relator or the respondent, were drilling in anticipation of a desperate conflict. Wordy quarrels were frequent upon the streets, but the partisan managers, who would have been held responsible for an outbreak, were doing their best to quiet the more boisterous of their followers.

News of Bashford's intent quickly spread. Early in the day not only residents, but country people from as far as ten miles out of town, for the most part Bashford's adherents, crowded into the statehouse, fully expecting a sanguinary fight. At eleven, Bashford and a small bodyguard of friends proceeded to the rooms of the supreme court and obtained the waiting writ, which the Dane County sheriff was charged with serving. Sheriff and governor made their way through the throng, which encouraged them by friendly cheers, and rapped for admittance at the door to the executive chamber, wherein were McArthur, his private secretary, and a few friends.

Bashford was a portly, dignified, pleasant-mannered man of the "old school." When bidden to enter, he leisurely took off his top-coat, hung it and his hat in the official wardrobe, and blandly informed the irate McArthur that he had come to take charge of the office. The latter demanded to know whether force would be used, whereat Bashford quietly asserted that "he presumed no force would be essential; but in case any were needed, there would be no hesitation whatever, with the sheriff's help, in applying it." McArthur said that he "considered this threat as constructive force," and thereupon promptly left the office with his secretary and adherents, passing between rows of Bashford's supporters, who now were guarding the building throughout. There was a shout of triumph, and in a few minutes Governor Bashford was being congratulated by the crowd.[1]

The Republican senate received Bashford's opening message with enthusiasm, and passed a congratulatory vote; but the Democratic assembly at first refused (thirty-eight to forty-four) to hold communication with the new executive. Finally, thirty Democratic members withdrew after filing a protest, and the assembly then voted (thirty-seven to nine) to recognize the governor. The incident

[1] This description of the scenes accompanying the accession of Bashford is the substance of what was, several years ago, related to the present writer by the late General David Atwood, editor of the *Wisconsin State Journal*, himself a prominent friend of Bashford, and an eye-witness of every phase of the affair.

was of much importance in the history of the state, for there is no doubt that for a time the factionists were close to the verge of civil war, and grave danger threatened the system of government by the people.

Another unfortunate state event created widespread interest. In January, 1853, Levi Hubbell, judge of the second judicial circuit, and one of the most prominent men in Wisconsin, was charged before the assembly, by a private citizen, with "high crimes, misdemeanors, and malfeasances in office." A committee of the assembly reported on the matter a month later, preferring about fifty charges, with accompanying specifications, and recommending the judge's removal from office. The accusations included bribery, adjudicating cases in which he was interested, inflicting slighter punishments than required by law, undue partiality, arbitrariness, misapplication of funds, immoral conduct, allowing himself to be approached and influenced out of court on suits pending before him, borrowing money from contestants before his court, and interfering with suits in other courts.

The senate sat as a court of impeachment, from June 6 to July 11, the sharply-contested trial attracting large audiences and arousing much factional bitterness. The newspapers of the state, freely taking sides, and discussing the affair with characteristic acrimony, appear to have been about equally divided in their sympathies. The contending lawyers included some of the most distinguished members of the Wisconsin bar; but especially prominent was Edward G. Ryan, of Milwaukee, who headed the assembly's counsel. His closing argument for the prosecution was in some respects the most acute and brilliant of its kind ever heard within the state, and is still studied in some law schools as a remarkable example of legal invective. The verdict of the senate was "not guilty," a judgment commented on by press and people according to individual predilections. While Hubbell was certainly placed in an unpleasant light, and appears to have been lacking in judicial manner, much of the evidence was of a flimsy character, and personal animus seems to have played some part in the proceedings. The trial is " an isolated episode in Wisconsin history." [1]

Allusion was made in a previous chapter to the legislative act of January 5, 1838, organizing " at or near Madison, the seat of government," the " University of the Territory of Wisconsin." It had been the custom for Congress to bestow upon each new territory seventy-two sections (46,080 acres) of public lands as a university endowment, and Wisconsin received the usual grant. These lands were officially selected, but throughout the territorial period remained untouched, for no steps were then taken to organize the proposed institution.

[1] See J. B. Sanborn, " The Impeachment of Levi Hubbell," in Wis. Hist. Soc. *Proceedings*, 1905.

In fact, but few citizens of the territory were much interested in the cause of higher education. To the great majority of frontiersmen, engaged in wresting a somewhat meagre livelihood from soil, forest, lakes, and mines, the proposed university seemed an enterprise far removed from the necessities of Western life.

The state constitution provided for "a state university, at or near the seat of state government." In July, 1848, it was duly incorporated, and appraisers of school and university lands were appointed. But at once the question arose, What should be the policy of the state, in this endowment of higher education by the federal government? Immigrants were fast pouring in, and lands must inevitably rise in value. Should the trust sections be kept until higher prices prevailed, and the university of the future thus be assured a worthy income? or, should they be sold at once, on terms so low that immigration would be encouraged, and the university itself be left to the care of the next generation, which doubtless would be quite able to support such a school by taxation?

Each state carved out of the Old Northwest had faced the same problem. Of the five, Michigan alone kept faith with the national government. Maintaining possession of her lands until 1837, she received prices averaging $22.50 per acre, and to-day the fund accruing from their sale brings to the university a considerable income. Wisconsin chose to use the federal gift as a bait for immigrants, selling most of the university's acres at prices much below ruling market rates, and thus seriously crippling the college during the first twenty years of its existence.

In 1848 a second land grant of seventy-two sections was made by Congress, but this was not available until 1854, the year in which the university graduated its first class of two young men. The first grant having been wasted, it might have been supposed that the second would be treated with respect. But in neighborhoods where $10 to $20 an acre was the customary price, the new university lands, despite the indignant protests of the board of regents, were offered for three dollars, the seventy-two sections thus bringing but $138,240.

To make a bad matter worse, the fund produced by the sale of both land grants was recklessly invested. Upon the plea of assisting settlers, the state land commissioners — again the secretary of state, the state treasurer, and the attorney-general — made loans from all of the educational funds to thousands of individuals, largely political friends of those officers, and many of these quite irresponsible, and it is still unknown how great was the loss. In 1861 there was an investigation of the wretched business by the land commissioners then in office, and an exposure was made in their annual report: " Truth compels the confession that this trust has been, and is now, of necessity, most unfaithfully administered. The best of the school lands have been disposed of with eager haste and in disregard of the interest of the funds for which they were dedicated."

Thus the state university started upon its career in a condition of extreme weakness. Sadly hampered for funds and obliged to erect buildings from the wasted endowment given by Congress solely for support and maintenance, its early management was not popular and was beset by numerous enemies in the legislature. A drastic reorganization occurred in 1858, and under improved business management public confidence was gradually restored. Not until 1872, however, was a state tax levied for the benefit of the university — and then in distinct official recognition of the fact that the institution had suffered " serious loss and impairment by such sales of its lands, so that its income is not at present sufficient to supply its wants." [1] Since then, the University of Wisconsin has received generous aid from each recurring legislature, which has in this manner paid the debt imposed upon the state by the errors of its predecessors of a half century ago. [2]

In February, 1849, the Wisconsin legislature requested the state's representatives in Congress " to oppose the passage of any act for the government of New Mexico and California, or any other

[1] Preamble to chapter 100, Laws of Wisconsin for 1872.
[2] See Thwaites, *History of the University of Wisconsin.*

Territory now belonging to the United States, or which may be hereafter acquired, unless it shall contain a provision forever prohibiting the introduction of slavery or involuntary servitude into said territories, except as a punishment for crime." Later, a bill to organize the territories of New Mexico and California, with this so-called " Wilmot proviso," was passed by the House of Representatives, but defeated by the Senate; upon the last night of the session, however, the latter attached to the general appropriation bill a " rider " erecting these territories without the anti-slavery clause. Isaac P. Walker, one of the Wisconsin senators, took part in this questionable proceeding, which was, however, opposed by his colleague, Henry Dodge. The state legislature thereupon passed resolutions approving Dodge's course, but calling on Walker to resign his seat, he having " outraged the feelings and misrepresented those who elected him to that station, and openly violated the instructions " of the legislature. Walker made no answer, and kept his seat, but thereafter cautiously voted upon the anti-slavery side.

On September 18, 1850, the President approved the federal Fugitive Slave Law, which provided for using the machinery of the United States courts in apprehending runaway slaves and returning them to their masters. This act—which denied to the bondman a trial by jury, the writ of *habeas corpus*, the right of appeal, and the summoning of wit-

nesses in his own behalf — met with general con-
demnation in the free states. Various political
conventions in Wisconsin denounced it as "odious
and offensive," and adopted resolutions refusing
aid in carrying out its provisions. But this state
was not on the usual route between the South and
Canada, so that few slaves were transported across
its borders by the "underground railroad," although that widely-ramified institution did not
lack agents in Wisconsin, who courted a larger
traffic of this character. There was, therefore, infrequent opportunity here for a clash over the
matter between federal and state authorities; but
when a fugitive slave case did arise, the conflict
attracted national attention, and again aroused the
strong state-rights sentiment which appears to have
existed in Wisconsin in *ante bellum* days.

Joshua Glover, a runaway negro slave, was in
the winter of 1853–54 employed in a sawmill some
four miles north of Racine, on the high road to
Milwaukee. Just before dusk on the night of March
10 he was in his house, playing cards with two
other negroes. Their game was suddenly inter-
rupted by the entrance of seven heavily-armed
white men, who had driven thither from Racine.
Two of the intruders were federal deputy marshals,
who had with them four assistants, the seventh
trespasser being Benammi W. Garland of St. Louis,
who claimed to be Glover's master. In the attempt
to arrest Glover a desperate fight ensued, in the

course of which his negro friends escaped; but single-handed he displayed great strength, and was only overcome by being knocked on the head and manacled while insensible.

The kidnappers had intended returning to Racine; but realizing that news of the encounter would soon reach that hotbed of abolitionism, they feared a rough reception, so determined to drive across country to Milwaukee, twenty miles northward. The night was bitterly cold, but the bleeding fugitive was thrown into an open wagon, without covering, and throughout the night-long ride was frequently kicked and clubbed, and threatened by the brutal Garland with still worse punishment when he reached "home." At daylight, the poor black was cast into the Milwaukee jail, where his wounds were bandaged by a physician.

The anti-slavery leaders of Milwaukee were at once aroused. One of the most prominent among them was Sherman M. Booth, editor of a small paper called "Wisconsin Free Democrat." Learning of the Glover affair, Booth, during the morning of the eleventh, rode on horseback up and down the streets of the city, and like a town crier shouted: "Freemen, to the rescue! Slave-catchers are in our midst! Be at the courthouse at two o'clock!" At the appointed time, five thousand citizens gathered in the courthouse square, where men of local prominence made impassioned speeches against the fugitive slave law and negro-kidnapping.

The Milwaukee county judge issued a writ of *habeas corpus* in favor of Glover; but the sheriff, advised by Federal Judge A. G. Miller, who had issued the warrant for the slave's arrest, refused to serve the paper. Excitement grew hourly. At five o'clock a contingent of a hundred persons arrived by steamboat from Racine, where a large mass meeting had been held that morning, at which it was resolved that "We, as citizens of Wisconsin, are justified in declaring and do hereby declare the slave-catching law of 1850 disgraceful and also repealed." The delegation of a hundred were sent to Milwaukee to insist on fair play for the negro. In the course of the afternoon the Milwaukee local militia were ordered out to preserve the peace, but failed to obey the summons.

At six o'clock, following a glowing appeal by Booth, the mob demanded that the sheriff give up his prisoner. Refusal following, the jail door was battered in with a ram of timber. Glover was then taken out and handed over to the "underground railroad" agency, which put him aboard a schooner clearing for Canada, where he arrived safely. As for Garland and the deputies, they were arrested for assault, but Judge Miller released them.

Soon after this event, a number of anti-slavery meetings were held in various free states, to take action against the Nebraska bill. At gatherings of this character it became customary to adopt a resolution clearly indorsing the affair at Milwaukee;

in Wisconsin, a resolution was generally added, expressing the opinion that the obnoxious federal law was unconstitutional. As for the Wisconsin press, it generally sympathized with the movement, although there was in most editorials a cautious note of deprecation against the use of mob violence, save under great provocation.

Public interest now centred in Booth, who became the victim of a long and expensive series of legal actions as the principal inciter of violence against the federal authority. Four days after Glover's jail delivery, Booth was arrested on a warrant from the United States commissioner, charging him with "aiding and abetting" in the former's escape; but the state supreme court discharged him (July 19) on a writ of *habeas corpus*. In his opinion on the case, Associate Justice A. D. Smith held that Congress had no power, under the federal constitution, to legislate on the subject of persons held to labor or service, that being a state function; he also denied that the federal judiciary was "the sole and exclusive judge of its own powers," and advised the general government to "abstain from interference" with state affairs. The full bench, in supporting this opinion, held further that the fugitive slave law was "unconstitutional and void."

Booth was promptly reindicted by the federal authorities, and haled before the United States District Court, which in January (1855) condemned him to a month's imprisonment and a fine of a thousand dollars. Public meetings were now held throughout the state, at which money was raised for continuing the defense of the popular agitator, who was himself a man of indomitable courage and perseverance. Some of the fervid resolutions adopted at these gatherings remind one of Wisconsin Territory's nullification address to Congress, ten years previous.

As soon as practicable, the case of Booth was, amidst great popular excitement, again presented to the state court, which once more issued the *habeas corpus* writ, this time accompanied by a decision from Chief Justice Edward V. Whiton, distinctly declaring the Fugitive Slave Law " unconstitutional and void." Mr. Justice Smith filed a still stronger individual opinion, reiterating his former contentions. These decisions were cheered to the echo throughout Wisconsin and other Northern states. Charles Sumner, of Massachusetts, writing to a Wisconsin correspondent under date of Washington, June 18, 1856, says : " I have read Judge Smith's opinions. He has placed the lovers of constitutional freedom under renewed obligations. . . . Judge Smith's opinion showed the true metal."

The United States Supreme Court, as might be expected, in 1859 reversed the action of the state court, which was ordered to return Booth into federal custody. This, however, the state refused to do, and Booth was rearrested on federal warrant, March 1, 1860. Again was the aid of the state supreme court invoked, but meanwhile there had been changes in the composition of that body, and the application for a new writ failed.[1] The prisoner escaped from confinement, on the first of August, and fled to the northern part of the state; but being rearrested at Berlin, October 8, he remained in confinement until pardoned by President Buchanan just previous to Lincoln's inauguration.

In 1857, as the result of this protracted disturbance, the legislature passed an act "to prevent kidnapping." District attorneys in each county were instructed "to use all lawful means to protect, defend, and procure to be discharged . . . every person arrested or claimed as a fugitive slave," and to throw around the bondsman every possible safeguard. Two years later the spring election of 1859 for justice of the state supreme court turned on this issue. Byron Paine, Booth's principal counsel, ran upon an anti-slavery platform, which also involved state-rights, for in his argument in behalf of Booth, Paine had quoted the Virginia and Kentucky nullification resolutions, and boldly declared: "The states should have the right to judge, in the last resort, when their sovereignties are encroached upon, and to take measures for their protection." After an exciting campaign, in which "state-

---

[1] Chief Justice I .xon held the Fugitive Slave Law constitutional and valid; Associate Justices Orsamus Cole and Byron Paine were of the contrary opinion, — but as Paine had been of Booth's counsel, he declined to act, which left the vote a tie.

rights" was the slogan of Paine's managers, he won by about two thousand majority in a total vote of seventy-nine thousand. Writing from Rome in May, Sumner fervidly congratulated Paine, in his ecstasy crying, " God bless the people of Wisconsin who know their rights and knowing dare maintain ! " [1]

Thus the growing insolence of the slave power at last introduced a distinctly moral issue into public discussion, and swiftly brought about the desirable readjustment of parties upon great national issues. Thereafter was noticeable in this, as in other Western states, a marked improvement in the quality of public service, and in every walk of life a loftier standard has since been adhered to. The scandals of fifty years ago have never been repeated in the history of Wisconsin, whose public affairs are in our day conducted on a plane immeasurably higher than in the period treated in this chapter.

[1] Vroman Mason, " The Fugitive Slave Law in Wisconsin, with reference to Nullification Sentiment," in Wis. Hist. Soc. *Proceedings*, 1895.

CHAPTER XV

THE WAR CLOUD

In 1860 Wisconsin contained a population of somewhat over three quarters of a million, a gain of three hundred fold in twelve years. In his message to the legislature, delivered January 12, Governor Alexander W. Randall, then entering upon his second term, called attention to the fact that the finances of the fast-growing young commonwealth were never in so excellent a condition: "The difficulties and embarrassments under which the state has labored for some years have been outgrown. . . . Wisconsin has paid for her public improvements, such as the erection of prisons and charitable institutions, without creating a permanent state debt for such purposes." There was not even a floating debt, and a satisfactory balance remained in the treasury. The business of the state was being conducted, he declared, at less expense and with lower taxes than that of "any other Northern state out of New England, with a single exception." Among the evidences of a healthful condition was the existence of 4331 school districts, and schoolhouse property valued at $1,185,-181.

But there was a cloud in this otherwise promising sky. The insurrectionary aims of the slaveholders were becoming more and more evident, and the governor discussed them with a due sense of the gravity of the situation. Quite ignoring the nullification sentiments but recently applauded within his own state, on the occasion of the boundary and the Glover affairs, his message clearly placed Wisconsin on record as now a stanch and unquestioned supporter of the federal authority. "The disunion sentiments avowed in portions of the country, and sometimes in our halls of national legislation, are," the chief executive declared, "unpatriotic, undignified, and disgraceful. Every *threat* of *disunion* should be held up to public reprobation in all sections of the Union, and every *attempt* at disunion rewarded with a halter. . . . If any state forgets its allegiance, it must be brought back."

Language such as this might not have been favorably received, anywhere between 1854 and 1859, at public meetings in Wisconsin called to support Booth. But here, as elsewhere in the North, stress of events had caused a sudden revulsion of popular sentiment in regard to federal loyalty. Now that a crisis was imminent, but few citizens of Wisconsin found themselves opposed to the attitude of the entire state administration — not only were all of the governor's colleagues (the department chiefs) of his own party and way of thinking, but the legislative majority was also of the same opinion.

In Congress, Senator James R. Doolittle of Wisconsin made (December 27) a learned and convincing speech against secession, which attracted the attention of the country. He pointed out to his Southern colleagues that: " Your right of secession involves the right of expulsion; " and plainly told them that, instead of injustice, " you have had your full share, and more than your full share, of the territories we have acquired from the beginning up to this hour. . . . We deny you no right which we do not deny ourselves." Senators Doolittle and Timothy O. Howe, serving Wisconsin as such throughout the war, were men of commanding importance in those stirring days. Howe's maiden speech in the Senate (March 22, 1861), attacking the secessionists, was eagerly read at the time, particularly for its skillful passage-at-arms with Stephen A. Douglas and others of his opponents.

Of the Wisconsin members of the House of Representatives throughout the war period, the most conspicuous were Amasa Cobb, Charles A. Eldridge, Charles H. Larrabee, John F. Potter, A. Scott Sloan, Ithamar C. Sloan, and Cadwallader C. Washburn. Potter, a bluff, outspoken man of considerable ability, was, during the early days of secession talk (1860), challenged to fight a duel with Congressman Roger A. Pryor, a Virginian somewhat inclined to " fire-eating." Under the

" code of honor," Potter as the challenged party
had the privilege of choosing weapons for the contest, and in a spirit of grim humor selected a pair
of particularly vicious-looking bowie-knives; whereupon Pryor indignantly withdrew, declaring that
he was not a butcher. In the superheated political
atmosphere of the time, this otherwise amusing incident became at once a national event. " Bowie-
Knife Potter " was the hero of the hour among the
most violent of the anti-Southern element; and to
his dismay, poor Pryor, on whose shoulders were
placed all the supposed iniquities of the South,
found himself posted above Mason and Dixon's
line as " a typical Dixie coward." [1]

The result of the presidential election in November following was practically an announcement to
the South, on the part of the North, that the slave
power was doomed. Wisconsin made a distinct
contribution to this verdict, for out of 152,180 votes
cast in this state, the Republican presidential elec-
tors received a plurality of 21,089 over the Democratic candidates.

The threatened Southern revolt was not long
delayed. December 20, the South Carolina convention unanimously passed an ordinance dissolving
the union between its own and the other states; in
this being followed by Mississippi (January 9,

---

[1] Potter's bowie-knives, together with several others presented
to him by admiring Northern friends, are now in the museum of
the Wisconsin Historical Society, at Madison.

1861), Florida (January 10), Alabama (January 11), Georgia (January 18), Louisiana (January 26), and Texas (February 1). Upon the day of Florida's secession, Governor Randall again addressed the Wisconsin legislature at length upon the national situation. " The right of a state to secede from the Union," he declared, " can never be admitted. . . . A state cannot come into the Union as it pleases, and go out when it pleases. Once in, it must stay until the Union is destroyed. . . . Secession is revolution; revolution is war; war against the government of the United States is treason." His closing paragraph was stilted, but typical of much of the political oratory of that day: " Wisconsin is true, and her people steadfast. She will not destroy the Union, nor consent that it shall be done. Devised by great, and wise, and good men, in days of sore trial, it must stand. Like some bold mountain, at whose base the great seas break their angry floods, and around whose summit a thousand hurricanes have rattled, strong, unmoved, immovable — so may our Union be, while treason surges at its base, and passions rage around it, unmoved, immovable — here let it stand forever."

The state legislature was overwhelmingly Republican, but party lines were no longer drawn; all united in support of the Union. Affairs moved swiftly in the South. February 18, General David E. Twiggs, commandant of the Military Department of Texas, then including the largest body of

federal regulars, surrendered to the agents of the
Confederacy a million and a quarter dollars' worth
of government property in his care at San Antonio ;
together with nineteen posts, navy yards, arsenals,
and a vast quantity of military stores in various
parts of the state ; while the 2700 men in his charge
were ordered to depart from the commonwealth, being for the purpose given transportation and food
to the coast. For this service the Texas convention
voted, " That the thanks of the people of Texas are
due and are hereby tendered to Maj.-Gen. David
E. Twiggs for his patriotism, moral courage, and
loyalty to the Constitution of the United States,
embracing the rights and liberty of his native
South."

Wisconsin pioneers were particularly interested
in this incident, because, as major of the Fifth
United States Infantry, Twiggs had served for
several years as commandant of Forts Howard
and Winnebago, respectively, and had been a
prominent character in our pre-territorial history.
One of his lieutenants at the latter post was Jefferson Davis, then a young graduate from West Point,
and now provisional President of the Confederate
States.

The retirement of President Buchanan, who had
allowed the revolt to gather head, and the inauguration of Lincoln, pledged to preserve the Union,
meant henceforth a vigorous policy both at Washington and at the several state capitals. On the

13th of April, anticipating a call from President Lincoln for volunteers, the Wisconsin legislature passed an act giving to Randall practically *carte blanche* in the adoption of such measures " To provide for the defense of the state, and to aid in enforcing the laws and maintaining the authority of the federal government," as to him should seem appropriate. For this purpose, a hundred thousand dollars were voted. But on the 14th (Sunday) came news of the surrender of Fort Sumter in Charleston harbor. On Monday the President called for seventy-five thousand three-months' volunteers to aid in executing federal laws in the seceding states. The next day the Wisconsin governor issued a proclamation urging prompt response on the part of the people of the state, especially by uniformed militia companies, and at a later hour the same day the legislature doubled the sum previously appropriated for use in the great emergency.

On Wednesday noon, according to a previously adopted resolution, the legislature adjourned *sine die*, but the members at once resolved themselves into a public meeting, held in the chamber of the assembly. This gathering was addressed by members, lobbyists, and citizens generally, Democrats as well as Republicans, the proceedings being marked by intense enthusiasm and unstinted expressions of loyalty.

The heroes of the occasion were the men of the Madison Guard, a local militia company that had unanimously tendered its services to Randall as early as January 9, the day of Mississippi's secession. Immediately upon signing his proclamation of April 16, the governor sent for the captain of this company and accepted the tender. Thus this organization was the first in Wisconsin to enlist. While its members were being cheered at the meeting in the assembly chamber, the telegraph brought similar offers from Milwaukee and other cities throughout the state, as well as news that Virginia had that day taken steps to withdraw from the Union.

Within a week Governor Randall had on his hands an embarrassment of riches; for while Wisconsin's assigned quota was but one regiment, thirty-six companies had volunteered. "In six days from the issue of my proclamation of the 16th," the governor officially announced, "the first regiment called for by the President of the United States, for the defence of the Union, is enrolled and ready. . . . It is to be regretted that Wisconsin is not permitted to increase largely her quota, but her loyal citizens must exercise patience till called for." Of the ten companies accepted, four were from Milwaukee, two from Madison, and one each from Beloit, Fond du Lac, Horicon, and Kenosha.

On the 18th and 19th of April, Northern troops passing through Baltimore on their way to Washington were attacked by mobs, which on the latter day drew the first blood that was shed in behalf of the Union. The First Wisconsin infantry regiment, recruited up to standard and thoroughly organized, was tendered to the War Department on the twenty-second. Going into camp at Milwaukee five days later, the men were on the 17th of May mustered into the United States service for three months. On June 7, the regiment received marching orders, and two days later left for the capital of Pennsylvania. Its progress eastward elicited warm greetings. Contemporary newspaper reports spoke of their "comparatively perfect equipment," and their "splendid appearance." A New York "Tribune" correspondent prophesied that "The clarion voice of their martial-looking Colonel [John C.] Starkweather, will ring the knell of the traitors who get within rifle distance."

Despite the amiable compliments of ill-informed newspaper correspondents on the martial appearance of the First Wisconsin, it must be confessed that, in common with other Northern militia regiments now hurrying to the front, our representatives were soon to discover that they were but ill provided for the stern necessities of camp and field. The War of Secession found the people of the North quite unprepared. Few of its military organizations were worthy of the name. Wisconsin's militia system, probably as good as that of its neighbors, was weak and ineffective ; the most important public service rendered by the fancifully uniformed and sometimes artistically drilled com-

panies had heretofore been to parade on public
holidays and at gubernatorial inaugurations. The
officers knew nothing of the conditions of actual
service. There was abundant patriotism, and at
first no lack of either men or money, but in Wisconsin as elsewhere confusion reigned; people in
authority worked at cross purposes; only inade-
quate supplies of military stores could be obtained,
and generally these were ill adapted to the purpose
designed, and managed by an untrained commis-
sariat.

Governor Randall developed a quite unusual
capacity for hard and efficient work. He sent
agents to Washington to collect expert information as to the handling, outfitting, and general care
of troops, so far as military men then understood
that branch of their work; but in these matters
none were then really proficient, as judged by the
standards of our own time. In the first week of
May he was a prominent member of a conference
of governors of Western and Border states held at
Cleveland, and was selected to lay the results of
this convention before the President; he organized
the women of the state in their important task of
coöperation with the army, a helpfulness which
soon assumed large proportions; conducted a wide
correspondence with the national authorities and
his fellow state executives; addressed patriotic
meetings; and in general supervised in person even
the minutest details of management. But do what

he might, — and under like circumstances no man could have effected larger results, — Wisconsin troops had their full share of such trials as in those early months arose from insufficient and improper food, clothing, and equipment, and wretchedly unwholesome camps.

The governor complained to the War Department because Illinois, with not quite double the population of Wisconsin, had been called on for six regiments while his own state was restricted to one. Secretary of War Cameron, reflecting the opinion of the federal cabinet, that had not yet risen to an appreciation of the magnitude of the task before it, replied that one regiment was all that could be used, and suggested canceling all enlistments beyond the required number. Randall, however, thought that he knew better, and began forming regiments of reserves, which, he declared, would soon be needed. In this manner the Second, Third, and Fourth Infantry were organized and made ready for camp before the authorities at Washington had expressed any desire for them.

While the Cleveland conference was in session, President Lincoln issued his second call for troops — this time asking for forty-two thousand for three years. Wisconsin's quota under this levy was two additional regiments. Randall dispatched the Second and Third, and again begged the privilege of adding others, only to have his offer once more declined.

However, he had not long to wait. On the 4th of July the President was authorized to call for five hundred thousand men. By November, sixteen Wisconsin infantry regiments had been organized, and were being drilled at central camps in Madison,[1] Milwaukee, Fond du Lac, and Racine ; and the early three-months' commands, now veterans of several engagements, had reënlisted for long periods. Besides these, the state had put into the field two cavalry regiments, seven batteries of artillery, and a company of sharpshooters. The quota of Wisconsin had thus far been placed at twenty thousand, but she had exceeded this by three thousand.

The legislature, meeting in special session from May 15 to 27 (1861), took vigorous measures for promoting Wisconsin's part in the war. The expense entailed was startlingly large for so small and new a state; but rigid economy was forced upon every department of the public service, in order that the one great end might be served. Thenceforward Wisconsin promptly and efficiently met every demand made upon her during the gigantic struggle ; her quota of troops was always more

[1] Camp Randall, at Madison, then the fair grounds of the Wisconsin State Agricultural Society, was the principal training field. Of the 91,379 troops contributed by Wisconsin to the war, 70,000 were at various times quartered in or drilled at this camp. In 1893 the ground was purchased by the state as an athletic field for the University of Wisconsin, with a view to securing its proper maintenance as an historical site.

than full; and although at times the fiscal situation
seemed desperate, no question arose as to the wisdom of making liberal provision for the military
chest.

Never was the financial outlook in our state more
foreboding than at the outset of the struggle. We
have seen that during the fifties " wildcat " banks
were prevalent in the West. Many of these institutions had fallen in the crisis of 1857, and there
was still a shortage of commercial capital in Wisconsin. The one hundred and nine state banks
within the limits of the commonwealth, in the spring
of 1861, had a circulation of four and a half million
dollars, two thirds of which was secured by the
bonds of Southern and Border states, now sadly depreciated. Consequently, business paralysis seemed
imminent.

Within a fortnight after the fall of Fort Sumter,
thirty-eight weak banks suspended payment on their
bills (aggregating somewhat over two millions of
dollars), leaving only seventy-one on the list. On
Friday, June 21, the Milwaukee bankers, seeking
to save something from the wreck, threw out ten
other tottering concerns. This action was, however,
not published until after banking hours on Saturday, the general pay-day for workmen. When the
latter discovered that many of the bills handed to
them as wages on Saturday were now discredited,
they considered this action of the financiers as fraudulent, and on Monday stormed banks and brokers'

offices with bricks and paving stones, causing a
total loss in furniture and windows of about forty
thousand dollars. During an entire week business
was suspended at the metropolis, and for a month
much disorganized. Before the close of the year the
state made an arrangement with the bankers by
which the Southern bonds were sold at a sacrifice
and replaced by state securities; all bank paper
not already retired was again received at par; and
the holders of the bills of discredited banks were
compensated for whatever loss they had sustained.

Nevertheless, public confidence was not wholly
restored until after the great Union victories in
1863, that practically decided the result of the war.
Until then, the volume of business in the state, and
correspondingly its general wealth, had noticeably
declined from the standards of 1860.[1]

It has been shown that immigration from Europe
was the chief cause of Wisconsin's rapid growth
during the twelve or thirteen years just previous to
the war. Had it not been for this tragic event, the
population of the state would doubtless have been
still more markedly German in its origin. Conditions in Germany were such, in the early years of
our contest, as greatly to increase the tendency towards emigration. But the war and the correspond-
ing financial depression in the United States at
once largely diverted the general tide of Europeans

[1] Carl Russell Fish, "Phases of Economic History of Wisconsin, 1860–70," in Wis. Hist. Soc. *Proceedings*, 1907.

towards South America, and in consequence the
German migration to Wisconsin particularly suffered. On the other hand, Norwegian immigration
hither increased materially during this period of
stress, and in several counties large groups of Norwegians now supplanted Germans in the ownership
of the soil. There was throughout the war a considerable movement toward this and other Middle
Western states of farmers from New York and
New England; but meanwhile many restless Wisconsin people were moving to still newer states in
the farther West. The net result was, that from
1860 to 1865 the total growth of population of the
commonwealth was but twelve per cent; whereas
the census of 1870 revealed that during the succeeding five years of peace, with European immigration revived upon a large scale, there was an
increase of twenty-one per cent.

The fact that Wisconsin contained large and
varied groups of settlers of European birth gave a
certain picturesqueness to her troops at the front.
The Ninth, Twenty-sixth, and Forty-fifth infantry
regiments were almost wholly German; the Canadian French were largely represented in the
Twelfth; the Fifteenth was distinctly Scandinavian (chiefly Norwegian); the Irish were strongly
centred in the Seventeenth; while our Indian
wards, now eager to serve the once-hated "Bostonnais," were enrolled in considerable numbers in
the Third, Seventh, and Thirty-seventh. It was

noticeable that European immigrants, inheriting a
martial spirit, made unusually effective soldiers,
and won laurels on many hard-fought fields.

Indeed, most Wisconsin volunteer commands
were fortunate in earning and maintaining excellent reputations during the great war. One cause
for this was the recruiting policy of the state, which
differed materially from that of many other commonwealths. Says General Sherman in his " Memoirs: " " I remember that Wisconsin kept her
regiments filled with recruits, whereas other States
generally filled up their quota by new regiments;
and the result was that we estimated a Wisconsin
regiment equal to an ordinary brigade." They were,
also, participants in most of the great operations
in all parts of the theatre of war. This resulted
from the wise practice of the federal authorities in
making up brigades and divisions from regiments
representing widely-separated states, thus breaking
down the sectional spirit which up to that period
had been a serious hindrance to the growth of na-
tionalism. Wisconsin regiments served in each of
the great armies, and fought in every Southern
state save Florida; many patrolled the Rio Grande
during the threatened invasion from Mexico; and
others were engaged in quelling Indian uprisings
in the trans-Mississippi.

CHAPTER XVI

NEWS from the front soon came to have grave significance for the people of Wisconsin. On July 2, 1861, her First Regiment of infantry, a part of Abercrombie's brigade and employed in a vain attempt to prevent Johnston from reinforcing Beauregard at Bull Run, was engaged in a skirmish at Falling Waters. In this engagement George Drake, a Milwaukee private, was killed, he being not only Wisconsin's first sacrifice to the Union, but the first soldier to fall in the Shenandoah Valley, which so soon was to be drenched with American blood.

At the first battle of Bull Run (July 21), the Second Wisconsin was conspicuous in the contest for Henry Hill, and therein lost over a seventh of its numbers in killed and wounded. Sherman praised the command for steadiness and nerve, qualities afterwards winning for it a wide reputation. This organization stands first in the list of regimental losses in the Union army; of its total enrollment of 1203, no less than 238, or 19.7 per cent, were killed or died of wounds throughout the long contest, "which indicates the extreme limit of danger to which human life is exposed in a war similar in duration and activity." [1] Nearly 900 members of this regiment, in all, were either killed or wounded, leaving but few of the actual fighting strength unharmed — for it must be remembered that the term "total enrollment" includes many non-combatants, such as musicians, teamsters, hospital staff, quartermaster's men, detailed men, sick, and absentees of various sorts, besides cooks and servants.

The Seventh Wisconsin stands third in the maximum tables of losses in killed and mortally wounded, and together with the Twenty-sixth is fifth in the percentage table, their death losses being alike 17.2 per cent of their total. The Thirty-sixth lost 15.4 per cent, and has the sixteenth place in the percentage roll of honor. In the maximum table the Sixth Wisconsin has tenth place, and the ill-fated Second the thirteenth.

The Third Regiment was at Frederick, Maryland, in September (1861), being sent thither to capture the so-called "bogus" legislature assembled for the purpose of voting that state out of the Union. This task the Wisconsin men accomplished, keeping the Maryland legislators under guard until the latter consented to abandon their intent.

By the close of his term, Governor Randall had made a brilliant record. Admirably organizing the fighting machinery of the commonwealth, he had

[1] W. F. Fox, *Regimental Losses in the American Civil War*, p. 9.

placed Wisconsin troops upon as good a footing as those of any of the older and wealthier states. His constituents would have been glad to elect him for a third term, but he preferred to follow the American custom in this regard, and declined to be a candidate.

Louis P. Harvey, his successor, who took office January 6, 1862, was a man of ability and power ; yet his task lay in continuing the work along lines laid down by Randall, for he was destined to remain at the helm but a brief period. At the battle of Pittsburg Landing, Tennessee (April 4), some of the Wisconsin regiments had received severe handling by the enemy, and there was much suffering among the wounded. The Sanitary Commission — formed in 1861 for nationalizing the sanitary interests of the several Union armies, and distributing clothing, medicines, sanitary supplies, and delicacies among camps and hospitals — was not as yet properly organized, and it became necessary for Wisconsin to look after her own men. The governor, heading a relief party, set out immediately for Mound City, Paducah, and Savannah, and was returning home when the steamboat bearing him collided with another in the Tennessee River (April 19), and he lost his life by drowning.

His widow, a woman of noble impulses and unusual ability, entered the ranks of the Sanitary Commission as visitor and hospital nurse. She soon won deserved prominence in that highly effi-

cient organization, through which the energetic
women of the North proved a valuable adjunct to
the Union armies. Her advice and encouragement,
the fruit of long and arduous hospital service at
the front, were among the strongest assets of the
Commission's auxiliary in this state, the Wisconsin Soldiers' Aid Society, with its two hundred
and twenty-nine branches.[1] As a ministering angel,
particularly among the " boys " of her own state,
Mrs. Harvey's career is still cherished by them as
a sacred memory. It was owing chiefly to her un-
tiring intercession with President Lincoln that the
federal authorities somewhat reluctantly consented
to establish soldiers' hospitals in the more healthful North.[2] Three such were opened in Wisconsin

[1] There was also a Central Freedmen's Aid Society in Wisconsin, with many branches. This sought to aid the refugee blacks
who had settled in the state, and to encourage them to enlist in
the army.

The United States Christian Commission was another powerful
organization, formed in November, 1861. During the early years
of the war, Wisconsin's contributions thereto were made through
the Northwestern Branch, at Chicago. A Wisconsin branch was
organized October 8, 1864. Its forty-five representatives were
often in the field, more than half of them being with our troops
during the campaign ending in the surrender of Lee. During the
nine months of its existence the Wisconsin branch expended about
$75,000.

[2] Objection lay in the fear that the armies might suffer by the
long absence of invalids at points far distant from fields of action;
also, that desertion might thereby be encouraged. In practice,
however, it was found that these fears were ill grounded.

Many ailing Confederate prisoners were sent to hospitals in connection with Northern military camps. During a wild storm in

— at Madison in the autumn of 1863, and at Prairie du Chien and Milwaukee the following year. That at Madison was, in her honor, called Harvey Hospital, being immediately after the war converted into a soldiers' orphans' home. There were, in 1866, eight thousand such orphans in Wisconsin alone.

Lieutenant-Governor Edward Salomon, a Prussian by birth, who succeeded Harvey in the executive office (1862–63), had had but slight experience in the public service, but soon displayed unexpected energy in the management of military affairs. Under his effective leadership new regiments were quickly raised and equipped, and several relief expeditions were sent to the sick and wounded in the field. In recognizing the services of Wisconsin's several war governors, — and the commonwealth was eminently fortunate in its chief executives during this trying period, — it is but just to state that they had upon their practically-unchanged military staff two men of unusual strength: Adjutant-General Augustus Gaylord

the night of April 6, 1862, the Confederates lost to the Union forces Island Number Ten, in the Mississippi River, near New Madrid, Missouri. Several hundred of the retreating forces, chiefly of the First Alabama Regiment, were captured and sent to Camp Randall, at Madison. Being in wretched condition, they were for the most part placed in hospital; one hundred and thirty-nine died there, being buried in Forest Hill cemetery. The Confederate Veterans' Association has recently erected a suitable monument over their carefully marked graves.

and Surgeon-General E. B. Wolcott. Gaylord's
annual reports are monuments to his industry and
capacity for details. As for Wolcott, he was
throughout the war nearly always promptly on the
battlefield with assistants and supplies, whenever
Wisconsin troops had suffered heavily, for the
state continued thus to supplement the work of
the Sanitary Commission; he kept closely in touch
with our regimental surgeons, and frequently visited military hospitals in the South, ministering to
the wounded and dying from his own state.

At Shiloh, Tennessee (April 6–7), the Fourteenth, Sixteenth, and Eighteenth Wisconsin won
unusual recognition. This was the first engagement for the last named two commands, but they
held their ground with admirable nerve, and the
war correspondents commended them highly. The
Fourteenth had not arrived until the second day's
battle, but at once was in the thick of the fight.
Their daring charge of a Confederate battery, after
a Kentucky regiment, preceding them, had been
repulsed with heavy loss, elicited Grant's especial
admiration. Three times driven back, the Wisconsin men, under Major John Hancock, gallantly
carried the work and inaugurated a rout that resulted in a complete Union victory.

In the Peninsula campaign of 1862, Wisconsin
was represented by the Fifth and by Company
G of Berdan's famous sharpshooters. At Williamsburg, the Fifth, in Hancock's brigade, splen-

didly charged the enemy, and at the bayonet point
turned the wavering fortunes of the day in favor
of the Union. "Through you," said General McClel-
lan, in addressing the regiment, " we won the day,
and Williamsburg shall be inscribed upon your
banner. Your country owes you its grateful thanks."
To the War Department he telegraphed that the
" charge was brilliant in the extreme."

The Third was prominent in the Shenandoah
Valley campaign of the same year. Speaking of
the work at Gainesville, Virginia (August 28), of
the celebrated Iron Brigade, — the Second, Sixth,
and Seventh Wisconsin regiments constituted the
greater part of its membership,[1] — Pope said that
they were " among the best troops in the service."
In this, one of the sharpest and most disastrous of the
minor battles of the war, the Second Wisconsin,
leading the brigade, suffered casualties amounting
to sixty per cent of its rank and file ; the loss sustained by the entire brigade was nine hundred
men.

In the second battle of Bull Run (August 30),
the Iron Brigade again won distinction, successfully
covering the retreat of Pope's army. Two weeks
later, at South Mountain, Maryland (September
13–14), these war-worn veterans drove the enemy

---

[1] Besides these regiments, the brigade contained the Nineteenth Indiana until October, 1862, when the Twenty-fourth
Michigan was added. This command sustained in the war the
heaviest aggregate loss by brigade.

from the national road at Turner's Gap, and in chasing them through Boonesboro led the entire Army of the Potomac, while receiving the enemy's retreating fire.

At the battle of Antietam, Maryland (September 16–17), characterized by Greeley as " the bloodiest day America ever knew," the Third Wisconsin — which five weeks before had opened the battle of Cedar Mountain, Virginia (August 9) — stood in an exposed position, firing steadily, " until the fallen cartridge papers, for months afterwards, showed by a strange windrow its perfect line of battle," and losing nearly two thirds of the men it took into the fight. One of the features of the day was the galling fire of the Sixth Wisconsin, of the Iron Brigade, from behind a rail fence. The Fifth stubbornly supported a battery during the heaviest fighting; and Battery B of the United States Heavy Artillery (largely Wisconsin men) suffered on this field the heaviest loss met by any battery on either side in any single battle of the war.

In the operations at Corinth, Mississippi (October 3–4), the Fourteenth, heroes of Shiloh, was, the brigade commander reported, "the regiment to rely upon in every emergency ; always cool, steady, and vigorous." The Seventeenth distinguished itself in what was declared by the brigadier to be " the most glorious charge of the campaign." The Eighteenth received praise for "most effective service," and the Eighth and Sixteenth were also honorably mentioned in the reports. The Fifth, Sixth, Eighth, and Twelfth batteries all " did noble work."

At Chaplin Hills, Kentucky (October 8), General Rousseau reported of the First Wisconsin, which had captured a stand of Confederate colors and were heroes of the day : " They drove the enemy several times with great loss, and until their ammunition gave out bravely maintained their position." Of the Tenth, Rousseau declared, " Repeatedly assailed by overwhelming numbers, after exhausting its ammunition it still held its position. These brave men are entitled to the gratitude of the country." Sergeant William Nelson of Company I of the Tenth, with a detail of twenty-two men, for two hours held Paint Rock railroad bridge, near Huntsville, against a force of nearly three hundred Confederate cavalry, " repulsing them in the most signal manner." The Fifteenth captured heavy stores of ammunition and many prisoners. The Twenty-first, also, was an important factor in the fight; and the Fifth Battery was thanked on the field by General McCook, for having thrice turned back a Confederate charge, thus " saving the division from a disgraceful defeat."

On the seventh of December, at Prairie Grove, Arkansas, Wisconsin troops were conspicuous. The Twentieth made a charge on a Confederate battery, in common with the Nineteenth Iowa, which Herron declared was " a glorious sight. Better men never went upon the field." The loss of the Twentieth was eighty-six in killed or mortally wounded, the largest death loss sustained by any Union regiment in any one battle in the war. Of the Second and Third Wisconsin Cavalry, who sharply attacked the Confederate left wing, Herron reported that they had proved themselves "worthy of the name of American soldiers."

From December 11 to 15, in the battle of Fredericksburg, Virginia, the Iron Brigade, on the extreme left of the Union line, was constantly under severe artillery fire.

Wisconsin was represented at Stone's River, Tennessee, during the final week of the year (1862), by the First, Tenth, Fifteenth, Twenty-first, and Twenty-fourth Infantry, and the Third, Fifth, and Eighth batteries. In his report, General Scribner said that "the Tenth Wisconsin would have suffered extermination rather than yield its ground without orders." Rousseau declared that when his supply trains were attacked by the enemy's cavalry, "the burden of the fight fell on the Twenty-first Wisconsin, who behaved like veterans." Sheridan alluded to the "splendid conduct, bravery, and efficiency of the Twenty-fourth Wisconsin." The Fifth and Eighth batteries were also highly complimented for "determined bravery and chivalrous heroism."

While Wisconsin troops were thus creditably serving the nation at the front, and thereby winning honors for the commonwealth, the year 1862 was far from a cheerful one at home. Thousands of the state's most useful and vigorous citizens, the sort of men who in time of peace would have furnished the elements of commercial and industrial success, had either yielded up their lives, or been permanently disabled upon battlefields or by disease contracted in unsanitary camps. It is estimated that an aggregate of seventy-five thousand Wisconsin men, half of the voters of the state, were for a period of over three years taken into the army directly from the ranks of productive industry. Their loss was in large measure compensated by the increased employment of women and children in the field and at the bench; and crops were now being garnered by newly introduced labor-saving machinery, notably the reaper.[1] Nevertheless, the cost of the war, which had assumed quite unlooked-for proportions, was, in the form of direct taxes, or in increased prices and low wages, or by reason of rapid depreciation of the

[1] The report of the United States Commissioner of Agriculture for 1862 asserts that owing to the absence of so many farm laborers at the front, it would have been quite impossible to harvest the wheat crop for that year, had it not been for the increased use of mechanical reapers, each of which effected a saving of the labor of five men.

In his message to the Wisconsin legislature, dated January 15, 1863, Governor Salomon said: "It is an occasion for congratulation that, notwithstanding the withdrawal from peaceful pursuits of so large a number of our citizens, who have volunteered in the country's behalf, the area of our cultivated crops has been increased rather than diminished during the past year."

national currency, weighing heavily upon the people; and as usual the burden was most severely felt by the poor. Anxiety was graven on every face.

A minority of the Democratic party was much dissatisfied with the necessarily arbitrary war measures of the federal government. The state convention of that party, held at Milwaukee, September 3, 1862, adopted as its platform (ayes 112, nays 12) a long, argumentative appeal to the people (commonly called the " Ryan address," because prepared by Edward G. Ryan, the eminent jurist), in which various acts of the administration were severely criticised, notably the suspension within loyal states of the writ of *habeas corpus* and of the freedom of the press. There was, in the convention itself, a storm of dissent from this address; and " War Democrats " throughout the state promptly held indignation meetings at which they branded the document as disloyal, while many of them openly joined the ranks of the Republicans. In fact, a large majority of our people, quite regardless of party predilections, adhered to the war policy of Lincoln, and determined that the struggle should be maintained to the bitter end.

While at first Wisconsin had more than met her quota by volunteers, eager to join the new regiments as they were formed, the drain became at last so great that only by conscription could enough men be secured. But among some of the newly

arrived European immigrants, not as yet suffi-
ciently Americanized, there were many who, having
escaped from militarism at home, objected to being
forced to join the American army, and risk their
lives in a quarrel concerning whose merits they
were uninformed. In August, 1862, the President
had called for three hundred thousand new troops,
of which Wisconsin's share was twelve thousand.
The draft began in November. Some of the Belgians of Ozaukee and Washington counties became
riotous. Scenes of violence were enacted by them
at Port Washington and West Bend, respectively;
but a bold front and arrests of leaders saved the
day. At Milwaukee threatening mobs were easily
overawed by troops who patrolled the streets of the
city. No further armed opposition to this stern
necessity of war was experienced within the state;
but, as elsewhere in the North, hundreds of able-
bodied citizens who were subject to conscription
secretly fled to Canada or to Europe, to "avoid the
draft."

In neighboring Minnesota, Little Crow's band
of rebellious Sioux for a time aroused grave alarm
among the settlers (September, 1862), and it was
feared that this Indian uprising might become
general throughout the Northwest. Minnesota lost
heavily in slaughtered families and ruined farms;
but Governor Salomon's prompt shipments of arms
and ammunition to threatened counties in northwestern Wisconsin convinced the restive Chip-

pewa of that quarter that it would be unwise to
repeat such outrages in the country east of the St.
Croix.

The Army of the Potomac's "mud campaign,"
in the early months of 1863, was participated in by
many of the Wisconsin regiments. At Fitzhugh's
Crossing, Virginia (April 29), the Iron Brigade
did brilliant service in protecting the pontoon-
layers, and in one of its bayonet charges carried
Confederate rifle-pits and captured hundreds of
prisoners.

At ill-fated Chancellorsville, a few days later,
the Third Wisconsin was the last to withdraw
before the crushing advance of Stonewall Jackson;
while near by, on Marye's Hill, at Fredericksburg,
the Fifth Wisconsin, together with the Sixth Maine,
was leading the forlorn hope detailed to capture
that famous height whereon six thousand Union
soldiers had in the preceding December been
slaughtered by the intrenched enemy. It was a
wild and bloody scramble up the slippery, bowlder-
strewn hill. The men from Wisconsin and Maine,
although supported by New York and other regiments, were alone upon the first firing line, and
captured redoubt after redoubt amid a terrible
storm of grape and canister. Finally reaching the
summit, although sadly depleted in numbers, they
were rewarded by the generous cheering of the
victorious army. When the Confederate commander handed his sword and spurs to Colonel

Allen of the Fifth, he declared it the most daring assault he had ever seen, and said that he had supposed there were not men enough in the Army of the Potomac to carry the works. Horace Greeley wrote: " Braver men never smiled on death, than those who climbed Marye's Hill on that fatal day." And the correspondent of the Southern-sympathizing London "Times," writing from Lee's headquarters, said that " never at Fontenoy, Albuera, nor at Waterloo was more undaunted courage shown."

In the campaign leading to the fall of Vicksburg (1863), — probably the most decisive of all the Union victories, — Wisconsin was represented by thirteen infantry regiments, three batteries, and the Second Regiment of cavalry. Of the infantry, however, only the Eleventh, Fourteenth, Seventeenth, Eighteenth, Twenty-third, and Twenty-ninth "shared the entire preceding campaign and were in the line of investment from the beginning to the surrender;"[1] but all of the batteries served conspicuously throughout, and Wisconsin men won high praise in the official reports. The Twenty-third, skirmishing in advance of the Union army, was the first regiment to enter Port Gibson (May 2), and in recognition of this served as provost guard

---

[1] William F. Vilas, "A View of the Vicksburg Campaign," *Publications* of Wisconsin History Commission, 1908. This state commission is charged with the publication of data concerning Wisconsin's part in the War of Secession.

of that town for the day. An officer of the same
command received (July 4), at the base of the
works, General Pemberton's offer to surrender.
To the Fourteenth — " every man of whom is a
hero," reported General Rousseau — was given the
post of honor when that general's division entered
Vicksburg after the surrender; this regiment had
in the great struggle suffered a loss of nearly half
its men.

The battle of Helena, Arkansas, culminated on
the day when Vicksburg surrendered. General
Frederick Salomon, a Wisconsin man (formerly
colonel of the Ninth), planned the defenses that
assured victory, and the Twenty-eighth Wisconsin
was awarded special honors. Salomon reported that
" the bravery and valor displayed by the officers
and men of my gallant little command stand unparalleled." When, five days later, Port Hudson,
Louisiana, surrendered its garrison of six thousand,
a charge into a ditch by the Fourth Wisconsin
caused Greeley to declare that " never was fighting
more heroic."

While these deeds were being accomplished in
the Mississippi valley, other events of great importance were occurring in the East. The bloodiest
engagement of the war was fought at Gettysburg,
Pennsylvania, during the first three days of July.
Although wasted by a tedious march of a hundred
and sixty miles, from which it had been given no
time to recuperate, the Iron Brigade plunged into

the thickest of the fight. The Second Wisconsin, of that command, led its corps on the 1st of July, and began the infantry part of the battle, receiving an opening volley that mowed down over thirty per cent of its rank and file. Eventually, this famous regiment lost in this titanic combat sixty per cent of the men it brought upon the field. The remainder of the Iron Brigade — save the Sixth Wisconsin, busy elsewhere, capturing a Mississippi regiment — was, on this opening day, close upon the heels of the Second, and took eight hundred prisoners. The entire loss of the brigade, which throughout the three-days' battle remained in an extremely exposed position, was 64.3 per cent of those it took into action. The Third Wisconsin was decimated under a heavy cross-fire, but drove Ewell from Culp's Hill. Of the officers of the Twenty-sixth, only four remained unhurt. The Wisconsin company of sharpshooters were an important element in opposing the final charge of the enemy. Company F of the Seventh was the command to which Bret Harte's hero, the picturesque "John Burns of Gettysburg," since known to declamatory youth the country over, attached himself. "In swallow-tailed coat with smooth brass buttons," and with pockets filled with cartridges, this village character of a famous day nonchalantly "sniped the rebels who had driven away and milked his cows." [1]

[1] A picturesque account of the battle of Gettysburg was written a few days after the event, by Lieutenant (later Colonel) Frank

On the Georgian field of Chickamauga (September 19, 20), the First, Tenth, Fifteenth, Twenty-first, and Twenty-fourth Wisconsin Infantry, and three of our batteries, suffered heavily; some of these commands participated in the operations that won for General Thomas the sobriquet, "The rock of Chickamauga." Later, the same troops were besieged at Chattanooga and encountered much hardship, being in November relieved by Sherman with the famous Fifteenth Corps, to which the Eighteenth Wisconsin was attached. At the subsequent battle of Mission Ridge these Wisconsin troops proudly shared in the fearful charge to the summit, with them being now joined the Twenty-sixth Infantry.

Among other notable military events in the closing months of 1863 was the affair at Warrenton, Virginia (November 7). Here the Fifth Wisconsin and the Sixth Maine, heroes of Marye's Hill, led the Fifth and Sixth corps in a gallant charge which

Aretas Haskell of the Sixth Wisconsin, then aide-de-camp to General John Gibbon, commander of the Iron Brigade. First published as a pamphlet, it was reprinted in October, 1908, by the Wisconsin History Commission. Haskell distinguished himself on the third day by a feat of great valor, thus described by General Winfield S. Hancock in his official report: "At a critical period of the battle, when the contending forces were but 50 or 60 yards apart, believing that an example was necessary, and ready to sacrifice his life, he rode between the contending lines with a view of giving encouragement to ours and leading it forward, he being at the moment the only mounted officer in a similar position. He was slightly wounded, and his horse was shot in several places."

resulted in the capture of sixteen hundred prisoners and a large quantity of munitions of war. At Carrion Crow Bayou, Louisiana, in the same month, the bravery of the Twenty-sixth Wisconsin alone saved the Union forces from complete destruction in a forest ambush; although in this brief but terrible conflict the fighting strength of the regiment was reduced from two hundred and twenty-six men to ninety-eight.

On the night of February 9, 1864, a hundred and nine Union officers escaped from dreaded Libby Prison, at Richmond, Virginia, by means of a tunnel dug by a contingent of prisoners under Colonel Thomas E. Rose of Pennsylvania, who throughout this daring enterprise acted in conjunction with Colonel H. C. Hobart of the Twenty-first Wisconsin. Among the twenty-eight who were run down and recaptured by the Confederates was Lieutenant Charles H. Morgan, also of the Twenty-first. Sometimes Wisconsin soldiers were massed by hundreds in this as well as other Southern military prisons, and for months together suffered untold horrors in such dens of despair as Belle Isle, Danville, Cahawba, Florence, Macon, Salisbury, Camp Lawton, Camp Sorghum, and Andersonville.[1]

[1] A typical story of life at and escape from a Confederate prison, with consequent hazardous experiences of the fugitives, is told by General John Azor Kellogg, of the Sixth Wisconsin (later commander of the Iron Brigade), in his remarkably vivid narrative, *Capture and Escape*, published by the Wisconsin History Commission, 1908.

When, in March following, Banks set out boldly
to penetrate as far up Red River as Shreveport, Louisiana, the head of steam navigation, he had among
his troops the Eighth, Fourteenth, Twenty-third,
Twenty-ninth, and Thirty-third Wisconsin Infantry,
and its Fourth Cavalry. During this unfortunate
campaign Wisconsin men were prominent, and upon
the retreat from Sabine Cross Roads (April 8) were
the last to leave the field. The Eighth was also one
of the favorite regiments in this as upon several
other campaigns. Its sobriquet, "The Eagle Regiment," arose from the fact that the men of Company C, recruited in the Eau Claire neighborhood,
carried as a pet "Old Abe," a bald-headed eagle
—the nation's emblem. This spirited and apparently sagacious bird was usually borne upon a
perch, but in battle was fond of posing on a cannon and occasionally soaring and screaming far
above the field of conflict. "Old Abe" won a reputation in the Union army quite equal, in a way, to
that of any of its generals; and for many years after
the war was a popular attraction at national and
state army reunions and other patriotic celebrations.

The special honors of the Red River expedition
were, however, won by Lieutenant-Colonel Joseph
Bailey of the Fourth Wisconsin. While the fleet
was above the rapids at Alexandria, the stage of
water fell, making it impossible for the vessels to
descend, a perilous situation which encouraged the

enemy to swarm upon the banks and seriously to
threaten the little navy with destruction. Bailey
was serving on Franklin's staff as chief engineer,
and proposed the construction of a huge dam, by
which the water in the river should be raised to a
sufficient height; then, the obstruction being suddenly broken in the centre, the entrapped vessels
might escape upon the outrushing flood. The scheme
was familiar enough to Wisconsin lumbermen, who
in this manner still artificially " lift " stranded rafts
of logs; but his army colleagues laughed at Bailey,
although he was given three thousand men for the
purpose, and told to amuse himself with this vision-
ary experiment. His first requisition was for the
" lumber boys " of the Twenty-third and Twenty-
ninth Wisconsin, who appreciated what was needed
in this backwoods engineering scheme, and soon
trained their fellows to the task. Bailey's sappers
worked unwearyingly through the first eight days
of May, and on the morning of the twelfth the great
gun-boats plunged through the boiling chute, thus
triumphantly escaping the clutches of the discomfited Confederates, who had thought the expedition
an easy prey. Admiral Porter frankly acknowledged
that the fleet owed its safety entirely to the Wisconsin engineer's " indomitable perseverance and
skill; " he was further presented by the naval officers with a valuable sword and cup,[1] was thanked

---

[1] Now in the museum of the Wisconsin Historical Society, at
Madison.

by the Navy Department, and soon was brevetted brigadier-general.

In Grant's campaign against Richmond, the Iron Brigade served with the Fifth (Warren's) corps, and lost heavily in the Wilderness; in the support of Hancock, at the "death angle" of Spottsylvania (May 12), the brigade repulsed five successive Confederate assaults; at Hatcher's Run, the Seventh Wisconsin made a large haul of prisoners, while at Jericho Bridge (May 25), at Bethesda Church (June 1–3), and in the assaults on Petersburg (June 18 and July 30), the brigade was a leading factor. The newly-organized Thirty-seventh Wisconsin had the misfortune to lead the charging party into the Petersburg crater (July 30), losing a hundred and forty-five men out of the two hundred and fifty-one sent out. At Hatcher's Run, the Thirty-sixth, also freshly recruited, cut through a line of the enemy and captured three times their number in prisoners; but at Bethesda Church lost sixty-nine per cent of the men they took into the fight. At Fair Oaks (October 27) the Nineteenth lost over half their number in a splendid charge that brought them deserved fame.

Sherman's Atlanta campaign, opened in the spring of 1864, brought Wisconsin again to the fore, that general having selected for his model army fifteen regiments and three batteries from this state. From Chattanooga to Atlanta they were constantly under fire, and daily were represented on the skirmish lines thrown out in advance of the army. The Twelfth and Sixteenth were members of McPherson's "whip-lash corps," famed for quick flank movements that astonished and almost always overwhelmed the enemy. When, in September, after a long series of fierce battles — such as Dalton, Resaca, Kenesaw Mountain, Peachtree Creek, Allatoona Pass, and Leggitt's Hill — the Union forces marched victorious into Atlanta, Company A of the Twenty-second Wisconsin led the advance.

In November and December, Wisconsin infantry were figuring valorously, but with frightful loss of life, in operations around Nashville, Tennessee. Under Schofield, the Twenty-fourth had a fierce brush with Hood (November 29) ; but on December 16, while a part of Thomas's army, the Eighth, Twenty-fourth, and Thirty-third assisted in crushing Hood's left flank and creating wild havoc in the Confederate ranks.

When, in November, Sherman set forth from Atlanta on his picturesque "march to the sea," there were in his train eleven infantry regiments and three batteries from Wisconsin, all of which were conspicuous participants in this resistless charge through the heart of the South. The general always relied on them for the hardest work, and wherever discretion was most needed, and was not slow to sound their praise. In the subsequent siege of Savannah, and the difficult advance north-

ward through the Carolinas, in the early months
of 1865, the loss to Wisconsin commands was considerable, but they never suffered defeat.

It was quite evident early in April (1865), that
the war was nearing its end. Sherman's victorious
army was eager to join Grant and the Army of the
Potomac, and assist in making an end of Lee's
forces and of his stronghold, Richmond. The news
reached them at Goldsboro', North Carolina, on
April 6, that Richmond had fallen three days before, and that Lee was hurrying to join Johnston.
Sherman at once turned aside from the road to
Richmond, and thought to intercept Lee at either
Raleigh or Smithfield. However, a few days later a
horseman rode along the lines, shouting the bulle-
tin from Appomattox Court House (April 9), that
" Grant has captured Lee's army ! " The news of
Lincoln's assassination (April 14) soon followed ;
but this tragedy could not stem the tide, and
on the twenty-sixth Johnston surrendered near
Raleigh, his submission being followed in quick
succession by that of the other Confederate com-
manders.

We have of necessity followed more closely the
experiences of our infantry than those of other
arms of the service. But Wisconsin cavalry regiments were frequently heard from throughout the
war, and were no less famous than the infantry
commands. The First had at the outset been engaged in Missouri on scouting service. In Tennes-

see it led many gallant forays. It made its mark, also, at Chickamauga; was with Sherman on the Atlanta campaign; and with Wilson in his bold raid through Alabama and Georgia. At Fort Tyler it fought dismounted; and a detachment under Lieutenant-Colonel Henry Harnden coöperated with the Fourth Michigan Cavalry in the capture of President Davis (May 10, 1865). The Second marched and skirmished all over Louisiana, Texas, and Arkansas. The Third, while chasing guerrillas in Arkansas, engaged in many a brush with Quantrell's band, and made a particularly brilliant record at Prairie Grove. The Fourth was for two years a popular infantry regiment, but after September, 1863, had a dashing career as cavalry in Louisiana and Texas. It has been claimed that this command served the longest term of any volunteer regiment in the service. The Wisconsin batteries, also, won high honors on many fields of action, some of their deeds having already been mentioned. The state's representatives in the navy included several who achieved renown for individual valor.[1] Wisconsin was also represented in

[1] On the night of October 27, 1864, W. B. Cushing, a native of Delafield, Waukesha County, headed a party of fourteen men on an improvised torpedo boat, and in the face of apparently insuperable obstacles blew up the much-dreaded Confederate ram, Albemarle, in Albemarle Sound, North Carolina. His companions were captured, but Cushing made a daring escape. The naval historian J. R. Soley wrote: "It is safe to say that the naval history of the world affords no other example of such marvelous coolness

various companies of scouts, whose thrilling adventures alone would make an interesting volume.

James T. Lewis had succeeded Governor Salomon in January, 1864. To him fell the pleasure, on April 10, 1865, of formally announcing to the people of the state what was practically the close of the war. The legislature had previously selected that day as the time for final adjournment of its annual session; but just before the hour agreed upon, the following executive message was received with cheers: "Four years ago on the day fixed for adjournment, the sad news of the fall of Fort Sumter was transmitted to the legislature. To-day, thank God, and next to Him the brave officers and soldiers of our army and navy, I am permitted to transmit to you the official intelligence, just received, of the surrender of General Lee and his army — the last prop of rebellion. Let us rejoice and thank the Ruler of the Universe for victory and the prospect of an honorable peace."

Three days later, recruiting was discontinued in this state. During the summer the Wisconsin offices of the provost marshals were closed; and in the following autumn and winter, at intervals, our regiments were disbanded, a task not at once possible to complete, for on the fall of the Confederacy some of the Wisconsin troops were sent into

and professional skill as that shown by Cushing." The hero was thanked by Congress, congratulated by the Navy Department, and made a lieutenant-commander.

the Southwest to keep Mexican raiders from crossing the Rio Grande, and into the Northwest to protect the Indian frontier. By the close of the year, however, the greater part of our bronzed and war-scarred veterans had, after being joyously welcomed home by their grateful fellow citizens, quietly settled down again into civil life — on the farms, in the workshops and offices, at the counter and desk; or, through the acquiring of government lands in central and northern Wisconsin, extended the agricultural frontier.

On every hand was now heard but one desire, that of restoring prosperity to the "Badger State," after these four long and painful years of strife that seemed to have taxed to the utmost its resources of men and treasure. As Governor Lucius Fairchild forcefully said in his inaugural address (January 1, 1866): "A million of men have returned from the war, been disbanded in our midst, and resumed their former occupations. . . . The transition from the citizen to the soldier was not half so rapid, nor half so wonderful, as has been the transition from the soldier to the citizen. The citizen soldier has become the plain citizen," alive to the gravity of new political, financial, and social problems facing the nation and state, and eager to assist in their solution.

First and last throughout the war, the state had furnished, as reported by the governor to the legislature, a few days later, " fifty-two regiments of infantry, four regiments and one company of cavalry, one regiment of twelve batteries of heavy artillery, thirteen batteries of light artillery, one company of sharpshooters, and three brigade bands, besides recruits for the navy and United States organizations,[1] numbering in all 91,379, of which number 79,934 were volunteers, 11,445 drafted men and substitutes. The total quota of the state under all calls is 90,116. . . . The state stands credited with 1263 men, as an excess over all calls, a gratifying evidence of the devoted patriotism of the people of Wisconsin. The total military service from the state has been about equal to one in every nine of the entire population, or one in every five of the entire male population, and more than one from every two voters of the state. The losses by death alone, omitting all other casualties, are 10,752, or about one in every eight in the service." When it is considered that practically each death meant an empty chair in some Wisconsin home, to say nothing of many thousands of lives wrecked by disease or maiming (the gallant governor had himself lost an arm at Gettysburg), the chief executive's careful statistics become eloquent.

Governor Fairchild further reported that during the contest there had been paid out of the state treasury for war purposes — extra pay for soldiers supporting families, and the expenses of recruiting

[1] Wisconsin contributed 133 men to the navy and 165 to the colored troops, and was represented in various companies of scouts.

and of state military offices, being the largest items — the enormous sum of approximately $3,-900,000; counties, cities, and towns had raised by public tax a further $7,752,505.67, making an official total for Wisconsin of some $11,652,505.67. To this should be added large sums "paid by localities, by tax levied last year, of which the state has no account." In due time the general government gradually refunded to the state the amount it had itself expended on behalf of the war; but the still greater local burden was never lightened.

CHAPTER XVII

INCIDENTS OF ECONOMIC DEVELOPMENT

WE have seen that the *ante bellum* history of Wisconsin was profoundly affected by its remarkable geographical position. Lying between the Great Lakes and the Mississippi River, and abutting upon their respective headsprings, its territory is traversed by streams debouching into both drainage systems, and from time immemorial these furnished the aborigines with convenient portage routes between one and the other. This interesting fact induced the voyage hither of Nicolet, at a time when the remainder of what is now called the Middle West — the Northwest of early days — was quite unknown to white men.

Both French Canada and early Louisiana sought the trade of this land wherein was the keystone of the arch of French occupation in North America. By the Great Lakes and the Ottawa came Montreal and Quebec fur-traders, and Wisconsin peltries and lead reached the market of New Orleans upon the swift current of the Mississippi; while by means of the Mohawk and the lower lakes adventurous English traders from Albany occasionally poached upon this French preserve. Under the

English régime, and later while the American fur-trade was dominant in the Northwest, Green Bay was a dependency of Mackinac and Montreal, while Prairie du Chien was much influenced by overtures from St. Louis and the South.

In a previous chapter it has been shown that the earliest American miners in the Galena district, which includes southwestern Wisconsin, came by way of the Mississippi. Even after the irruption of operators from New York and New England, Southern goods and ideals were prevalent in this region, the product of which long sought Eastern markets by the roundabout route of New Orleans and the Gulf of Mexico. Its strong Southern connection noticeably differentiated the lead mine country from eastern Wisconsin, whose outlet to the world in the days before railroads was Lake Michigan. The *personnel* of the two districts was, in territorial days, quite as distinct as their trade relations, early giving rise to that political and social rivalry so strikingly typified in the careers of Doty and of Dodge, each the idol of his region, but by the other mistrusted and often maligned.

The opening of the Erie Canal made Eastern markets much more accessible to dwellers upon the Great Lakes, a factor materially assisting in the development of eastern and southern Wisconsin. A decreasing stage of water in the Mississippi, incident upon the demolition of forests on its headwaters, with consequent interruption to southward

navigation, caused the lead miners of the Galena
region to look enviously upon the Great Lakes and
the canal as a transportation route. It will be
remembered that attempts to deepen the old-time
Fox-Wisconsin waterway, with a view to relieving
the lead trade, early proved abortive ; as was also,
for other reasons, the scheme of a canal connecting
the Milwaukee and Rock rivers. An Illinois canal
between Lake Michigan and Illinois River afforded
some temporary assistance. The picturesque but
costly overland wagon caravans between the mines
and Lake Michigan ports have been described.

Just before the war railroads were pushed
through from the great lake to the great river, between Milwaukee and Prairie du Chien (1858) and
La Crosse (1859), so that at last the lead miners
had their long-sought outlet to the East, and settlers on the upper reaches of the Mississippi were
no longer entirely dependent on transportation
through the South. By the time, however, that this
result had been accomplished, the Wisconsin lead
industry had, from causes already explained, suffered a serious decline ; but the railroads, lacking
expected patronage from the mines, at once took
prominent part in developing the far more important agricultural interests of the state.

From a political and military point of view, these
new highways of commerce came soon to be
of still greater significance. The secession of
the Southern states resulted in the closing of the

Mississippi to Northern trade. The immediate effect of this action upon Western interests will best be appreciated, when it is reflected that before the war the Southern states themselves annually purchased many millions of dollars' worth of Western cattle, grain, and manufactures, and that New Orleans was the most important *entrepôt* for the millions of bushels of Western wheat and other exports seeking world markets.[1]

In any earlier decade this closing of the great river might well have given pause to all Northern states bordering thereon. It might possibly have induced some of them, following their exports, to cast lot with the South; as some Western communities had indeed been inclined to do when, seventy years before, the Spanish embargo was in force at New Orleans. But with the new railroad connection between river and lakes, in Wisconsin and Illinois, with a succession of bad crops in England creating

[1] The New York *Tribune* for June 13, 1861 (p. 4) strongly portrays the situation. Sixteen million dollars' worth of steamboats, it reports, are engaged in the Mississippi River trade — 1600 in number, giving " employment to thousands of men, and life and animation to entire cities. . . . No other river on earth has ever possessed a fleet so capacious, nor a traffic that could sustain it." This business had " a future of indefinite magnitude, when the blight of rebellion smote it with destructive palsy." Of Cincinnati's exports alone, annually aggregating $107,000,000 in furniture, clothing, whiskey, and foodstuffs, the South bought two thirds. "A thousand loyal communities " are similarly affected, and " the few boats which descend the river come crowded with fugitives from a common ruin."

a ready market abroad, through Eastern ports, for American foodstuffs, and with great Northern armies to supply at home, there was now no such thought. The effect in Wisconsin was to divert trade from the river to the lakes — a hastening, however, of what must, with the advent of railroads, soon have happened under normal conditions.[1]

Nevertheless, the reopening of the Mississippi to commerce was regarded by contemporary statesmen as an economic necessity of the utmost importance. Stephen A. Douglas had declared (April 20, 1861) that " the very existence of the people in this great valley depends on maintaining inviolate and forever the great right secured by the Constitution, of freedom of trade, transit, and of commerce, from the centre of the continent to the ocean that surrounds it." Governor Randall of Wisconsin, in a message to the legislature (May 15, 1861), said that " the vast lumber and mineral interests of Wisconsin, independent of her commanding produce and stock trade, bind her fast to the North, Border, and Northwestern states, and demand, like

[1] " The through freight from Prairie du Chien in the year before the war amounted to 9960 tons ; in 1861 it was 115,123 ; in 1865, 161,317 tons. That from La Crosse in 1860 was 28,627 tons ; in 1861, 89,940 ; in 1862, 89,882, clearly indicating the influence of the war in altering the channels of commerce." — C. R. FISH, *Phases of the Economic History of Wisconsin, 1860–70*, a thoughtful and helpful monograph, giving facts which we have freely used in this connection.

them, the free navigation of the Mississippi and all its tributaries." And when, in 1863, supreme efforts were being directed to force the river open, by means of the Vicksburg campaign, Governor Salomon assured the legislature (January 15) that " the opening of the Mississippi, in which, with other states, we have a direct interest even beyond that which the nation in general feels in the free passage of that great natural thoroughfare, would give new and additional life to our commerce."

The regaining of the Mississippi was of immense military importance to the Union arms, but not so vital, commercially, as had been expected. By the close of the war, the habit of using the railways had become so fixed among manufacturers, farmers, and travelers, that thereafter began a steady decline in steamboat traffic; as evidenced by the fact that Mississippi River tonnage amounting in 1860 to 468,000 tons had by 1870 fallen to 398,-000 — an advance in the latter year of only twelve per cent over 1863, when it had reached its lowest point. On the other hand, the tonnage on the Great Lakes increased thirty-five per cent between 1860 and 1863.

The effect of this sudden and remarkable development of Wisconsin's new east-going avenues of trade was greatly to enhance the growth and relative importance of Milwaukee. By the opening of the war this state had become one of the principal producers of wheat, and Milwaukee its chief port

for the shipment of surplus products. In 1862 the
tonnage of vessels using Milwaukee harbor was
25,844; but a twelvemonth following this figure
had leaped to 140,771. The population of the city
rose from 45,000 in 1860 to nearly 55,000 in 1865,
an increase of twenty-three per cent, which was
almost double that of the commonwealth itself
during the same period. The impetus thus given
to Milwaukee was such as to assure her future as a
great lake port. In due time she became a prominent centre for the influx and distribution of immigrants both from the Eastern states and from
Europe, her manufacturing interests grew to large
proportions, and her commerce and population
kept full pace with the growth of the sturdy state
of which she had early become the metropolis.

We have alluded to the slow but steady advance
in the state's population during the war period,
also to the considerable extension of the agricultural frontier in western and northern Wisconsin
by disbanded Union veterans. Even during the
years 1860–65 no less than 338,000 acres of wild
lands were sold in Wisconsin by the federal and
state governments, and by such railroad and canal
companies as had received aid through land grants;
whereas in the following five years the acreage sold
was 896,000. In the decade ending with 1870 the
total farm acreage had advanced from nearly
8,000,000 to about 12,000,000, or some forty-six
per cent; while the acreage of actual cultivation

had increased by fifty-seven per cent. The political defection of Virginia, with the closing of its tobacco fields to general commerce, greatly stimulated the growth of this crop in the North. Wisconsin was found to excel in soil and climate for the variety used for cigar wrappers; the result being that the 87,000 pounds raised in this state in 1860 had become 314,000 in 1865. As Southern cotton advanced in price, woolen goods had grown in favor, so that by the close of the war Wisconsin farmers were not only supplying the increased number of local mills, but were exporting wool in large quantities.

During the decade 1860–70 manufacturing establishments within the state had doubled in number, the capital engaged had increased two and a half times, and the number of factory employees was nearly 30,000 greater in 1870 than in 1860. These facts, in conjunction with the large increase in farming operations, explain the readiness with which the returning soldiers were absorbed into the industries of the commonwealth. On the whole, Wisconsin had made considerable economic and social advance during the harassing period of the war, although of course far less marked progress than would have been noted had there been continuous peace.

Despite this growth of our industrial boundaries, there was but slight extension of railway mileage in Wisconsin within the decade which included

the war. Scarcity of circulating medium was one
potent reason; but another was, that Iowa, Minnesota, and other trans-Mississippi regions were
insistently demanding transportation to the lake
ports of Chicago and Milwaukee, and seemed to
offer a more attractive field for speculative enterprise. Liberal land grants were being offered by
the federal government as an inducement to companies developing these newer districts, and immediately after the war both American settlers
and European immigrants rushed thither to break
the virgin soil. By 1870 it was recognized that in
the matter of railroad building Wisconsin was not
as enterprising as her neighbors to the west of the
river; but it should be taken into consideration
that the principal industry of the state, lumbering,
was almost exclusively using the abundant lakes
and rivers for the transportation of logs and rafts
both from forest to mill and from mill to the great
markets of Chicago and St. Louis.

We have already alluded to some of the legislative scandals associated with the granting of Wisconsin railway charters previous to the war. Not
only was the state government of that time impli-
cated in questionable practices in this regard, but
the feverish zeal of communities and individuals
to foster railway extension also gave rise here and
there to financial operations that left a sting. Farmers living along prospective " rights of way "
were induced by glib-tongued agents to mortgage

their farms in aid of these enterprises, being assured that enormous dividends would ensue and the
value of their land be greatly enhanced. It is estimated that in the aggregate there were issued for
this purpose nearly four thousand farm mortgage
notes alone, the face value of which amounted to
somewhat over four million dollars. Some of the
village and city governments were similarly hood-
winked, and freely bonded themselves to " help the
road." Sold to innocent purchasers, usually through
Eastern brokers, these individual notes and municipal bonds, despite the fact that many of the companies failed to construct the projected lines, came
soon to prove nightmares to their signers, and foreclosure suits followed quickly upon non-payment
of interest. Long and expensive litigation failed to
bring relief, for the contracts were astutely drawn,
and ruin was widely wrought.[1]

[1] In 1853, the city of Watertown bonded itself to the amount
of $80,000, at eight per cent, payable in ten years, to aid the
Milwaukee and Watertown Railroad Company, the latter guaran-
teeing payment of principal and interest, a promise supposed to
be secured by the deposit of collateral stock with the city. Again,
in 1856, the city issued $200,000 worth of bonds to the Watertown
and Madison, and a like amount to the Chicago, St. Paul, and
Fond du Lac. The bonds of the last-named company were paid,
but the other two lines were not constructed. The paper was,
however, sold in the open market at from five to ten per cent of
its face value. Watertown sought to evade payment. From 1872
to 1892 a curious method of evasion was practiced, by which each
newly elected city council would meet secretly and vote the taxes
for the year; then the mayor and junior aldermen would resign,
leaving the senior aldermen to form themselves into a board of

It is small wonder that these early experiences led many of the people of Wisconsin to look askance upon railway corporations, despite the undoubted fact that roads of steel largely contributed to the making of the state. Addressing the legislature on January 10, 1867, Governor Fairchild said : —

The strife which for years past has existed between a portion of our people and various corporations of the state has, I regret to say, in nowise abated. Complaints of injustice and oppression on the part of railroad companies are still heard. A portion of our people are still complaining that unjust discriminations are made by these corporations, and demanding the aid of legislative enactment to reduce the tariffs of freight to a more equitable standard. The companies, on the other hand, still earnestly assert that their charges are just and equitable. If the railroad companies are in the wrong, either in whole or in part, the fact should be ascertained, and the wrong corrected by proper legislation. I know of no better plan for procuring the data necessary to intelligent action, than by the appointment of a committee from your body, or by the appointment of a commission, to investigate thoroughly and carefully the whole question, and to submit the result of such investigation to this or a succeeding legislature. It is especially due to the people, and it is your peculiar province, as their chosen guardians, to stand between them and injustice

street commissioners, devoid of tax-levying power. The matter was finally adjusted by the city paying $15,000 as settlement for outstanding judgments aggregating $600,000.

and oppression, from whatever source they may come, and I am confident you will discharge this duty without fear or favor.

Nothing, however, then came of this suggestion of a commission. In 1869 there was a vigorous attempt to pass a bill to establish railway rates, but it was defeated. A like measure came before the legislature the following year, with further provisions regulating running connections, induced by the then common failure of rival roads to provide proper connections at junctions. The contest developed much bitterness; but the only railway legislation enacted was a bill authorizing cities and towns to lend their credit in the aid of new roads, to an extent not exceeding $5000 per mile, the municipalities to accept bonds as securities for the loan.

In January, 1873, Governor Cadwallader C. Washburn pointed out to the legislature that "vast and overshadowing corporations in the United States are justly a source of alarm, and the legislature cannot scan too closely every measure that comes before them which proposes to give additional rights and privileges to the railways of the state."

This warning came just previous to a financial panic that profoundly affected the commercial and manufacturing interests of Wisconsin, in common with those of other states. One result of the financial storm of 1873 was the customary defeat of the dominant party. The Democratic-Liberal Reformers came into power in January, 1874, with William R. Taylor as governor, supported by an assembly of his political faith; but the senate, owing to half of the body being hold-over members, remained Republican. The most conspicuous legislation was an act called the "Potter Law," or "Granger Law,"[1] which asserted the right of the state to regulate railroad freight and passenger rates within the commonwealth through a board of three commissioners clothed with almost autocratic powers.

The legislature adjourned on March 13. A fortnight later the presidents of the St. Paul and the Northwestern systems — then, as now, the principal companies operating in the state — officially informed the governor that their respective corporations would "disregard so much of the law as attempts to fix an arbitrary rate of compensation for freight and passengers." Their contention was, that the rates fixed by law would "amount to confiscation, as the working expenses could scarcely be paid under it." Governor Taylor issued a proclamation to the effect that, unless the companies

[1] Members of a widespread farmers' secret organization, the Patrons of Husbandry, expressing themselves through local lodges (or "granges"), had been particularly active in electing Taylor. They were commonly called "Grangers," and the term "Granger legislation" became attached to laws restricting the railroads. Senator R. L. D. Potter, of Waushara County, introduced the bill.

submitted, he would use to the utmost all the great powers of his office to compel them to do so. Action was thereupon brought in the state supreme court, in the nature of a *quo warranto*, for the annulment of the charters of the transgressing roads.

Application was also made to the supreme court by the attorney-general, for an injunction restraining the companies from further disobedience of the law. A long legal fight followed, that attracted national attention, with the result that the court granted the injunction, the decision in the case being written by Chief Justice Edward G. Ryan. Judge Ryan held that "in our day the common law has encountered in England, as in this country, a new power, unknown to its founders, practically too strong for its ordinary private remedies. . . . It comports with the dignity and safety of the state that the franchises of corporations should be subject to the power that grants them, that corporations should exist as the subordinates of the state which is their creator." The attorney-general was, on his part, instructed not to prosecute the companies for forfeiture of charters until the latter were given a reasonable time to arrange their tariffs under the new law.

In the United States District Court at Madison, a suit of stockholders of the Northwestern Railway, praying for an injunction against the state, on the ground that the value of their securities was being depreciated by the Potter Law, was decided against the petitioners, so far as the validity of the law was concerned. The question as to the state's right to interfere with interstate commerce, however, was left undecided, as the court desired to hear further argument.

Thus the companies were defeated at every point, so far as traffic within the state was concerned, and open opposition ceased. But more effective measures were now resorted to by them, to influence public opinion against the law. European capitalists, who at that time were chiefly relied upon for assistance in American railroad development, declined further investments in the stock of such roads as ran through the " Granger states " — some of the neighboring commonwealths having followed Wisconsin's example. Work on roads in course of building was suspended, projected lines were abandoned, some of the smaller towns were, on the plea of enforced economy, badly treated in the matter of service, and everywhere railroad employees were spreading reports that Grangerism was spelling ruin to the companies on whom Wisconsin so largely depended for prosperity. In 1876 the Reform party was buried beneath a mountain of opposition ballots, the sting in the railroad law was promptly removed by the new legislature, and the Granger movement became a closed chapter.

Throughout the eighties Wisconsin experienced

a remarkable revival of railway building. New iron and copper mines were discovered in northern Wisconsin and on the Upper Peninsula of Michigan. During this period large numbers of prosperous Wisconsin farmers sought the Dakotas and other trans-Mississippi states, and sprinkled the names of Wisconsin towns over the map of that new region; but the influx from Central and Eastern states and from Europe far outstripped the exodus, and central, northern, and northwestern Wisconsin, heretofore much neglected, now settled rapidly. Much of the railroad building was speculative; for, as usual in the West, lines were often projected far in advance of actual settlement. Some of the companies met serious reverses as the only reward of enterprise born of the splendid imagination of their founders; but in the end the prophets were justified. Great uninhabited stretches of cut-over forests were opened into farms, waterpowers were developed, quarries and mines were opened, miscellaneous industries were gradually introduced to replace the slowly-receding lumber mills, frontier shanty hamlets grew into small cities, and they into communities having more and more a metropolitan appearance.

In 1905, after some years of renewed agitation, recalling not a few aspects of the Grangerism of three decades previous, the state created a new railroad-rate-regulating commission, composed of three members with large powers. Two years later there were placed under the jurisdiction of this body the various other public utility corporations of the state, — those operating street and interurban railroads, sleeping cars, gas plants, electric power and lighting plants, waterworks, and the like. The constitutionality of laws creating this public utilities commission having been called in question, the state supreme court rendered a decision on June 5, 1908, confirming the validity of the commission and declining to hamper its operations so long as stockholders were allowed a " reasonable compensation " for their investment. Corporations of this character are now taxed by the state upon an ad valorem basis, the valuation of their tangible property being established by the State Tax Commission (created in 1899), which employs for this purpose a competent staff of engineers, appraisers, and accountants.

The extension of railways throughout the dense forests of northern Wisconsin was the chief factor in conquering that vast wilderness. But the building of towns in the heart of the " pinery," and the construction of sawmills both in such communities and at tiny milling hamlets scattered along the wooded shores of rivers and lakes, gave rise to grave dangers from fire. Frequently a town was hemmed in upon every side by dense, highly inflammable woods that for hundreds of miles extended in every direction ; the only openings being occasional watercourses and the narrow path of the railway that connected the settlement with both neighbors and market.

Towns and hamlets were themselves loosely, often shabbily, constructed of timber; the principal streets were apt either to be paved with pine planks or covered by a soft mat of sawdust; swampy places, as at Oshkosh and Fond du Lac, were filled with sawmill offal; in the cut-over portions, great piles of cast-off boughs ("slashings," in the vernacular), dry as tinder, encumbered the ground; and even where farms had been opened, there were haystacks, heavy fences of split rails, and piles of such forest products as hemlock bark, fence posts, and cord wood, all well calculated to assist in holding and spreading fire. The resinous forests and the wooden towns, blistering in the heat after a long midsummer drought, required but a spark from some passing railway locomotive, from some sawmill fueled with its own airy offal, or from a careless hunter's camp, to start a blaze that could not be extinguished until it had swept the country-side like a besom. Forests and towns went down before it like chaff, human beings were burned to a crisp in the leaping flames, and the financial loss was enormous.

On the 8th and 9th of October, 1871, following a drought of three months' duration, Wisconsin experienced one of the most appalling forest conflagrations in recorded history, the region affected being portions of Oconto, Brown, Door,

Shawano, Manitowoc, and Kewaunee counties. Over a thousand lives were lost, nearly as many persons were miserably crippled, and three thousand were beggared. The disaster centred at the town of Peshtigo, on the shores of lower Green Bay, hence is historically referred to as " the Peshtigo fire." Nearly $200,000 was raised for the immediate care of unfortunate survivors, and expended under state control. The United States government liberally distributed army stores among them ; even Europe sent contributions ; nearly every manufacturing or commercial interest in the country contributed liberally ; railway, express, and telegraph companies made no charges in the forwarding of relief and of messages, and probably few persons in Wisconsin failed in some manner to contribute their quota of assistance.

Other notable and typical forest or sawmill fires in Wisconsin have been those at Oshkosh, April 28, 1875, whereby about half of this prosperous manufacturing city was destroyed ; at Marshfield, June 27, 1887, that city of three thousand inhabitants being almost obliterated, fifteen hundred people being rendered homeless, and a loss entailed of from two to three millions of dollars ; at Iron River, forty miles southeast of Superior, July 25, 1892, where there was a loss of $200,000, and fifteen hundred persons were without food or shelter ; and at Fifield and Medford, July 27, 1893, the loss at the former place being $200,000, while the latter (a town of eighteen hundred) was practically destroyed. A year later, July 26–30, 1894, the then heavily forested counties of Douglas, Bayfield, Ashland, Chippewa, Price, Taylor, Marathon, and Wood were the scene of an extremely disastrous fire involving great loss and suffering. Phillips, the county seat of Price, a town of two thousand, was all but swept from earth (July 27), almost its entire population being rendered homeless, and thirteen persons killed. Medford, in Taylor County, was again threatened, and only saved by great exertions; so also Centralia, in Wood County. Mason, a railroad hamlet in Bayfield County, was destroyed, July 29; and in that vicinity seventeen persons were killed while seeking to escape by crossing a lake. Help was extended from many quarters, the state government lending its aid in organizing the relief. A widespread fire occurred September 29, 1898, in the western half of Barron and the eastern part of Polk counties, wherein a half million dollars in property was destroyed and large numbers of settlers made homeless. There were many thrilling escapes on the part of men and women caught in the blazing woods, and even townsfolk in the centre of the fire belt found great difficulty in reaching refuge. The military department of the state government efficiently administered the work of relief.

There was a disastrous drought throughout Wisconsin in the latter half of the summer of 1908, culminating in a phenomenally hot September. In every portion of the state much damage was wrought to pastures and root crops. In the dry and inflammable northern forests and on the cut-over lands a condition of extreme hazard prevailed. In the neighboring upper peninsula of Michigan, and in northeastern Minnesota, there was much damage from fire, the smoke from which befogged all of Wisconsin, Minnesota, Michigan, and much of Illinois, and endangered navigation on Lakes Superior and Michigan. While in Wisconsin the loss was less severe than in the more northern districts, nevertheless about $200,000 worth of timber was destroyed within our bounds, both on and off the state reserves; for several weeks many villages in Douglas, Bayfield, Sawyer, Lincoln, Oneida, and Oconto counties were in imminent danger of destruction; and some three thousand men were engaged under state control in fighting fire.[1] Relief was brought upon September 27, when the thermometer dropped fifty degrees in a few hours, accompanied by a heavy fall of rain, which latter, with accompanying sleet and snow, effectually placed the region out of danger.

Although apparently less liable to devastating hurricanes than are some of the states to the west of the Mississippi, Wisconsin has been visited by a

[1] An engine and small fire brigade were sent on September 20 by the city of Milwaukee to Rhinelander, the courthouse town of Oneida, to assist in saving the place.

few so-called "cyclones" that have wrought enormous damage. Evidences of early wind storms of
great severity were not infrequently encountered
in the northern woods by lumbermen. Occasionally
were to be seen half-mile-wide paths wherein trees
had been uprooted and the forest blasted for a distance of fifty or sixty miles ; but as there had been
no settlement of importance upon such devastated
strips, small account was taken of them.

Since record began to be kept of these terrifying
and destructive phenomena, there have been several
of sufficient importance to rank as historical events
of state-wide importance. On June 28, 1865, a
storm of this character wrecked the little city of
Viroqua, in Vernon County, killing fourteen persons and injuring a hundred. A similar storm began
to gather on July 4, 1873, some sixty miles west of
Princeton, and, passing eastward through Green
Lake, Fond du Lac, and Sheboygan counties,
exhausted itself upon Lake Michigan. Besides the
uprooting of trees and the destruction of farm crops
and other property, a large number of buildings were
shattered, especially in the cities of Fond du Lac
and Waupun, and ten lives were lost upon Green
Lake. The fury of the gale was felt as far south as
Milwaukee. Hazel Green, a Grant County village,
was wrecked on March 10, 1876, the list of dead
being nine, of maimed fifteen, and the property
loss $36,000. The entire west shore of Green Bay
was visited by a hurricane early in the evening of

July 7, 1877 ; six lives were lost and many persons injured, while the damage to property amounted to $200,000. The village of Pensaukee, five miles south of Oconto, was almost a total wreck. Another visitation of this sort, on May 23, 1878, devastated the country between Mineral Point and Oregon, a distance of nearly forty miles. The width of the path averaged a half mile, and the damage amounted to several hundreds of thousands of dollars ; a few lives were lost, and several persons sustained serious injuries. At the same time, furious storms visited northern Wisconsin (particularly along Flambeau River) and northern Illinois. The northern and western outskirts of the city of Racine were razed on May 19, 1882, by a cyclone whose path was not over twenty rods in width ; five persons were killed and eighty-five injured. The cyclone centring at New Richmond, on June 12, 1899, was, however, the severest of all. The storm lasted less than five minutes ; but when it had spent its fury the little city lay a mass of débris, property valued at well nigh a million dollars had been blotted out of existence, over fifty people were killed, and many scores were maimed. Fire broke out among the ruins, adding a new horror and greatly extending the financial disaster. In the neighboring country, also, particularly to the north, much damage was wrought ; Clayton, in Polk County, one of the centres of the great forest fire of the previous year, suffered severely. Again the state government skillfully organized the work of relief, and contributions in money and goods poured in from all over the commonwealth, as well as from the neighboring Minnesota cities of Minneapolis, St. Paul, and Stillwater. On the evening of Sunday, August 16, 1908, a severe wind storm wrecked buildings and crippled telegraph service at Pewaukee Lake, Waukesha Beach, Port Washington, and through a belt of country lying north of Milwaukee city limits.

Disaster of another sort was met by those who, in 1885–87, invested their accumulated savings in iron mines that were being "boomed" on the Gogebic iron range, crossing the boundary line between Northern Wisconsin and the Upper Peninsula of Michigan. Large deposits of high-grade ore had in the spring of 1885 been discovered between Penokee Lake and Gogebic Gap. There was at once a degree of excitement only rivaled by the experiences of early gold-mining camps in the Rocky Mountains. A hundred or more companies were soon selling stock at fanciful figures; railways were hastily projected into the region; the towns of Hurley, Bessemer, and Ironwood, centres of the district, grew with mushroom speed, for 15,000 people were soon upon the range; the entire country roundabout was pitted with prospectors' shafts; fortunes were made overnight by some of the first on the ground, and several of these speculators became millionaires. There seemed no limit to the possibilities, for one of the mines, the Norrie, shipped a million tons of ore in one season, showing that metal undoubtedly existed in large quantities. But, as usual, far more money was sunk in the majority of the pits than ever came out of them, and in the summer and autumn of 1887 there was a general crash; the speculative millionaires who had retained their holdings were again impecunious, and it was many years before the name of Gogebic ceased to be a bugaboo in thousands of deluded households. In due time, legitimate miners succeeded speculators, and the Gogebic still makes a goodly yield, although at present the Mesaba range, in northeast Minnesota, is a far greater producer of marketable ore.

With the all-too-rapid subjugation of her forests, and the opening of her farthest wilderness to settlement, it might be supposed that Wisconsin would by this time have small concern with the aborigines. But as a matter of fact, few states in the Union now contain as many Indians. In 1904 there were 10,520, not taking into consideration the civilized Brothertown and Stockbridge who own and work their own farms in Calumet County, and have been admitted to citizenship.

It will be remembered that by various treaties the Winnebago surrendered all of their rights to soil within the present limits of Wisconsin, being assigned to reservations lying west of the Mississippi. Nevertheless, a majority of these people remained in their old haunts along the water-courses leading into the Wisconsin and the Mississippi south of Black River and Wausau, which is still their habitat, although to-day they chiefly dwell in Adams, Jackson, and Waushara counties. A considerable Presbyterian mission school, for the education of their youth, was in 1835 established at Yellow River, Iowa, subject to frequent inspection by the commandant at Fort Crawford.

Owing to the timidity of white settlers, these gypsy Indians were, in the summer and autumn of 1848, induced, under pressure of thinly-veiled threats, to migrate to the reservation on Long Prairie in Minnesota. The federal government provided them with steamboat transportation from La Crosse to St. Paul, whence they were dispatched in wagon caravans to Long Prairie, a leisurely journey of four or five days. But the Winnebago did not like Minnesota, neither did they relish being placed in the neighborhood of their old and overbearing enemies, the Chippewa; the majority therefore trailed back to Wisconsin during the following winter, and resumed their former life.

In the spring of 1851 the Winnebago were again a source of alarm to white pioneers north of Wisconsin River, who pleaded for armed removal of these tribesmen. Governor Dewey, who did not share the popular fear of aborigines, sent an agent among the bands, who persuaded many peacefully to depart the state.

In 1870 there was another " scare." The Wisconsin legislature represented to Congress (March 15) that " the interests of the residents of the northern and northwestern parts of this state, as well as the interests of the stray bands of Indians therein, imperatively demand that the said stray bands of Indians be removed and located upon a reservation at or near the headquarters of the Eau Plaine River, in the northern portion of the said state." Congress responded (June 15) by appropriating fifteen dollars per head for " the removal of stray bands of Pottawotomies and Winnebagoes in Wisconsin to the tribes to which they respectively belong." During the following autumn and winter, persons under contract to effect this order succeeded, with military assistance, in removing to the trans-Mississippi several hundred Winnebago, but in most cases with quite unnecessary harshness and even cruelty. But by far the greater number of the inoffensive barbarians evaded pursuit and capture.

So insistent was the popular demand, however, that in May, 1872, Congress appropriated thirty-two thousand dollars for the further removal of the Winnebago, and a more wholesale deportation took place in the winter of 1873–74. Disgusted with reservation life, and pining for their old woods and streams, fully a half of them again returned to Wisconsin, where, to the number of some fifteen hundred, they have since been allowed to remain, receiving a small annuity per head from the federal government, and being assigned to inalienable homesteads of forty acres for each male adult, on which possessions, however, but few of them as yet abide. The remainder of the tribe, a somewhat larger number, are upon the reservation in Dakota County, Nebraska.

The latest Indian alarm in Wisconsin occurred in June, 1878. The Chippewa had been taught a new religious dance by a squaw visiting them from some reservation beyond the Mississippi,[1] and in order to practice this large bands gathered in Burnett County. With painted faces and bedecked with ornaments, the tribesmen spent whole days and nights in noisy and somewhat feverish ceremonial. The whites of this then sparsely settled district were chiefly Norwegians and Swedes but lately arrived from Europe, and such unwonted disturbances on the part of these fiercely attired savages naturally gave them great uneasiness. A rumor spread that the Wisconsin Chippewa were about to join Indians west of the great river in a general war on the settlers. At once a wave of terror swept over the county, culminating on the eighteenth of the month. The poor frontiersmen fled precipitately, often without food or proper clothing, and took shelter in neighboring towns, both in Wisconsin and across the line in Minnesota, chiefly at Taylors Falls and Rush City. The

[1] Possibly the " ghost dance " described by James Mooney in Bureau of Ethnology *Report*, 1892–93.

adjutant-general of the state, in company with an officer of the federal army, at once proceeded to the scene of disturbance; but, discovering that alarm was groundless, they gently chided the astonished dancers, and restored quiet among the pioneers. The officers officially recommended, however, that hereafter the Indians be more closely restricted to their reservations, and forbidden to wander into white neighborhoods, where such protracted dances could but arouse fear.

CHAPTER XVIII

SOME NOTABLE CONTESTS

AT various times within the history of the state there have been more or less serious proposals to remove the capital from Madison; for the most part these have emanated from Milwaukee. In the legislative session of 1858, a bill to provide for transplanting the seat of government to that city had, in its preliminary stages, developed in the assembly a favorable majority of six; but when the measure came upon the order of passage (May 15), it was lost on a tie, every member voting. In 1868 the assembly, while in the horse-play attitude sometimes assumed during the last days of the session, actually passed a bill giving the capital to Milwaukee; but on the following day (March 5) the measure was recalled from the senate and indefinitely postponed. Two years later a similar project was killed in the assembly, after a spirited debate, by a vote of fifty-six to thirty. Similar attempts were made at intervals thereafter, particularly following the destruction of a large part of the statehouse by fire (February 27, 1904), the most persistent claimant at that time being Oshkosh. But the legislature of 1907 placed what doubtless will prove a quietus on further efforts of this character, by making provision for a new statehouse at Madison, to cost six millions of dollars. Further, a constitutional provision places the state university " at or near" the capital, and the investment in the present plant for that institution is now so large that suggestions for its removal are also quite improbable.

The first serious labor disturbance in Wisconsin, necessitating the interference of state troops, occurred at Eau Claire, in September, 1881. Workmen in the then large and numerous sawmills at that place had been employed for twelve hours daily during the cutting season, but struck for a ten hours' day at the old wage. This concession being refused by the mill-owners, a strike ensued, with some rioting and destruction of property. Eight companies of militia were called out to keep the peace, and the " sawdust war," as it was derisively called, quickly ended in a victory for the employers.

In the first week of May, 1886, contemporaneously with the Haymarket massacre in Chicago, a labor riot of considerable magnitude broke out in Milwaukee. Some time previous, the national Federation of Trades had adopted resolutions advising organizations of wage-earners "to so direct their laws that eight hours should constitute a legal day's work on and after May 1, 1886." The Knights of Labor were particularly prominent in this movement. Their attractive slogan, " Eight hours' work for ten hours' pay," enabled them to gather in their ranks large numbers of both men and women, especially unskilled laborers. In Milwaukee, the knights had enrolled ten thousand members, pledged to carry out this eight-hour programme, and in the large lumber-manufacturing towns of the state the order was proportionately successful. In the face of what seemed to be a tidal wave, several Milwaukee manufacturers yielded, and the aldermen, influenced by great mass meetings, decreed that eight hours should thereafter constitute a legal day for all laborers employed by the city. But many large concerns, particularly machine shops and rolling-mills, flatly refused to grant the demand; strikes followed, and by the night of Monday, May 3, fourteen thousand men had ceased work.

Upon the afternoon of that day rioting began at establishments where laborers had declined to go out. The aggressors were largely Poles, whose passions had been played upon by Socialist leaders lately arrived from Europe, who advocated what looked suspiciously like anarchy. The wildest disorder prevailed, and red flags were appearing in the impromptu parades incident to such a situation. The police being powerless to protect property or persons, several regiments of state troops were ordered to Bay View, the centre of disturbance. On the following day (Tuesday), the militia responded to ugly assaults of a mob of fifteen hundred strikers by firing into their midst, eight persons being killed. The riot promptly subsided, strikers quietly resuming work under the old conditions. But although many of the agitators were arrested and a few sentenced to hard labor in the house of correction, a boycott was maintained for several months against both militiamen and hostile employers, and it was years before the effect of the uprising was wholly obliterated in business and social life.

Three years later (1889) a dispute arose between workmen and their employers during the construction of the Superior Air Line Railway. The laborers struck because they failed to receive their pay at the time stipulated ; this tardiness was the cause of much hardship, and considerable violence was manifested at West Superior. Militia were sent to the scene of disturbance and promptly restored order ; but popular sympathy was this time with the wage-earners, and Governor Rusk gave picturesque expression to the general sentiment when he declared, " These men need bread, not bullets ! " His influence was successful in compelling the company at once to pay their discontented employees.

Oshkosh was the scene of a labor war during the summer of 1898. Differences relative to hours and wages arose between thousands of wood-workers in that city and their bosses. In the course of the ensuing strike, there was the customary violence, with some bloodshed. Again were state troops summoned, being encamped in the city June 24-30, preventing further outrages; but much bad blood was displayed during the fourteen weeks through which hostilities continued. Towards the close of August, a compromise was effected; but the manufacturers had lost a season's trade, and the workmen suffered much from prolonged loss of pay.

Even in territorial days the liquor question was prominent in Wisconsin politics, and since the organization of the state it has not infrequently come to the front. It is impracticable here to mention more than a few of the many and diverse features of the anti-liquor movement. In 1850 the legislature adopted what is known as the Bond Law, which provided that every retail dealer in intoxicants should execute to his city, town, or village a bond in the sum of a thousand dollars, conditioned to pay all damages that might be sustained by the community or individuals " by reason of his or her vending intoxicating liquors." Three years subsequent, the people of the state voted, on referendum, in favor of a prohibitory law — ayes 25,579, noes 24,109; but the succeeding legislature declined to adopt a measure designed to carry these instructions into effect. The legislature of 1855 passed such a law, but it was vetoed by Governor Barstow.

The next important enactment was that known as the Graham Law, adopted amid much excite-

ment at the session of 1872. This act declared
drunkenness unlawful; dealers in intoxicants were
made responsible for the care of intoxicated persons; and any one, whether a relative or not, might
in his own name sue the dealer for damages to person or property, or because of loss of support, occasioned by the intoxication of any third person. On
his part, the dealer must execute to the community
a bond for two thousand dollars, conditioned for
the payment of all possible damage suits. The
Graham Law awakened much bitterness during the
brief period of its existence, being among the many
causes contributory to the political upheaval of
1873, that resulted in the triumph of Grangerism.

The prohibition leaders were persistent, however, and in 1878 presented to the legislature a
petition signed by fifteen thousand persons, asking
that the people be allowed to vote on a prohibition
law; but this was denied, as were also similar petitions sent up in 1879 (40,000 names), 1880, 1881,
and 1882. The result of this long-continued effort
was, that the minimum of the liquor license fee
was quadrupled, and cities were allowed thereafter
to vote once in three years on the question of rais-
ing this fee in their own communities. At present
there are various forms of local option, including
one applicable to small city neighborhoods.

At its session of 1889 the Republican legislature passed a bill introduced by Assemblyman
Michael J. Bennett of Iowa County, and com-

monly known as the Bennett Law, that gave rise
to a remarkable political disturbance. The state
educational authorities had called attention to
the fact that fifty thousand Wisconsin children
between the ages of seven and fourteen were not
attending schools of any sort, and there was a
general feeling that the laws of the state providing for compulsory education should be made
more effective. Bennett's bill was designed to accomplish this result.

At the time of its passage no one appears to
have discovered anything revolutionary in the
measure; but early in 1890 a writer in a German Catholic paper in Milwaukee called public
attention to certain of its provisions that were
most unfortunately phrased. A fierce discussion
at once arose in the press, and in several public
meetings held for the purpose. Both Roman Catholics (chiefly Irish and Germans) and Lutherans
(Germans and Scandinavians), having many and
strong congregations in Wisconsin and conducting
numerous parochial schools, academies, and colleges, united in vigorous objections to two clauses
that to them seemed designedly aimed against their
excellent and far-reaching educational systems.

The first of these provisions stipulated that
" every parent or other person having under his
control a child between the ages of 7 and 14
years, shall annually cause such child to attend
some public or private day school in the city,

town, or district in which he resides." Coupled
with this were certain further regulations, fixing
the minimum school year at twelve weeks, and
placing upon public school boards, clothed for this
purpose with large authority, the responsibility for
the education of each child in the commonwealth.
The objectors urged that under their systems, in
which boarding schools played a large part, it was
quite impracticable for all their children to be
educated in the city, town, or district of each
child's home ; that the enforcement of such a provision would result in closing two thirds of the
parochial schools in the country districts. While
considering public schools necessary, they declared
that parents had " the right to send their children
to a better or more suitable school outside the district." Moreover, they said that the law " compels
parochial and other private schools to observe the
time or times of attendance, fixed by school boards,
without regard to the rights or customs of churches
or their schools. . . . The State and its officers
have no right to interfere with the management of
parochial or other private schools." [1]

The second objectionable clause read : " No school
shall be regarded as a school under this act unless
there shall be taught therein, as part of the ele-
mentary education of children, reading, writing,
arithmetic, and United States history in the Eng-

---

[1] Quoting from resolutions adopted by the "Anti-Bennett State
Convention," held at Milwaukee, June 4, 1890.

lish language." This came to be regarded by both
German and Scandinavian opponents as a thinly
veiled attack on their native languages, which
largely prevailed in their denominational academies and parochial schools. The Democratic platform of 1890 declared: "To mask this tyrannical
invasion of individual and constitutional rights,
the shallow plea of defense of the English language is advanced. The history of this state, largely
peopled by foreign-born citizens, demonstrates the
fact that natural causes and the necessities of the
situation are advancing the growth of the English
language to the greatest possible extent." At a
state convention held at Milwaukee (June 4, 1890),
for the purpose of organizing all shades of opposition to the law, it was resolved that while the
delegates had "no enmity to the English language," they nevertheless were "opposed to all
measures tending to oppress the immigrated citizens, or to suppress their native tongue," and
asked "those who cherish liberty, regardless of
party or nationality, to join us in the effort to
have this unnecessary, unjust, and discord-breeding
measure repealed."

The Democratic party thus promptly espoused the
cause of "anti-Bennettism," and skillfully rallied
the forces bent on repeal. In their state platform
the Republicans branded the published objections
to the act as "gross misrepresentation," declaring
that they had no "purpose whatever to interfere

in any manner with private and parochial schools supported without aid from public funds, either as to their terms, government, or branches to be taught therein;" but on the other hand believed that "adequate provision should be made for the care of children incorrigibly truant." A general state election occurred in November, after a somewhat violent campaign, and Governor William D. Hoard, who had signed the Bennett Law, was, together with the entire Republican ticket, defeated. George W. Peck, heading the Democratic ticket, received 30,000 plurality. The Bennett Law was repealed by the next legislature, and not until 1894 were the Republicans again placed in control of the government.

While agitation over the Bennett Law was in its early stages, the state supreme court was engaged in hearing a protracted and learned discussion of the constitutionality of Bible-reading in the public schools of the commonwealth. In school district number eight of the city of Edgerton, six taxpayers formally objected to the fact that teachers read each day to the children certain portions, selected by themselves, of the King James (Protestant) version of the Bible; whereas the parents of many of the children were Catholics, who did not believe that the Scriptures should be indiscriminately read to youth by persons not authorized by the Church to expound them. They further contended that to select the King James to the exclusion of the Douay (Catholic) version was essentially sectarian instruction; that the reading of the Protestant Bible transformed the public-supported school into a place of sectarian worship, with no liberty of conscience to those of other denominations; and " that the practice complained of disturbs domestic tranquillity, and therefore does not promote the general welfare of our people."

The school board having declined to interfere with the teachers in this matter, the circuit court for Rock County (Judge John R. Bennett) was requested by the plaintiffs to issue a mandamus commanding the board to cause the teachers to refrain. The court held that the practice was not unconstitutional; whereupon the plaintiffs appealed to the supreme court, before which argument commenced on February 1, 1890. In one aspect or another this question had arisen in many of the states of the Union; hence the Wisconsin test case attracted national attention. Several attorneys of much ability appeared before the court, pro and con, and the public press bristled with articles on the subject.

On March 18 the court handed down a unanimous decision, written by Justice William P. Lyon, declaring that the reading of the Bible in public schools was undoubtedly sectarian instruction and an act of worship, thus a practice uniting the functions of Church and State, and therefore contrary to the inhibition of the state constitution on that point. Justices Cassoday and Orton rendered separate, but confirmatory, opinions. The action of the court elicited strong protests from several Protestant ministerial conventions; but in the face of this definitive interpretation of the constitution, the state department of public instruction promptly gave notice to boards and teachers that Bible-reading must at once cease in all public schools within the commonwealth.

The constitution of the state provides that after each federal or state census there shall be a fresh apportionment of the senate and assembly districts; "such districts to be bounded by county, precinct, town, or ward lines, to consist of contiguous territory, and be in as compact form as practicable."

In the session of 1891 the new Democratic legislature, elected as a result of the Bennett Law agitation, adopted a reapportionment of the state based on the federal census of the preceding year. The Republican leaders charged that this measure was a particularly pernicious "gerrymander," and if allowed to prevail would ensure the continuous election of Democratic legislatures. For instance, it was shown that in the senatorial apportionment, especially, the matter of proportionate population cut little figure, some Democratic senate districts having far below the unit of representation, and certain Republican strongholds having far above this number. The Republican county of La Crosse, to cite but one of several like examples, was given

but one assemblyman, while Manitowoc County, a
Democratic seat, having practically the same population, was awarded three. It was further shown,
by means of maps, that many of the new districts
did not " consist of contiguous territory " in " compact form," but were curiously shaped, and obliged
voters to make long and unnecessary trips to reach
their nominating conventions and polling centres.

Action against this law was begun (February 9,
1892) in the state supreme court by the Republicans, nominally acting through the Democratic
attorney-general. On March 22, the court (composed of three Democrats and two Republicans)
unanimously decided that the apportionment act was
unconstitutional, therefore null and void. County
lines, the justices held, could not be divided in
forming assembly districts, senate districts must
be composed of convenient contiguous assembly
districts, and there must be substantial equality
of representation. Governor Peck called a special
session of the legislature on June 1 to adopt a new
apportionment that should meet the requirements
of the court as to uniformity of population and
contiguity of territory. The second act, approved
July 1, was, however, almost equally distasteful to
the Republicans, and they again asked the attorney-general to bring suit to vacate it. But that
officer now declined to act, being convinced, he
said, that the new apportionment was quite in accord with the rules laid down by the court. After

much legal sparring, the court granted permission to a private person, acting in the name of the attorney-general, to bring such suit. Like its predecessor, the new appointment was declared improper by a majority of the court (September 27). The legislature was again convened in special session (October 27), and this time adopted an apportionment that was not contested; under its provisions the succeeding legislature was elected.

From the earliest years, state treasurers in Wisconsin had personally collected interest on state funds deposited in the banks, and had regarded this as a proper perquisite of their office. During the decade 1880–90, the treasurers thus obtained from twenty-five to thirty thousand dollars a year in addition to their legal salaries. Attacks on the practice began in 1882 and were repeated from time to time; but as the censured officials were expected to subscribe liberally to campaign funds, and the office was regarded as a special reward for high political service, politicians at first paid small attention to criticisms of so time-honored a custom. The treasurers themselves justified their conduct by declaring that, having given heavy bonds for the safe-keeping of such of the state's money as came into their hands, it was sufficient if the actual sums paid to them were properly accounted for.

When, however, the Democrats came into power in the first week of January, 1891, it was decided by the party leaders that such of the treasurers as were not exempt under the statute of limitations should be prosecuted and the interest collected by them returned to the state treasury. Two test cases were brought before the circuit court for Dane County, which decided, after a suit attracting wide attention, that interest earned on the funds of the state belonged to the state, and should have been accounted for by the treasurers at the expiration of their several terms of office. Appeal was taken to the state supreme court, which handed down an elaborate opinion (January 10, 1893) practically confirming the decision of the lower court. The treasurers were acquitted by the court of criminal intent, deposits not having been made by them as investments; but failure to pay over the interest was declared to be non-performance of all the duties of the office as guaranteed by bondsmen. Judgments amounting to $725,000 (including interest on the sums retained) were secured against the treasurers and their sureties; but subsequent legislation released some of the persons proceeded against, so that the net sum returned to the state treasury was $373,385.95.

From the time of the introduction of such public utilities, railway, telegraph, and express companies operating within the state fairly showered free passes and franks upon public officials of every grade, particularly members of the legislature. There is no doubt that this practice was long an effectual barrier to attempts to regulate public utility corporations, and not until after it was made illegal did the regulation policy become effective.

Public protests against railway passes were heard as early as 1871, when an unsuccessful attempt was made to pass a bill making it a felony for a commissioner or a juror in a railway damage case to accept such favors. Three years later the Potter Law contained a clause forbidding state officers, judges, and members of the legislature, or persons elected to such offices, to accept either passes or reduced rates; but it will be remembered that the entire law was repealed in 1876.

The agitation was renewed in 1892, and considerable effort was at that time made to arouse the somewhat indifferent public to an appreciation of what was considered by many as a serious political evil. Five years later the agitation was vigorously renewed; but it was not until 1899, and in the face of persistent opposition, taking frequently the form of ridicule, that there was adopted an anti-pass law, with stringent provisions. This was supplemented at the general election of November 4, 1902, by a constitutional amendment, adopted by a large popular vote, providing that: "No person, association, copartnership, or corporation, shall promise, offer, or give, for any purpose, to any political committee, or any member or employee thereof, to any candidate for, or incumbent of any office or position under the constitution or laws, or any ordinance of any town or municipality of this State, or to any person at the request or for the advantage of all, or any of them, any free pass or frank, or any privilege withheld from any person, for the traveling accommodation or transportation of any person or property, or the transmission of any message or communication." The legal authorities of the state have from the outset construed this mandate as including every manner of public official, state or local, whatever his grade, even janitors, school teachers, and the trustees of public libraries and schools.

This drastic legislation had been preceded by a corrupt practices act (1897), one of the most stringent in the Union, compelling political committees and candidates, under severe penalty, to file statements of campaign receipts and disbursements. An act was passed in 1905, placing the regulation of appointment to the civil service of the state in the hands of a commission of three members. After one of the most protracted and bitter political controversies in the history of any Western commonwealth, the Wisconsin legislature adopted in 1905 a sweeping primary election law, which was, on referendum vote, confirmed by the people at the succeeding general election. Under its provisions nominating conventions have been abolished, and by this means the legislature is informed which candidate for the United States Senate is approved by his party.

CHAPTER XIX

On May 29, 1848, President Polk approved the act of Congress admitting Wisconsin to the Union. The first general officers of the new state took the oath of office at Madison on June 7. The semi-centennial anniversary of these two events, occurring in 1898, was made the occasion for fitting celebrations by the people of the commonwealth.

As May 29 in that year fell on Sunday, and the 30th was Memorial Day, the observance of the signing of the act of admission was fixed for Saturday, May 28. Acting on the suggestion of the Wisconsin Historical Society, numerous local ceremonials were held on that day at county seats and other centres of population, these largely partaking of the character of pioneer reunions, at which were delivered reminiscent speeches and papers. Several local historical societies were the outgrowth of such meetings.

On June 7–9 there was a three days' celebration at Madison, the programme consisting chiefly of assemblies of pioneers of the territory, signers of the state constitution, students of Wisconsin history, and the like; at large evening meetings, addresses were made by distinguished citizens and visitors. Concerts, parades, boat races, and fireworks were among the popular attractions. During the week ending July 2, Milwaukee conducted a separate celebration, in which a carnival and historical pageants were the principal features, illustrating the commercial and industrial advancement of the state since territorial days.

While these events were in progress, Wisconsin was participating with her sister states in the Spanish-American War. On April 28, the day following the receipt of final orders from Washington, three twelve-company regiments of Wisconsin infantry, chiefly recruited from her national guard, were mobilizing at Camp Harvey — the state fair grounds, on the outskirts of Milwaukee. On May 14 the Third Regiment (1353 strong, Colonel M. T. Moore) was forwarded to Camp George H. Thomas near Chattanooga, Tennessee; being followed next day by the Second (1349 men, Colonel C. A. Born), destined for the same camp; while on the twentieth the First (1357 men, Colonel S. P. Shadel) was sent to Camp Cuba Libre, near Jacksonville, Florida. The Fourth (1301 men, Colonel H. M. Seaman) and a battery of 109 members (Captain B. H. Dalley) were later added to the quota of the state, thus making a total Wisconsin enlistment of 5469 men.

Although the First was the best equipped and best

drilled of these several commands, its colonel was outranked in seniority by those of the Second and Third, with the result that it remained inactive throughout the war, in camp at Jacksonville, and subsequently at Pablo Beach. Although asked for by General Lee, to serve with the proposed army of occupation in the West Indies, the First was ordered home early in September because of the length of its sick roll, induced by shamefully unsanitary conditions at the Jacksonville camp. The Fourth and the battery were quartered at the state's permanent military reservation — Camp Douglas, in Juneau County — until the close of the war, when the former was ordered to Anniston, Alabama, to prepare to join the army of occupation; the battery, however, never left the state.

On July 21 the Second and Third sailed from Charleston, South Carolina, under General Miles, for Porto Rico. Arriving at Ponce on the 27th and 28th respectively, they took part in the peaceful capture of that place. They were thereafter in almost daily engagement with the enemy, having been with the Pennsylvania Sixteenth, with whom they were brigaded, selected as the advance guard of the army. Detachments from these Wisconsin regiments played a conspicuous part in General Roy Stone's dashing raids northward toward San Juan.

Upon several occasions Wisconsin men distinguished themselves: particularly at the capture and holding of the little inland town of Yauco, a perilous enterprise conducted by Lieutenant Cochrane of Company E of the Third, and seventeen of his men, all from Eau Claire; at the mountain fortress of Lares, where Lieutenant Bodemer of Sheboygan and a small detachment had a sharp brush with the enemy while carrying a flag of truce; at Coamo, where a battalion of the Third was engaged; and at the mountain pass of Asomanta, — the final engagement between Spanish and Americans on the island, — where the Second was the last regiment in conflict, losing two men killed and two wounded, the only field casualties sustained by Wisconsin during the war. The total loss from death sustained by our regiments, almost wholly from camp diseases, was 131.[1] The state's military expenses aggregated $139,364.49, but these were later refunded by the federal government.

With the exception of the Fourth, Wisconsin volunteers returned to the state in September, being first welcomed as regiments at Milwaukee, and later as companies in their respective towns. In due course they were formally mustered out of federal service, the majority of them rejoining the several militia organizations from which they had been recruited.[2]

[1] The First lost from disease 45; Second, disease, 38; Third, disease, 29, killed and died from wounds, 2; Fourth, disease, 17.

[2] The First was mustered out October 19, 1898; Second, November 11–21, 1898; Third, January 4–17, 1899; Fourth (at Anniston), February 28, 1899; Battery A, October 8, 1898.

The reader of this brief historical review of the region now comprising the State of Wisconsin has discovered that up to about 1830 the fur-trade was its leading industry. After that, the lead-trade played a considerable part in the development of the country; then farming — at first wheat-raising, but later mixed crops, live stock, and dairying — assumed large proportions. But with the growth of settlement in the West, Wisconsin's forests came to be exploited by lumbermen on a large scale, and for several decades the annual output of her pineries nearly equaled in value that of her agricultural products. So rapid of late has been the work of the lumbermen, however, that Wisconsin's timber industry is fast dropping in the scale, the principal operators having already withdrawn to the South and far Northwest; but we still lead all other states in lumber and planing-mill products.

The area of the state comprises some fifty-six thousand square miles, of which but thirty-four per cent is as yet improved, and the present population is approximately two and a quarter millions, a half of whom are dwellers in cities. It is computed that even with the present system of "extensive" agriculture, six and a half millions of people could easily be accommodated here, and the wealth of the state might readily be increased threefold. "Intensive" agriculture, in the European manner, would add vastly to this capacity. Conscious of the ability of the state to sustain a far larger population than is found at present within our borders, the authorities have put forth strong efforts to "attract public attention to the many sources of wealth of the state which are not utilized or are practically unknown." It is thus hoped to accelerate immigration.

The amount of capital now invested in Wisconsin's miscellaneous manufacturing establishments is upwards of four hundred million dollars. Ranked in importance according to the following order are lumber and timber products, and the products of flour and grist mills, foundries and machine shops, cheese factories, creameries, condensed milk factories, leather works, breweries, iron and steel works, paper and wood-pulp factories, furniture factories, and sash, door, and planing-mills. Manufacturing is not concentrated in a few localities, as in many states, but is well distributed, and for materials is largely dependent upon local products. Lead, copper, iron, and zinc occur abundantly and are profitably mined, while the shipments of building stores and mineral waters are considerable.

As there are within our bounds some two thousand small lakes, most of them of great purity and beauty, and as all portions of the state exhibit much pleasing scenery, with a climate rendered equable through proximity to the Great Lakes, the summer-resort business is assuming large proportions. The state is to its great profit much frequented by sportsmen during the fishing and hunting seasons. Fishing as an industry is also lucrative, the state's annual products on the Great Lakes alone being valued at nearly $300,000, while there are also extensive inland fisheries that advance the total to considerably over half a million dollars. A State Fish Commission effectively controls these interests, and annually restocks the lakes and rivers.

Wisconsin's geographical position, already shown to have played a large part in her history, is still of great importance in the marketing of her exports. The products of her forests, farms, factories, mills, mines, and quarries are readily shipped to the East from ports on lakes Michigan and Superior. On the west, the Mississippi has, since the war, carried but a relatively small freightage, because of railway competition ; but its possibilities are still great, and potent forces are at work that must inevitably cause the great river and its leading tributaries in time to regain some measure of their former economic importance. The railways of the state now show a trackage of somewhat over seven thousand miles, fairly meeting the needs of nearly every section ; and interurban electric systems are fast pushing into the most populous districts in the eastern and southern counties. There is also a promising field for the greater utilization of the state's waterpowers, for manufacturing, transportation, and lighting purposes.

The commonwealth makes ample provision for the education of its youth. During the year 1906 the aggregate disbursements for common schools amounted to $8,982,992, for normal schools $372,-572, for the state university $1,022,548, and for other forms of popular instruction (teachers' institutes, day schools for the deaf, manual training departments, agricultural schools, and county training schools for teachers) $175,559 — a magnificent total of $10,553,571. In the same year there were 371,929 children between seven and fourteen years of age (limits of compulsory attendance), of whom 62.2 per cent were enrolled in the public schools of the state and 16.2 per cent in private schools, while 21.6 per cent did not attend any school. There were 7731 schoolhouses in the state, with a seating capacity of 569,169. Seven state normal schools (at Platteville, established in 1866 ; Whitewater, 1868 ; Oshkosh, 1870 ; River Falls, 1875 ; Milwaukee, 1885 ; Stevens Point, 1894 ; and Superior, 1896) give instruction to four thousand pupils. In 1908 there were two hundred and sixty-five free and fourteen independent high schools, with a total enrollment of 21,453.

The system of popular education in district, ward, high, and normal schools is fittingly crowned by the University of Wisconsin at Madison, founded, we have seen, in pioneer days. This institution, which at present has over four thousand students, of both sexes, is supported by the income from five distinct federal land grants,[1] by state taxation, and in part by private gift. At present the university receives the product of an annual tax of two sevenths of a mill· on each dollar of the assessed valuation of the state, besides specific legislative appropriations. Gifts have chiefly come in the form of foundations for certain chairs, fellowships, and scholarships.[2]

The university consists of colleges of letters and science, engineering, law, agriculture, and medicine, besides a largely-patronized graduate school, and fast-developing departments of university extension and correspondence study. The university extension division offers lecture courses in all parts of the state, to women's clubs, study clubs, home study groups, and teachers' conventions and institutes; it also aims to assist debating societies and all manner of local educational activities. The correspondence study department, now on a well-established basis, offering a large variety of courses, endeavors " to give every man a chance to get the

[1] The basic two-township grant, 1848; supplementary two-township grant, 1854; Morrill grant for the support of studies pertaining to agriculture and mechanic arts, 1862; Hatch grant for support of agricultural experiment stations, 1887; and supplementary Morrill grant, 1890.

[2] The most important of these benefactions are thus far the bequests of Charles Kendall Adams and William Freeman Vilas; the former is already operative in part, but the latter (which it is hoped may eventually reach thirty millions of dollars) is not yet available.

highest education possible at the smallest practical cost, to bring the university and the home in close touch." In short, the university, as at present organized, seeks to be "the centre of every movement that concerns the interest of the state." The widely-extended system of farmers' institutes, held simultaneously at many points in the state, and of short agricultural courses given at Madison to both youth and adults, is an exceptionally popular branch of university instruction, and has already immensely benefited Wisconsin agriculture; indeed, the college of agriculture and the state experiment station in connection therewith, have won national reputation for breadth of view and administrative skill. The effect of some of the station's practical experiments has been to revolutionize the dairy business of the entire world.

The principal Protestant denominational colleges in Wisconsin are at Milton (Seventh Day Baptist, established 1844), Waukesha (Carroll College, Presbyterian, 1846), Beloit (Congregational, 1846), Appleton (Lawrence University, Methodist, 1847), Ripon (Congregational, 1853), Watertown (Northwestern University, Lutheran, 1865), and Milwaukee (Concordia College, Lutheran, 1881). Milwaukee-Downer, an unsectarian college for women, at Milwaukee, is on the joint foundations of Milwaukee College (founded 1848) and Downer College (Congregational and Presbyterian, 1853). The Roman Catholics support Ste. Clara's Academy (Dominican, 1847) at Sinsinawa Mound, St. Francis Seminary (1853) at St. Francis, St. Lawrence College (Capuchin, 1861) at Mount Calvary, Marquette University (Jesuit, 1864) at Milwaukee, and Pio Nono College (normal, 1871), besides several efficient institutions of lesser rank.

Since the Wisconsin Library Commission was organized in 1896, the public library movement in the state has had a remarkable development. Free municipal libraries, supported by local taxation, are now established in a hundred and fifty communities — over half of them owning their own buildings or being comfortably established in city halls ; there are, in addition, several owing their support to individuals, associations, and school boards. The commission circulates nearly seven hundred well-selected traveling libraries in those sections as yet too sparsely settled to purchase their own book collections. It also conducts an advisory service, for giving assistance and advice of every sort to such public libraries as are in need thereof ; an instructional service, which includes a school for library training, the conduct of library institutes in various parts of the state, and practical instruction on the spot in the organization and conduct of small libraries ; a legislative reference library (in conjunction with the State Historical Library) for gathering and classifying material bearing on current questions of public moment and subjects of pending legislation, for the use of members of the legislature, state officers, citizens, and students of public affairs; and a document and magazine clearing house for the benefit of local libraries.

In this connection should be mentioned the well-known library of the State Historical Society, at Madison. This institution, founded by members of the first state legislature (January 30, 1849), has long been the most industrious and successful agency west of the Appalachians, for gathering and publishing material bearing upon American history, more especially that of the West and South. Its well-selected reference library, comprising more than 300,000 books and pamphlets, and occupying one of the most beautiful and best-equipped of American library buildings, is a favorite workshop for scholars, while its publications rank with those of similar societies in Massachusetts and Pennsylvania. Within the society's building are also housed the fast-growing libraries of the state university and the Wisconsin Academy of Sciences, Arts, and Letters. The excellent law library of the state is maintained at the capitol.

The penal and charitable institutions of Wisconsin are managed by the State Board of Control. There are state insane hospitals at Mendota (near Madison) and Winnebago (near Oshkosh); a School for the Blind at Janesville; a Workshop for the Blind at Milwaukee; a School for the

Deaf at Delavan; an Industrial School for Boys (reformatory) at Waukesha; a Home for the Feeble-Minded at Chippewa Falls; a School for Dependent Children at Sparta; a State Prison at Waupun; a State Reformatory at Green Bay; and a Tuberculosis Sanatorium at Wales — these several institutions costing the state, for current expenses alone, about half a million dollars annually. The incurable insane are cared for in county asylums supported by both the state and the county. The Wisconsin Veterans' Home, at Waupaca, while managed by the Wisconsin department of the Grand Army of the Republic, is liberally aided by the state. The National Soldiers' Home at Milwaukee is of course supported and managed by the federal government. The Industrial School for Girls (reformatory) at Milwaukee is partly under state control. There are also in Wisconsin many orphan asylums, hospitals, homes for the aged, and other private benevolent institutions, for the most part under ecclesiastical management; when specially incorporated, they are regularly inspected and reported on by the Board of Control — but the number thus incorporated is but a small proportion of those in existence.

Despite the wholesale and often wasteful lumbering operations of the past decades, there still remain in Wisconsin some large tracts of forest, chiefly hardwoods. A State Board of Forestry was authorized in 1905, and a technically trained state forester, who is also state fire warden, is now employed in a systematic attempt to prevent forest fires and acquire forest reserves. Over three hundred local fire wardens have been appointed in the northern counties. As sixty per cent of forest fires are caused by carelessness of settlers in clearing land and burning for pasture, it is hoped gradually to eliminate this factor. Thus far, the several reserves include 234,000 acres in northern Wisconsin; but in the immediate future it is hoped very largely to increase this area, from gifts of cut-over pinery lands, the sale of certain state lands, and receipts from the sale of forest products emanating from the reserves. The board expects incidentally to assist in diminishing disastrous floods along the Mississippi and to conserve valuable water-powers.

Reference has already been made to the work of the State Railway (public utilities) Commission, the Tax Commission, the Board of Assessment, the Board of Control, the Library Commission, the Commissioners of Fisheries, the Civil Service Commission, the Board of Forestry, and the State Historical Society, which last is practically a commission. The Bureau of Labor and Industrial Statistics, State Banking Department (essentially a commission), Diary and Food Commission, Board of Agriculture, Geological and Natural History Survey, Board of Examiners for Admission to the Bar, Boards of Dental, Medical, and Veterinary

Examiners, Board of Health and Vital Statistics, Live Stock, Sanitary Board, Board of Pharmacy, Tuberculosis Commission, Grain and Warehouse Commission, Board of Arbitration and Conciliation, and Board of Immigration — to make merely a selection from the list — are all of them useful agencies of state administration, and suggest the great breadth and complexity of the practical problems affecting a modern American commonwealth. Two recently created commissions are of peculiar interest: The Wisconsin History Commission, which seeks to collect and disseminate information concerning Wisconsin's part in the War of Secession; and the State Park Board, whose object is to select and report on park sites that, from considerations either of beauty or of historic association, should become the property of the state.

Sixty years ago, when Wisconsin entered the Union, it was relatively a crude community. It has slowly but surely advanced to the front rank of trans-Appalachian states. Fertile, healthful, and beautiful, with vast natural resources as yet but slightly drawn upon, it has come to be recognized as among the most energetic, enterprising, and prosperous of American commonwealths — perhaps most markedly enterprising in the matters of popular education and the science of government. Much of its material success is owing to favorable geographical position, and to abundant products of earth and water; but quite as great is the intellectual debt Wisconsin owes to her cosmopolitan population that has brought to her service the best of many lands. Both intellectually and materially, she faces none but pleasing prospects.

INDEX

INDEX